"Driving thousands of miles, along every motorway in France, looking at the service stations, restaurants, picnic areas and other facilities at all the 'aires', may seem an odd way to spend a summer. But I found much to enjoy in the France of the motorways; driving on the well-designed and landscaped roads was a pleasure, the scenery was varied and often spectacular.

"I discovered an astonishing range of facilities, ate some memorable meals and found many excellent places to stop for a picnic and to relax. Despite being a regular visitor, I also learnt quite a lot about France and the French. It was to share all this with other travellers that I wrote this book; I do hope that it will give you pleasure as well as help you to make the most of your motorway journey and to discover another not-so-hidden part of France."

Anna Fitter

BONNE ROUTE

Discovering French Motorways

Anna Fitter

Anthony Nelson

First published 1995
by Anthony Nelson Limited
P.O. Box 9, Oswestry, Shropshire
SY11 1BY England

ISBN 0 904614 56 5

Contents

Introduction

A French Motorway Guide! Why should I need one? If you ask yourself the question, you have probably never travelled on the motorways of France.

In the UK, and in most European countries, you use motorways in order to get from A to B as quickly as possible! In France, too, motorways provide the quickest, and safest, way of reaching your destination, but there is much more to them than that.

Every 10 to 15 kilometres there is an 'aire', a place to stop, beside the motorway. There is an astonishing range of facilities at these aires; quite apart from the essential services you would expect to find, there are picnic areas to suit all tastes, childrens' play areas, and exercise circuits for the energetic. Try your hand at fencing, sailing or mountain biking, or relax in the sun to the strains of medieval music. There are opportunities to take a stroll through an arboretum, beside a lake, or to inspect a nearby Roman pavement or a fortified castle. How about visiting the museum of rugby and prunes at Agen, a traditional olive mill in the Midi, the Archeodrome at Beaune, or the memorial to villagers shot during the war near Poitiers. At Nimes there is a set of columns from the old theatre beside the motorway. You will also find modern sculptures, works of art, innovative and exciting designs. The list of surprises is endless.

In the provision of all these aires, the French have had two major aims; firstly to increase safety by providing plenty of good facilities to make travelling more relaxing, and secondly to include a celebration of French culture, heritage and achievement, a window on the world for travellers. Most of these are French, looking in from a different region, but for the traveller from another country, the motorways provide an unexpected, and fascinating, insight into what it means to be French.

Along the motorway are large brown panels of tourist information, 'les panneaux marrons'. Most alert you to places or features of interest which are within easy reach if you leave the motorway at the next junction. They might mention aspects of the economic life of the region you are passing through, its agriculture, wines or industry; maybe a place of historical interest or an area of outstanding natural beauty. Possibly you already know something about the chateau, the mountain or the wildlife illustrated on the panel, or it may be quite new to you; your motorway journey could become a lesson on the history and geography of France! Bonne Route provides you with enough information to send you hunting for your regional guide to find out more; it does not intend to replace either your guide book or your maps, but to complement them.

This is the only guide of its kind, covering the whole network of motorways in France, and it is an essential source of independent information which will make the journey more comfortable, interesting and rewarding for every member of the family. Follow it as you drive along and see!

How to Use The Guide

The main section of the Guide is arranged in motorway number order. On each double spread you will find:

- A diagram showing the section of motorway covered.
- A list of aires either side of the diagram to correspond with the direction in which you are travelling.
- Information about the places mentioned on the *brown signs* in a shaded column on the right.

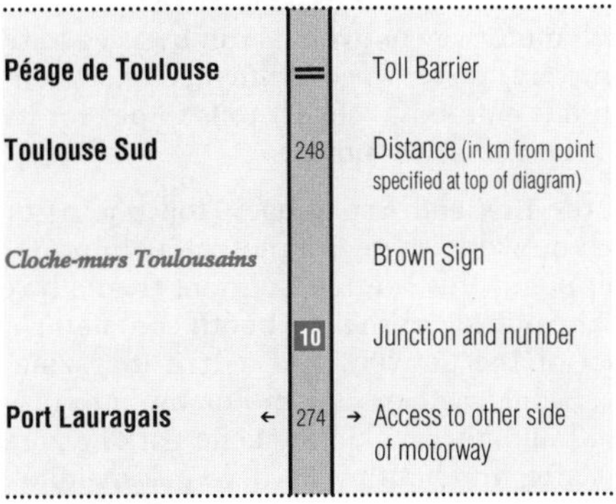

General Information

Just after most toll barriers there are WCs and a cardphone; many have a picnic table or two, but you are advised to drive on to an aire if you want to have a break. Consult the main section of the guide for details of other facilities at toll barriers.

You can expect all fuel stations to have WCs, with baby changing facilities, a shop, drinks machines and telephone.

Wherever there is a restaurant or caféteria, there will be a WC block, facilities for changing a baby, and telephone

Every aire has a WC block and a picnic area, unless I have indicated to the contrary. A few aires are very basic, and I have indicated where this is so; assume that all the others are reasonable places to stop.

Key to Diagrams

Péage de Toulouse	=	Toll Barrier
Toulouse Sud	248	Distance (in km from point specified at top of diagram)
Cloche-murs Toulousains		Brown Sign
	10	Junction and number
Port Lauragais ←	274	→ Access to other side of motorway

Picnic Areas

For picnic areas only, I have used a star system for those which I personally like best.

★★★ A picnic area of exceptional beauty with a wide range of facilities.

★★ A picnic area with good facilities, strongly recommended.

★ A very acceptable picnic area.

Symbols used in the guide are:

- Fuel
- Workshop
- Food
- Disabled facilities
- Children's play area
- Shade in the picnic area
- Showers (or open air brumisateurs)
- Card telephones
- *i* Tourist information kiosk/board
- Bureau de change
- Hotel

On The Road

Motorway networks

Each motorway network is run by a separate company, under a government concession, and it is entitled to collect tolls to pay for its upkeep and development.

At the first and last 'péage' (toll booth) of each network, there is a motorway information point; this is often no more than a box on the outside of the toll booth containing a map of the network and a free magazine. Occasionally, there is a motorway information building, or a kiosk, at the parking area just after the booths, so, if you want information, keep a look out for these. You can obtain free motorway maps from

Autoroutes Information
3 rue Edmond Valentin
75007 Paris

You can obtain information on roadworks on Minitel 36.15 (at many service stations), and the weather forecast and up-to-date traffic news (in French) on 16 (1) 48 94 33 33. There is also a motorway radio station, the frequency is advertised along the way.

These are the different networks:

SAPN	Autoroute Paris - Normandie
SANEF	Autoroutes du Nord et de l'Est de la France
SAPRR	Autoroutes Paris - Rhin - Rhone
COFIROUTE	Compagnie Financiere et Industrielle des Autoroutes
ASF	Autoroutes du Sud de la France
ESCOTA	Autoroute Esterel - Cote d'Azur
AREA	Autoroutes Rhone - Alpes
STMB	Tunnel Routier sous le Mont Blanc

Paying the tolls

Tariffs vary according to the type of vehicle you are driving; all cars are charged at the same rate.

There are two systems in operation. In the first the driver, or in the case of right hand drive cars, the passenger, takes a ticket from a machine, sometimes after pressing a button, at a booth on entering a network. Payment is due either on leaving the motorway (there is a 'péage' at each exit), on reaching a free section of motorway (often near a large town) or sometimes on joining another network. French francs or a credit card, including a UK one, can be used for this. If you use your card, you will find that the system is simple and rapid, and on receiving the bill you will find that you have not been charged an excessive rate of exchange. You are asked not to use a credit card for amounts of less than 50F.

In the second, the tolls are calculated for each section and you pay regular small sums along the way. Machines are often automatic and give change. However, it is useful to have plenty of small change, and to look out for those booths which have nets to throw the correct amount into; quite a speedy operation when you get used to it! There are always manned booths (go to the right) if you have no French francs.

There is a third system, Télépéage, available for regular users on busy sections of some networks. An electronic badge on the windscreen causes the barrier at specific booths, clearly marked 'Télépéage', to rise automatically.

Electronic display panels

These panels, found on many motorways, and situated about 2 kms before an exit, give information about road and traffic conditions on the next stretch of road, and, when there is no particular message to be relayed, they indicate the time of day and the temperature.

Patrols

There are regular security patrols, day and night, along the motorways. There is also daily cleaning, upkeep and gardening at the aires.

Speed limits

130 kms/hr in dry weather, 110 kms/hr if wet. Minimum speed limit of 80 kms/hr in the outer lane in good visibility.

Safety

French motorways are claimed to be 4 to 5 times safer than main roads. On 3 points in particular drivers are regularly cautioned:

1.Keep your distance from the vehicle ahead; on many motorways there are reminders of this, and road markings to demonstrate just how far away you should be.

2.Take regular breaks; once again, you will be reminded of the need for this as you drive along and, as you see from this book, there are so many places to stop, and so many activities to distract you that you will not find it difficult to follow this advice.

3.Make use of the opportunities along the motorway to check your tyre pressures free; apart from at fuel stations, there are facilities after the toll barriers at many 'péages'. Low pressures can lead to burst tyres.

Never overtake on the right.

With most motorways 2-lane, and with driving speeds in general higher than in the UK, it is important to return promptly to the right hand lane after overtaking.

Share the driving if you can.

At night

If you become tired whilst driving at night, you should pull into an aire for a rest. The majority of aires have lighting in the area near the toilet block, and that is where I would recommend you to stop, with the car doors locked. Overnight parking is not officially allowed on any layby in France, but it appears to be condoned on motorway aires, especially in the south. Some of the larger aires have plenty of space, and facilities, of course, but you do not have the security of a patrolled campsite. Camping cars and caravans are welcomed at the Aire de Cambarette on the A8 and at the Aire de Beaune on the A6.

Breakdowns

Stop on the hard shoulder, as far over to the right as possible. Put on the hazard warning lights, display the warning triangle, and have the passengers get out from the right hand side of the car. Go to the nearest emergency phone. These are sited every 2 kms and calls are free. Just press the button, wait for a reply and speak. Be as precise as possible about where you are, the nature of the breakdown and the details of your car. The police will send an approved mechanic, a repair will be done on the spot if possible, or your car will be towed either to a garage of your choice or to a motorway garage. The cost of the roadside repair or the tow is laid down by French law, and is higher at night and at the weekend.

Emergency Phones

Most of these orange SOS phones are beside the motorway; some of them are situated in an aire. On some motorways these SOS phones have a strobe light built into their top which flashes to alert drivers to dangers ahead.

Services

Fuel Stations

Fuel is available day and night, and a credit card is probably the simplest thing to use for payment. Prices are displayed clearly on the motorway, well in advance and, although in general fuel is expensive on the motorway, some stations are cheaper than others, so it is worth checking up.

Most fuel stations have a shop selling a wide variety of goods: drinks, fresh food, regional products, wine, cassettes, books, maps and motoring accessories. Staff will heat a baby's bottle if asked. There are drink machines, often ones which give change. These all produce excellent fresh coffee, and more; one I used recently offered coffee in six different ways, strong or weak tea, four ways of having cocoa, two soups and cold drinks as well! You will find telephones and sometimes Fax and Minitel machines. Many shops remain open at night, but not all.

Lavatories.

In large fuel stations, WC facilities are generally excellent, sometimes quite luxurious. You should find disabled facilities and a place for changing a baby; sometimes there are showers. On older motorways, where the fuel station has not been modernised, the facilities are sometimes just not large enough to cope, particularly when a coach party arrives, and this is frequently the case in cafétéria/restaurant buildings. Better to drive on to the more basic, but less crowded, picnic area facilities.

Lavatories at most picnic areas are 'squattoirs' but, thanks to daily maintenance, they are generally clean. Their design usually includes a gap between the roof and the concrete shell of the building, allowing a useful circulation of air. Standards drop on August weekends, so be prepared for this. Newer toilet blocks have better facilities, occasionally including showers. The British may find it surprising, though, that some of the most modern will have, say, electronic flushing, automatic lights, stained glass windows or attractive murals – and still no lavatory pan! You are more likely to find lavatory pans on the ASF network; toilets on their section of the A11, for example, have all been fitted with them.

The disabled driver and passenger

Minibuses which have been adapted for the use of the disabled pay the same toll as private cars.

At fuel stations there are attendants who will serve you on request.

Emergency telephones along the motorway are not accessible for people in wheelchairs, so if you happen to break down you will need to enlist the help of someone to phone for assistance for you.

Where I have indicated the existence of facilities for the disabled, you can assume that there is at the least access to a restaurant (if there is one), to a telephone and to toilet facilities, but there may be some parts of an aire which are inaccessible. I have pointed out where I have noticed a specific problem, such as a lack of access over a bridge.

Relais Bébé

At a few aires, indicated in this guide, hostesses are on hand to feed and change baby's nappy during the summer, in bright blue and white Nestlé caravans, with a terrace and awnings outside. Facilities ranging from reasonable to luxurious exist at most service areas for you to change baby yourself! In fuel station shops you will also find that they will warm a bottle for you.

Keeping Fit

Some aires on the Paris-Rhin-Rhone network have simple exercise facilities aimed at helping the driver to be more relaxed on a long journey; 'point relaxe'. A good idea, created by an organisation called the Back Institute.

At other aires you will find exercise circuits, generally of 200 to 500 metres in length and in wooded areas, with exercises to do along the way; 'parcours de santé' or 'parcours de détente'.

Many aires have a large grassy space suitable for ball games; there are table tennis tables at several, a pétanque pitch at an aire on the A72 and a swimming pool on the A9.

There is organised sport at summer weekends at some larger aires, including a surprising range of activities, from 'boules' through sailing to mountain biking. I have not tried these out at all, not through laziness but because I prefer to travel during the week, but I have seen the facilities. I imagine that some knowledge of French would be necessary to get the best out of these opportunities.

If all this exercise makes you rather warm, there are open air mist sprays called 'brumisateurs' at many aires in the south; on one particularly hot day, driving down to the Mediterranean coast, I found myself doing as the French do, stopping frequently for a quick shower; no time, or need, to take off shorts and T-shirt, nor to dry myself afterwards. What could have been a difficult journey was made quite bearable!

Telephones

Many aires have telephones but these are almost always card phones, taking only French phonecards. You can buy these from the AA in the UK, or in shops and boutiques in service stations in France.

There are pay phones in service stations and in restaurant buildings.

Making a Telephone Call

If you want to phone the UK:

- dial 19
- wait for the dialling tone
- dial 44
- dial the STD code minus the first 0
- dial the number

For example:

19 44 181 344 1234 (a London number),

19 44 1258 123456 (outside London)

If you want to call a number within France:

from the Paris region:
dial 16 + 8 digit number

to the Paris region:
dial 16 + 1 + number

Changing money

Apart from bureaux de change, generally at tourist information offices, there are cash dispensers at a growing number of aires. They are easy to use, with instructions in several languages, including English.

Where to Eat

There are a variety of places to eat, ranging from waiter service restaurants to kiosks selling snacks in summer only.
Smoking in any covered public place, including restaurants and cafés, is forbidden by French law, but facilities for smokers are provided.

Restaurants

Often advertised as 'Grill', these are open for lunch and dinner, generally from 11h00 - 15h00 (although you might not be served if you arrive much after 14h00) and from 19h00 - 22h00. Out of season they may not open in the evening. Service is usually efficient, friendly and speedy. There will be fixed price, à la carte, and children's menus, in English and French. There is sometimes a terrace for outdoor eating. Prices are higher than in a self service restaurant. The most common are Arche Grills and Relais restaurants, both of which are of a consistently high standard. An Arche steak or chop will be good quality meat, but may not be cooked enough for your taste unless you specify 'bien cuit' (well-cooked); the Relais menu offers an imaginative choice, especially of regional dishes. Grills sometimes have a 'take away' facility.

Self service restaurants

Often advertised as 'Caféteria', these are bright, well designed restaurants, usually with a terrace, which serve a good choice of food throughout the day. Arche are generally open from 06h00 -23h00; Relais 06h30 - 22h30. Some are open throughout the night; see the guide. Prices are comparable with those on UK motorways; quality is often better. A favourite of mine, usually on the Arche menu, is braised ham; try it with Madeira sauce and potato purée. The Relais regional speciality is generally delicious, too. On the debit side, caféterias are sometimes rather crowded, especially when a coach party is there. Avoid the peak eating period of 12h30 - 13h30 if you can.

Menus are in English and French, and there are clear photographs of main courses, either at the entrance or along the top edge of the walls as you walk through to make your choice. After taking a tray and cutlery, you will probably walk past cold drinks, starters, cheese, desserts and then main courses. One vegetable is usually included in the price of the main course; you pay extra for a second one, but you might like to do as the French do and take a roll instead of potatoes. You can sometimes find low-fat butter, 'beurre allégé', but I have not seen margarine.There will be a cheaper, childrens' menu.

Don't forget to buy a 'jeton' at the till (English currency is often accepted, and a UK credit card always is) and use it after the meal at the automatic coffee machine. Large and small cups cost the same ; the coffee in the smaller cup is stronger. It is consistently good. Near the coffee machine there will be a microwave oven for you to reheat your main course if you wish, a bottle opener, water, jugs and ice.

Prices for breakfast in a caféteria are reasonable. There will be fruit juices, fresh fruit, a variety of breakfast yoghourts, warm croissants and pains au chocolat, cheese and cold meats, and, often, bacon and egg! In Arche caféterias your coffee cup is refilled at the table. Why not make an early start and breakfast 'en route'?

Toilet facilities at caféterias are usually well-appointed and clean, but they can be inadequate at busy times. There will be disabled, and mother and baby, facilities.

If you are at an Arche caféteria, there will be a fountain, a giraffe maypole and some pigeons in a cage outside!

Snack bars.

Their minimum opening hours are 07h00 - 21h00, but many are open longer, and some for 24 hours. They are basic, but often have their own terrace. 'Caféroute' is the best known (see below). Aubepain offers a Drive-In service, and there are various 'sandwicheries' and 'Restauration rapides' too.

Many aires have seasonal snack bars, in temporary buildings, and these, too, will have a terrace.

Some fuel stations have a snack bar at one end of the shop; most are quite basic, but they do include Caféroutes, and one or two offer a wide choice of hot meals. You would be unlucky not to find at least a coffee machine in a fuel station shop.

Look out for a Caféroute if you want a snack. They are bright and stylish. They serve breakfasts, rapid meals, snacks and take away food. Food is served with a paper napkin or in a disposable container directly onto a tray; you clear your tray away when you have finished. It's rather less basic than it sounds; it is quite possible to have a three course meal, say, salad, chicken and chips followed by fruit tart. As in a caféteria, buy a jeton for your coffee when you pay for your meal. Quite acceptable if you want to eat quickly and don't mind a limited choice, and reasonably priced.

Vocabulary and Phrases

Abonnés	Season ticket holders
Achèvement	Completion
Aire	Area
Aire de repos	Rest area
Allée pour voitures	Track for cars
Animation	Activities
Appuyez sur le bouton	Press the button
Autoroute	Motorway
Bande d'arret d'urgence	Hard shoulder
Bocage	Farmland with hedges and trees
Bonne Route	(Have a)good journey
Bouchon	Traffic jam
Bouton	Button
Brouillard	Fog
Buzes	Buzzards
Céder le passage	Give way
Ceinture de sécurité	Seat belt
Ceinture attaché, vie protégé	Seat belt attached, life protected
Cerf	Stag
Chantier	(Road)works
Chaussée	Roadway
Circulation	Traffic
Colline	Hill
Convoi exceptionelle	Wide load
Dépannage	Breakdown
Détente	Relaxation
Diffuseur	Interchange, junction
Eau Potable	Drinking water
Echangeur	Interchange, junction
Elevage	Cattle breeding
Embouteillage	Traffic jam
Entretien	Maintenance
Essence	Petrol
Feux	(Traffic)lights
Feux clignotants	Flashing lights
Fluide	Moving (traffic)
Gabarit	Size
Gendarmerie	Police station
Giratoire	Gyratory (roundabout)
Gonflage	(Tyre)inflation
Gratuit	Free
Hors Gabarit	Outsize (vehicles)
Marquage axial sonore	Rumble strip
Monnaie	Change (given)
Noeud	Knot(m/way junction)
Oiseaux migrateurs	Migratory birds
Ouvert	Open
Ouverture	Opening
Panne	Breakdown
Panneau	(Road)sign
Parc d'activité	Business park
Parcours	Course, route
Parcours de santé	Health course
Parcours sportif	Sport course
Patrouille	Patrol
Paysage	Scenery
Péage	Toll
Périphérique	Ring road
Piétons	Pedestrians
Plomb	Lead
Pluie	Rain
Pneus	Tyres
Point Relaxe	Exercise area
Polyculture	Mixed farming
Poubelle	Bin
Prenez votre ticket	Take your ticket
Prochaine sortie	Next exit
Ralentissez	Slow down
Renard	Fox

Renseignements	Information
Restez sur votre file	Stay in lane
Sanglier	Wild boar
Sans monnaie	Without cash
Sans Plomb	Lead free (petrol)
Santé	Health
Sens	Direction
Serrez la droite	Keep to the right
Serrez la gauche	Keep to the left
Sortie	Exit
Station service	Service station
Toutes les deux heures, la pause s'impose	Have a break, every 2 hours
Travaux	(Road)works
Troisième voie	Third lane
Trop vite, trop près	Too fast, too close
Usine	Factory
Utilisez	Use
Vehicules lents	Slow vehicles
Verglas	Ice
Vers	Towards
Vignoble	Vineyard
Ville nouvelle	New town
Vitesse	Speed
Vitesse réduite	Reduced speed
Voie de détresse	Escape lane
Voie rétrécie	Road narrows
Zone Artisanale (ZA)	Crafts area
Zone Industrielle (ZI)	Industrial estate

Alternative Routes

Motorway routes to consider

1. From Calais to the south
   A26 to Troyes
   A5 to Langres
   A31 Beaune , A6
   use A46 to avoid Lyon centre.
2. From Calais to the south
   A26/A1 to just south of Charles de Gaulle Airport, Roissy
   A104, La Francilienne, direction Bordeaux/Nantes/Lyon
   (This outer Paris ring road links with A4, A5, A6 & A10).
3. From Le Havre or Caen to the south
   A13 to Triangle de Roquencourt
   A12, then N10, N191 to A10
   A10 to Orléans
   A71 to Clermont Ferrand
   then either A75 to St Flour, N9
   or A72 to St Etienne
   A47 or N82 to the A7.
4. From Paris to the south-west
   A10 to Orléans
   A71 to Vierzon
   N20/A20 to Montauban via Limoges/Brive la Gaillarde
   A62 to Toulouse.
5. From Paris to the south
   The A5 provides an alternative to the A6 out of the capital. Easiest way to get onto it: A4, A104 La Francilienne, A5.

On Saturdays in August avoid the A7 and, preferably, the A6, A8, A9 and A10; the approaches to Paris on Sunday afternoons are liable to delays, too.

If you arrive in France at Dunkirk I would recommend you to use the A16/A26 route south. The A25, a non-toll motorway, gets very busy and is used by a lot of lorries.

If you are looking out for signs to direct you to a particular motorway, acquaint yourself with the names of important towns on it. Signs often omit the motorway number, using the names of towns instead. You may see one saying LYON; if it is blue, take that direction for the A6. Likewise, the A4 is often signed METZ, the A1 LILLE.

New motorways

A network of motorways is developing north of Paris. The A16 will eventually provide the capital with another route to the Channel; the A28 and A29, sections of which are already open, will link Calais with Rouen and Le Havre and those towns with eastern France. The A16 is complete from Boulogne to Dunkirk, linking the Channel Tunnel exit to the main motorway south from Calais, the A26.

Further sections of the A75, which will link Clermont Ferrand with the south coast A9 motorway are open, making the A10/A71/A75 route to the south an attractive option, especially if you are travelling at the weekend in high summer.

The A20, l'Occitane, is progressing towards linking the A71 at Vierzon with Brive-la-Gaillarde. It is already a useful route to the Dordogne and the south-west. There are good picnic areas, the Aires de Coulerolles, on each side of the motorway just north of junction 24 (Bessines), about 30kms north of Limoges.

Two useful roads to look out for if you have to circle Paris are the outer eastern ring, the A104/N104 La Francilienne, which I have already mentioned, and the inner, but less complete ring, the A86. Not for the faint-hearted, they carry a lot of traffic, have more bends than one would like and have to narrow occasionally, on bridges for example. They have regular service stations.

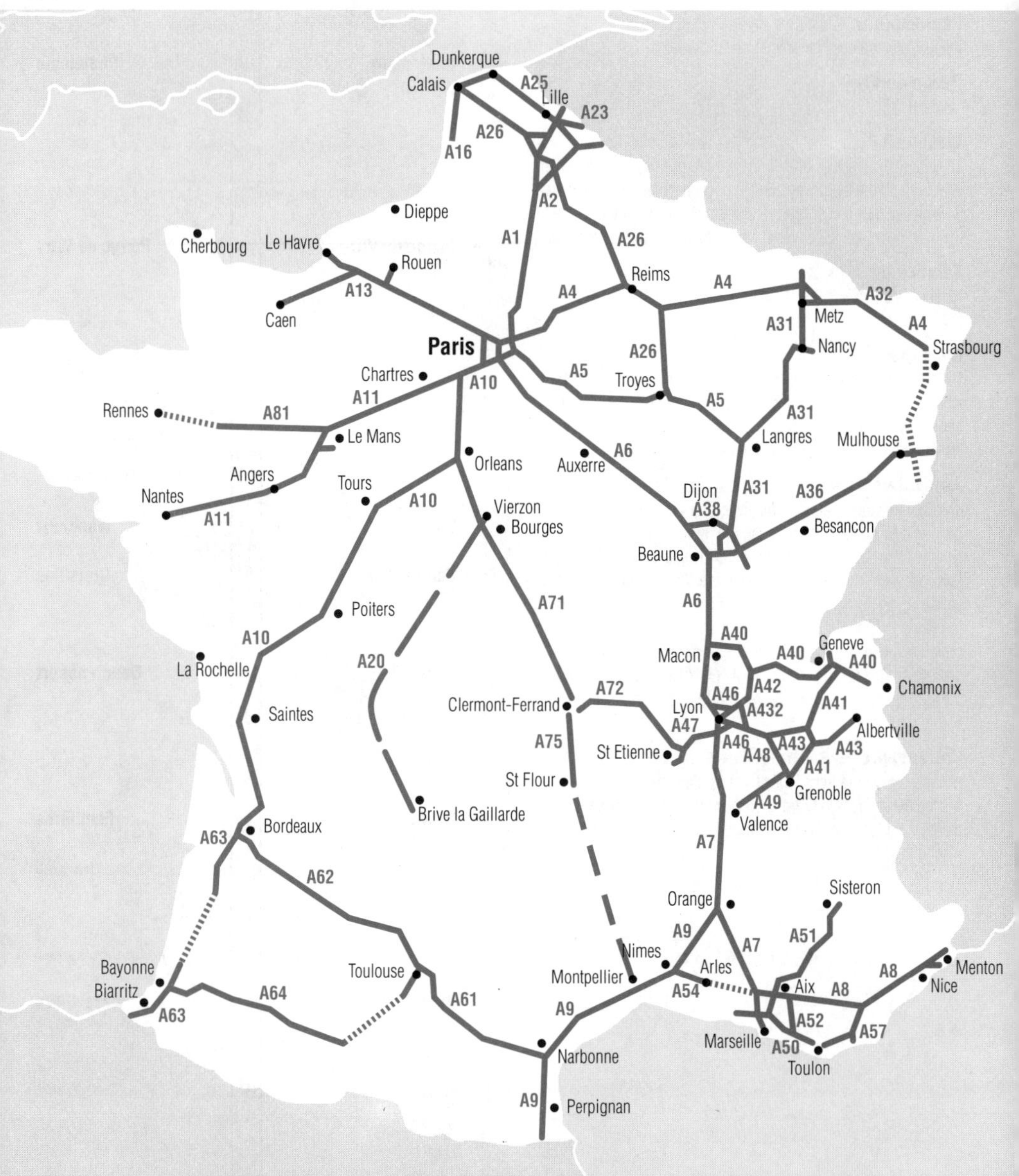
Dunkerque
Calais
A25
Lille
A23
A26
A16
A2
Dieppe
A1
A26
Cherbourg
Le Havre
Rouen
Reims
A4
A32
A13
A4
Metz
Caen
A31
A4
Strasbourg
Paris
Nancy
A26
A5
Troyes
Chartres
A10
A11
A5
A31
Rennes
A81
Le Mans
Langres
Mulhouse
A6
Orleans
Auxerre
Angers
Tours
Dijon
A31
A36
Nantes
A10
A38
A11
Vierzon
Bourges
Besancon
Beaune
A6
Poiters
A71
A40
A10
Geneve
Macon
A40
A40
La Rochelle
A20
A42
Chamonix
A72
A46
A41
Clermont-Ferrand
Lyon
A432
Saintes
A47
Albertville
A75
St Etienne
A46
A43
A48
A43
St Flour
A41
Grenoble
A49
Brive la Gaillarde
Valence
Bordeaux
A63
A7
A62
Sisteron
Orange
A9
A7
A51
Nimes
Bayonne
Toulouse
Arles
A8
Menton
Montpellier
Biarritz
A64
A54
Aix
A8
Nice
A61
A9
A52
A63
A57
Marseille
A50
Toulon
Narbonne
A9
Perpignan

Phalempin
Relais Caféteria des Flandres; no picnic area.

Péage de Vitry
Take a ticket.

Wancourt
Leave the carriageway at exit 15; go straight on, not left, which takes you off the motorway. First you reach a pleasant picnic area with nice planting of shrubs. There is a WC block on this side of the motorway; use the covered footbridge to reach the caféteria.

Saint Leger
Sandwiched between the TGV line and the road, the picnic area is basic but OK.

Maurepas
On a steeply sloping site, cars are directed down to the back where there is a narrow parking area by the fenced-off TGV line, and steps and a ramp up to the WC block in the lorry area. If you want to stop, drive to the end of the site.

Assevillers
The TGV line tunnels under this lively aire which has lots of facilities, and is liable to be busy at lunchtime. There is a Mercure Hotel with a restaurant as you enter the aire; nice planting of lavender and roses along the road to the Arche facilities (24 hour caféteria and newsagents). There is a cash machine. A Caféroute is planned. There is a separate sandwich bar behind the Arche building, and a wooded picnic area at the end of the site. The fuel station is at the far end of the site. A very smart restaurant routier, the first 'specially-for-truck drivers', with an enormous lorry park, is round the back.

Hattencourt ★
A screen of mature trees hides this pleasant aire. A pity it's sandwiched between the TGV line and the motorway, it is nevertheless the best so far on this motorway. Picnic at the end of the site among the trees.

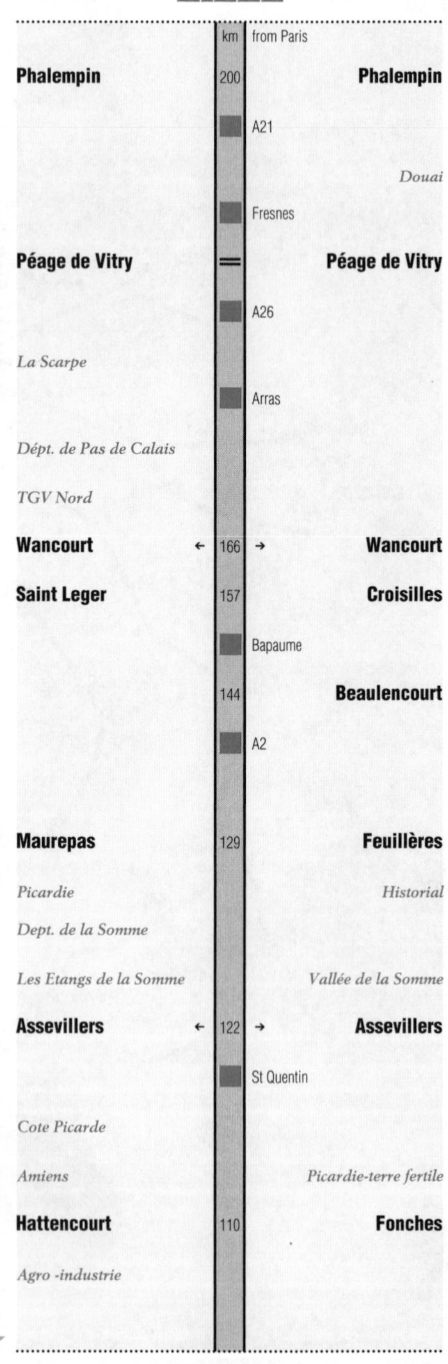

AIRES ROYE ~ LILLE

Phalempin
Relais Caféteria des Flandres.

Péage de Vitry
Pay here.

Wancourt ★
Go off at exit 15, and then bear right to get to the aire. The Relais d'Artois caféteria (open 24 hours) and other facilities serve both sides of the motorway. I couldn't see any space for cars beside the Relais; there is a lorry park there, so use that. Or walk back from car park, which is no fun if it is raining! The caféteria might get pretty crowded if several coaches arrived, but we ate there when it was quiet, and much enjoyed the regional dish, Porc de Picardie, and the local soft cows milk cheese, Maroilles. There is a picnic area beyond the car park.

Croisilles
No picnic area.

Beaulencourt
Despite the extra picnic area at the far end of the site, this is still a small aire.

Feuillères
A small, basic site.

Assevillers *i*
There is a Caféroute (open 24 hours in summer) as you enter the aire; then the Arche facilities which include a caféteria with a nice terrace and a newsagents. The Formule 1 hotel is on this side, Hotel Mercure on the other, and there is a footbridge. The fuel station is at the far end of the site.

Fonches
A good screen of trees, which is just as well as the car parking is all at the front of this fairly basic aire.

Some fine old houses in **Douai** escaped the damage of two world wars.

The slow waters of the Somme have meandered to form ponds, **Les Etangs de la Somme,** some of them strangely rectangular in shape. Around these are ancient peat bogs.

St Quentin became an early place of pilgrimage when a Christian was beheaded here. Portrait painter Quentin de la Tour lived here; his head figures on the brown sign. The town was behind German lines for most of the First World War. Within the ramparts of the castle at nearby **Péronne** is a remarkable modern museum, **L'Historial de la Grande Guerre**.

The sandy coast of Picardy, **La Cote Picarde**, north of the Somme estuary has several seaside resorts, of which Berck is the best known.

Amiens is the capital of the region and centre of the textiles trade. Given its position on the Somme, it is not surprising to learn that the town suffered badly in both world wars. It has the largest Gothic cathedral in France.

Picardie is a plateau crossed by the valleys of the Somme, the Authie and the Canche which flow into the English Channel. **Agro-Industrie**, farming, is intensive; crops, such as sugar beet and cereals on the plateaux, market gardening in the valleys.

Noyon was the birthplace of John Calvin.

The **Chateau de Blérancourt** is where a group of American women, under the leadership of Ann Morgan, based themselves in 1917, to offer what help they could to the devastated north of France. The chateau now houses a museum of Franco-American cooperation.

Goyencourt
Turn right down a narrow path just after entering the aire to the back of this pleasant, but small site.

Tilloloy
Truncated due to the building of the TGV line; well-landscaped , pleasant, but very small.

Ressons
The aire is 300 metres after exit 11. The Arche de Picardie caféteria and separate snack bar outside both have a terrace. No picnic area. The fuel station is at the end of the site.

Bois d'Arsy ★
A pleasant spot, even though the TGV line is very evident. There is a sharp turning right as you enter, leading into a small wood, and then plenty of space.

Longueil Ste Marie
Well back off the road, but small and basic.

Roberval
A pretty minimal aire.

Péage de Senlis
Pay here.

Vemars *i*
Relais Ile de France caféteria, open 24 hours, with a large terrace, and a newsagents. The Travelodge has a restaurant.

Chennevières
Small, but OK.

La Courneuve
No picnic area.

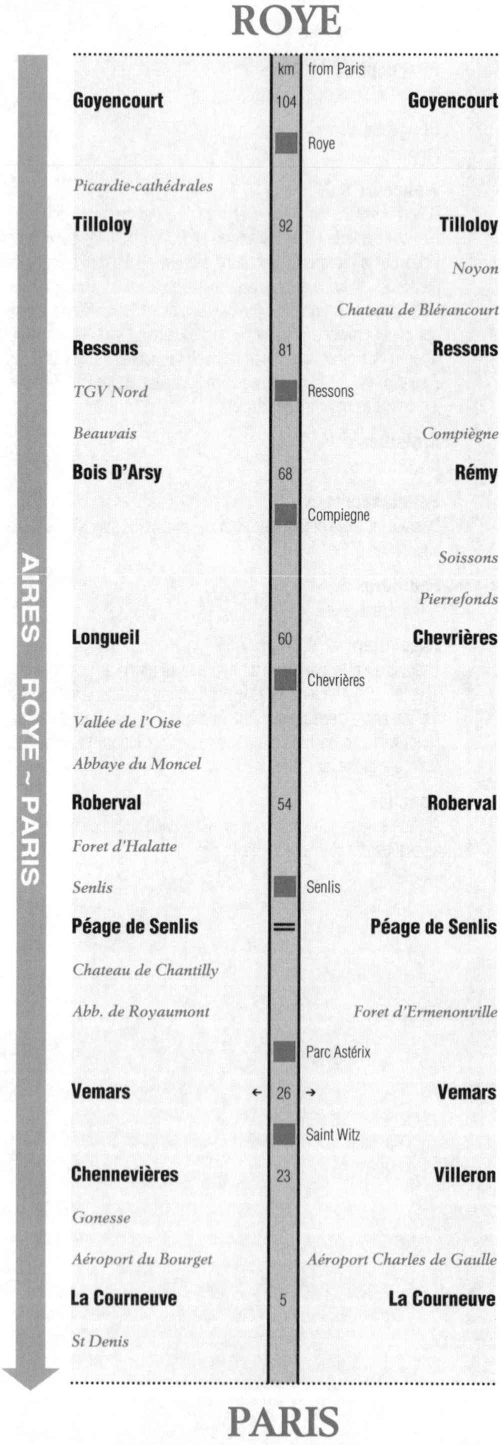

AIRES ROYE ~ PARIS

ROYE

	km	from Paris	
Goyencourt	104		**Goyencourt**
		Roye	
Picardie-cathédrales			
Tilloloy	92		**Tilloloy**
			Noyon
			Chateau de Blérancourt
Ressons	81		**Ressons**
TGV Nord		Ressons	
Beauvais			*Compiègne*
Bois D'Arsy	68		**Rémy**
		Compiegne	
			Soissons
			Pierrefonds
Longueil	60		**Chevrières**
		Chevrières	
Vallée de l'Oise			
Abbaye du Moncel			
Roberval	54		**Roberval**
Foret d'Halatte			
Senlis		Senlis	
Péage de Senlis	=		**Péage de Senlis**
Chateau de Chantilly			
Abb. de Royaumont			*Foret d'Ermenonville*
		Parc Astérix	
Vemars ←	26	→	**Vemars**
		Saint Witz	
Chennevières	23		**Villeron**
Gonesse			
Aéroport du Bourget			*Aéroport Charles de Gaulle*
La Courneuve	5		**La Courneuve**
St Denis			

PARIS

AIRES PARIS ~ ROYE

Goyencourt
A few tables among the trees; basic but OK.

Tilloloy
In a wooded area, with some mature trees.

Ressons
Go off the motorway at exit 11 and then straight ahead, not to the right. The Arche caféteria (open 24 hours) and sandwicherie have a terrace. There is a separate snack bar in summer only. No picnic area.

Rémy ★
A sharp, narrow entrance leads to a nice grassy picnic area among silver birch trees.

Chevrières ★ ★
This is a lovely, large aire in two sections, and the best so far for a picnic.

Roberval ★
A nice position, at a higher level than the motorway on a limestone outcrop; the aire is small, but drive round towards the end of the site to picnic.

Péage de Senlis
Take a ticket.

Vemars *i*
Relais Ile de France caféteria and snack bar, open 24 hours; newsagents; access to the Forte Travelodge and restaurant is by footbridge over the motorway.

Villeron
Small, but pleasant with a nice grassy slope above the aire..

La Courneuve
No picnic area

Fine tapestries were made at **Beauvais** from the 16th century to the outbreak of the Second World War . The cathedral is renowned for its height and apparent defiance of the laws of gravity; and of bombing raids, for when almost the entire centre of the town was destroyed by fire bombs in 1940, it escaped.

The **TGV, Train à Grande Vitesse**, is the celebrated French high speed train. The **TGV Nord** line between Paris and the Channel Tunnel follows the motorway for a major part of its journey.

A fine chateau, a lively town and a forest, where kings of France hunted; **Compiègne**, where the rich and famous guests of Napoleon 111 and Eugenie walked; where in a railway carriage in a clearing, on 11th November 1918, the armistice which ended the First World War was signed. Rebuilt in 1918, **Soissons** has a fine ancient abbey and a cathedral.

The 12th century castle of **Pierrefonds** was restored for Emperor Napoleon 111 by Viollet-le-Duc. This part of the **Vallée de l'Oise** is hardly cultivated, and the motorway passes filled-in and working gravel pits.

Trees from the **Foret d'Halatte** north of Senlis were felled in the 14th century to provide the oak for the roof timbers in the nuns' dormitory in the **Abbaye Royale du Moncel**.

Senlis has a cathedral, medieval streets, ramparts and towers.

In the **Foret d'Ermenonville** there is a pretty chateau where the nature-loving 18th century philosopher, **Jean-Jacques Rousseau** stayed.

Known to many as the capital of French horse racing, **Chantilly** also has a fine **chateau**, and park. In the Great Stables is the **Musée Vivant du Cheval et du Poney**.

The Cistercian **Abbaye de Royaumont** was taken over by a group of Scotswomen during the First World War and used as a hospital.

There is access to the **Parc Astérix** theme park from its own junction on the motorway; a Wild West stockade and Asterix himself, waving from a little hill, are there to entice you in.

The principal airport of Paris is the **Aéroport Charles de Gaulle** at Roissy. 20 years old, its design of central services and moving corridors and escalators leading to satellites is still innovative. It is mildly disconcerting to glimpse the tailfin of a British Airways jet and realise that the runways cross the motorway.

Wealthy 16th century Parisians insisted on having bread sent daily from **Gonesse**, until new methods of fermentation, developed in Paris in the 17th century, led to the manufacture of finer loaves in long moulds.

If you flew into Paris from London in the 1950s, you probably landed at **Le Bourget**; since the building of the Charles de Gaulle airport, its international traffic has gone.

Most of the kings of France were buried in the cathedral at **St Denis**.

La Sentinelle
Bar/buffet in shop.

Hordain
No picnic area; very basic.

Péage de Cambrai
Take a ticket.

Graincourt

Barastre

AIRES BELGIAN BORDER – A1

BELGIUM

	km	from border
		Valenciennes
	■	Lille, A23
La Sentinelle	56	**La Sentinelle**
		Canal à Grands Gaborits
Hordain	40	**Lieu Saint Amand**
Industrie Automobile		
	■	Hordain
L'Escaut		*Cambrai*
Péage de Cambrai	=	**Péage de Cambrai**
	■	Fontaine Notre Dame
	■	A26
Graincourt	20	**Havrincourt**
		Bois d'Havrincourt
		Canal du Nord
Barastre	6	**Rocquigny**

A1

Using your cash/credit card to obtain French francs

La Sentinelle
No picnic area

Lieu St Amand
No picnic area;very basic.

Péage de Cambrai
Pay here.

Havrincourt
Bar/buffet, La Grille
No picnic area.

Rocquigny

Valenciennes is an industrial town on the **Escaut**, a centre for processing sugar beet,

The **Canal à Grands Gabarits** takes extra-large loads.

The large complex just after the **Industrie Automobile** sign is a Peugeot factory.

Cambrai is an industrial town which had the misfortune to be devastated in both world wars.

Part of an extensive network of canals and canalised rivers in northern France, the **Canal du Nord** links the Somme and the Sensée.

Use the Relais Bébé facilities if you are travelling with a baby

Brumath ★ ⛽ 🔧 ♿
The picnic area is at a lower level at the end of the site.

Péage de Schwindratzheim ♿ *i*
Take a ticket here. Space for a picnic.

Gottesheim ♿
A small, neat and tidy aire with the pretty village of Gottesheim behind.

Saverne Eckartswiller ★ ⛽ 🔧 ♿ 🛝 🌳
Picnic in the orchard up behind the aire, but you are asked not to pick the plums!

Quatre Vents ♿
Below the level of the road; small, quite pleasant, with a grassy area at the end.

Schalbach ♿ 🌳
Pleasant but rather basic.

Berg ★ ♿ 🌳
Walk up into the woods to picnic.

Keskastel ⛽ 🔧 ♿ 🌳
Walk up into lovely beech and oak woods at the end of the site to picnic.

Petit Hambach ♿
Small, nice location, but basic.

Péage de Loupershouse *i*
Pay here. WC is in the motorway information building.

Péage de St Avold *i*
Pay here.

Longeville ⛽ 🔧 ♿
There is a vehicle bridge over to the facilities. No picnic area.

Narbefontaine ♿ 🌳
Small, but OK.

Landonvillers ♿
Small, with a nice grassy area.

STRASBOURG

AIRES STRASBOURG ~ METZ

	km	from Metz	
	■	Brumath Sud	
Brumath	140		**Brumath**
	■	Brumath Nord	
Péage de Schwindratz	=		**Péage de Schwindratz**
	■	Hochfelden	
La Plaine D'Alsace			
Gottesheim	122		**Lienbach**
			Canal de la Marne
	■	Saverne	*Saverne*
Saverne-Eckartswiller	112		**Saverne-Monswiller**
Quatre Vents	107		**Danne**
La Petite Pierre			*La Passerelle à Gibiers*
			Le Grès Rose
	■	Phalsbourg	
Parc Regional desVosges			
Schalbach	94		**Katzenkopf**
Berg	86		**Eywiller**
	■	Sarre Union	
Keskastel	74		**Keskastel**
			Canal des Houillères
Sarreguemines			*Sarralbe*
	■	Sarreguemines	
Petit Hambach	62		**Grundwiller**
			Puttelange
Péage de Loup.	=		**Péage de Loup.**
Foret de Farschviller			*Bassin Houiller*
	■	Farebersviller	
	■	Freyming A32	
Carling Petrochimie			*Foret de St Avold*
Péage de St Avold	=		**Péage de St Avold**
	■	St Avold	
Longeville ←	32	→	**Longeville**
Foret de Longeville			
Narbefontaine	24		**Brouck**
La Nied Allemande			
	■	Boulay	
Landonvillers	14		**Landonvillers**
Plateau Lorrain			*La Nied Francaise*

AIRES METZ ~ STRASBOURG

Brumath ★

An inviting grassy dell for picnicing. You have to return to the fuel station if you need the WC.

Péage de Schwindratzheim *i*

Pay here. Space for a picnic.

Lienbach

Small aire, basic but OK.

Saverne Monsviller ★ *i*

There is a tiny snack bar inside the fuel station shop. The picnic area is at the end of the site, overlooking the town. It is nicely kept, and you have a good choice of tables in the shade or in the sun.

Danne

A small, neat aire, well screened from the road; walk up into the woods to picnic.

Katzenkopf

What a varied display of shrubs! There is a view, too.

Eywiller

There is a pedestrian path into the trees; a small, pleasant aire.

Keskastel ★ *i*

A fenced play area, a large expanse of grass or, if you prefer, walk into the woods at the far end of the site to picnic. I was quite impressed by the cleanliness of the WCs in the fuel station; and its not often you find Eau de Cologne next to the liquid soap!

Grundwiller

Small, but pleasant.

Péage de Loupershause

Take a ticket.

Péage de St Avold

Pay here.

Longeville *i* £

Good Relais facilities; restaurant, caféteria, Petit Café (open 24 hours) and newsagents. Disabled access to the building is a bit steep. There is a very short lead in back onto the motorway.

Brouck

A pleasant aspect, the aire sloping to the south.

Landonvillers

Vous etes en Alsace; a landscape of rolling fields, farmed in large strips, and with an occasional hop field. On our journey to Strasbourg, we saw a group of storks in the plain east of the town, and were reminded of the place these birds traditionally have in the lives of Alsatians. Every Spring people ask whether the storks have arrived yet from Africa.

La Plaine d'Alsace is a corridor between the Vosges and the Rhine where the local dialect reminds one of the closeness of Germany; this was indeed part of Germany between 1871 and 1918. Cardinal Rohan (he of the Queen's necklace, shady Mme de la Motte and three musketeers fame) was responsible for the rebuilding of the splendid episcopal **Chateau de Rohan** at **Saverne** after a fire.

The **Canal de la Marne au Rhone** passes through the centre of Saverne.

The Northern Vosges are red sandstone, **grès rose**, those in the south are granite. Above the motorway, impressively landscaped as it cuts through the Vosges, is the **Passerelle à Gibier**, a wooden bridge enabling animals, and walkers, to cross to the other side.

The **Parc Naturel Régional des Vosges du Nord** covers a large area, including not only flora and fauna but ruined castles and fortresses and parts of the Maginot line fortifications. War memorials in this region are as likely to commemorate the war of 1871 as the wars of this century.

A famous 19th century French general by the name of Mouton (sheep) came from **Phalsbourg**; on one occasion Napoleon 111 is said to have exclaimed 'Mon Mouton est un lion!'

In a commanding position in the heart of the Petites Vosges, **La Petite Pierre** is a centre for tourists, especially walkers.

Sarreguemines has been famous for 200 years for its colourful enamelled earthenware.

I like the contrast of church spires and factory chimneys side by side against the sky at **Sarralbe**. There are important salt mines nearby.

The **Canal des Houillères de la Sarre** is the canal of the coal-mining region.

Quite a sight to the right of the motorway is the lake at **Puttelange aux Lacs**, its edge almost completely taken up by anglers cabins jutting out into the water on small square jetties.

The motorway sweeps down from the forests to the large coal-mining centre (**bassin houiller**) of **Freyming Merlebach** which has the highest yield in Europe. From the motorway you can see the cooling towers of the Emile Huchet power station which uses a combination of gas and coal. The vast **Carling petrochemical** complex in the **Foret de St Avold** includes several factories using coal, and a cokeworks.

The **Foret de Longeville** is part of the forest around St Avold. The small river **La Nied Allemande** rises in Germany. The **Lorraine plateau** is mainly forested; its towns, industries, villages and agriculture are in its basins and depressions.

Charly Oradour
A small, exposed site.

Metz St Privat
The bar/buffet is in the fuel station shop. Disabled access is to the WC only and there is no picnic area.

Péage de Briey
Take a ticket.

Bois St Martin ★ ★
You might pass this aire by; it looks very small. But there is a large, well-managed wooded area for walks and picnics at the back with lots of tables.

Bois de la Ronce ★
Turn into the woods as you enter the aire; not as large as the previous aire, but lovely.

Verdun St Nicolas *i*
Caféroute in the parking area, at the foot of the escalator up to the excellent facilities on the bridge. These include a sandwicherie, surprisingly spacious Arche caféteria and stylish grill-restaurant, and a newsagents, but they are not accessible to the disabled.

Les Genièvres ★
Turn into the wooded area to picnic, this is a lovely location.

Jubécourt ★
Another wooded site, but more grass here than in the last few aires.

Fontaine d'Olive ★
Drive into the dark spruce woods; a very large site.

Valmy le Moulin *i*
The bar/buffet is in the fuel station shop and has a terrace. When seen major work was in progress to provide a picnic area; it looked as if it would be very pleasant and should now be in use.

La Noblette ★
Drive back through the pine trees on the gravelled path which winds around the site, and you have a choice of wooded or grassy areas.

Reims Champagne *i*
The Relais facilities include a restaurant, caféteria (open 24 hours), and shop.

La Vesle
Close to the road, small but OK.

Péage de Reims

METZ

AIRES METZ – REIMS

	km	from Paris
Charly-Oradour	320	**La Crouée**
	■	A31
	■	Semecourt
Big Bang Schtroumph		
Metz St Privat	305	**Metz St Privat**
	■	Auboué
Fort de Fermont		
Péage de Briey	=	**Péage de Briey**
	■	Jarny
Briey		
Bois St Martin	291	**Le Bois de Labry**
Bois de la Ronce	276	**L'Epinotte**
Champ de Bataille		
	■	Fresne sur Woevre
Verdun St Nicolas ←	262	→ **Verdun St Nicolas**
Vallée de la Meuse		
	■	Verdun St Mihiel
Les Genièvres	245	**La Rouge Haie**
	■	Voie Sacrée *Voie Sacrée*
Jubécourt	223	**Rarecourt**
Foret d'Argonne		
Fontaine d'Olive	218	**Fontaine d'Olive**
Ste Menehould		*Vallée de l'Aisne*
Braux		
	■	Ste Menehould
Valmy le Moulin	208	**Valmy Orbeval**
Moulin de Valmy		
La Norette	186	**Charme**
	■	St Etienne au Temple
		N.D. de l'Epine
		Chalons sur Marne
	■	Chalons
	■	A26
Reims Champagne ←	160	→ **Reims Champagne**
La Vesle	151	**L'Espérance**
Péage de Reims	=	**Péage de Reims**
Reims		

REIMS

AIRES REIMS ~ METZ

La Crouée ♿
Basic, close to road.

Metz St Privat ⛽ ✕ ♿
4 Pentes grill and snack bar, the small first floor room is divided in two. OK, but in need of a facelift. Access is by outside steps; not possible for wheelchairs. The WCs are under the building; unisex, small and rather smelly, even though they had just been cleaned when we visited.

Péage de Briey *i*
Pay here.

Le Bois de Labry ★ ★
A neat, wooded aire, well screened from road, for walks or picnics. A track leads back into the woods to a parking spot beside each table.

L'Epinotte ★
There are sheltered picnic tables, a large grassy area and a good view back to the Ardennes.

Verdun St Nicolas ★ ★ ⛽ ✕ ♿ *i* £
This is a pleasant wooded aire; there are some tables among the trees, and you can walk into the woods. Use the escalator up to the bridge.

La Rouge Haie ★
A track leads into a small wooded area to the side.

Rarecourt

Fontaine d'Olive ★ ★
Drive back among the dense spruce trees. This is the best spot for a picnic or a walk in the woods so far coming from Paris; spoilt by litter the day we visited it.

Valmy Orbeval ⛽ ✕ ♿
The bar-buffet is in the fuel station shop.

Charme ★
Preceded by decorative coloured shaped panels alongside the road; to guard against boredom. Screened from the road by a bank of pine trees, this is a wooded picnic area. Globes, cubes, pyramids and totem poles join the panels after the aire! There are several sections of panels of this sort. One section gives the impression from an angle of being a bank of summer flowers; another is of autumnal colours.

Reims Champagne ⛽ ✕ ♿ *i*
Lorry park and fuel station only on this side of the motorway; the main services, Relais, are on the far side, with vehicular access by a bridge.

L'Espérance
A medium sized aire, quite OK.

Péage de Reims
Pay here.

Wallibi Big Bang Schtroumph is an amusement park 10 kms north of Metz.

The **Maginot Line**, a line of forts protecting the territorial gains of the First World War in the east of France was in place before the Second; when invasion came the line, of course, was not where it needed to be. The **Fort de Fermont** near Longwy is open to the public, and the visit involves a 2-hour tour by train.

One of the brown signs for **Briey** shows the church of St Gengoult and the new town, La Cité Radieuse, designed by Le Corbusier and built in 1960 to cope with the population growth due to the expansion of the iron and steel industry in the 1950s. The **Meuse**, cutting through the Ardennes, past Verdun and Sedan, continues northeastwards through Belgium and the Netherlands before reaching the sea.

Hundreds of thousands of French and Germans died in the First World War Battle of **Verdun**, which has left its mark not only visibly but in French consciousness. There is much to see and to think about if you drive up into the hills behind the town. Forests have replaced the lunar landscape seen in old film footage, but mine craters and trenches are still there among the trees. Forts, too, and command posts; but not villages. They disappeared in the fighting, and only memorial stones remain. **Voie Sacrée**, the 'sacred way'; the road from Bar-le-Duc to Verdun which was the lifeline of the French army during the battles in 1916, witnessed a constant stream of troops, equipment, munitions and supplies throughout the battle.

The valley of the **Aisne** marks the eastern edge of the Champagne region. To the west the land is chalk, to the east limestone. The **Foret d'Argonne** is on the border of Champagne and Lorraine.

The '**Ensemble 18ième siècle**' at **Ste Menehould** includes the Town Hall; its beauty didn't stop 19th century 'planners' putting the main road through the square in front of it.

Once a military headquarters, the chateau at **Braux Ste Cohière** is used today for a variety of cultural events. The **Moulin de Valmy** has been reconstructed on the hill where a famous victory by the French over the Prussian army took place in 1871.

Notre Dame de l'Epine is a fine, pale stone Gothic church on the scale of a cathedral, unusual for the uneven height of its two spires, which has been a place of pilgrimage since the Middle Ages.

Chalons sur Marne is an administrative and industrial centre, with sugar beet and champagne important products. The cathedral occupies an attractive site on a loop on the river.

A26 junctions are on either side of Reims; if you are turning off the A4 be careful to take the right one! For Calais the junction is to the west of the city. The motorway runs no more than 400 yards from the **cathedral**. Close to the motorway, too, the 11th century **Basilique St Rémi** is the one with spires, the cathedral having towers.

Pay here

Gueux ⛽ ✕ ♿
The bar/buffet is in the fuel station shop.

Lhery
Small but adequate.

Péage de Dormans
Pay here.

Le Tardenois ⛽ ✕ ♿
The Relais facilities include a caféteria with a terrace and a shop. Pleasant, spoilt by not having enough toilets to cope with both sides of the motorway, especially when a coach party turns up. No picnic area.

La Talmouse /⊓\
Small, but OK

Péage de Montreuil
Pay here.

Changis sur Marne ⛽ ✕
4 Pentes caféteria; disabled facilities at fuel station only. No picnic area.

Previlliers
The picnic area is basic but OK.

Péage de Coutevroult
Pay here.

Bussy St Georges ⛽ ✕ ♿
The bar/buffet is in the fuel station shop. No picnic area.

AIRES REIMS ~ PARIS

REIMS

	km	from Paris
	■	Reims Tinqueux
	■	A26
		Parc Rég Mont Reims
Gueux	130	**Vrigny**
Champagne Ardennois		
Lhery	115	**Romigny**
	■	Dormans
Péage de Dormans	=	**Péage de Dormans**
		Epernay
Le Tardenois ←	97	→ **Le Tardenois**
	■	Chateau Thierry
		Chateau Thierry
La Talmouse	77	**La Fontenelle**
Péage de Montreuil	=	**Péage de Montreuil**
	■	Montreuil
Changis sur Marne	57	**Ussy sur Marne**
Vallée de la Marne		
	■	St Jean
		Jouarre
Previlliers	43	**Vaucourtois**
Meaux		*Provins*
Ile de France		*Vallée du Grand Morin*
	■	A140
Péage de Coutevroult	=	**Péage de Coutevroult**
	■	Eurodisney
Bussy St Georges	27	**Ferrières**
A104 La Francilienne	■	
Guermantes		*Foret de Ferrières*
	■	A104 La Francilienne
Champs Sur Marne		

PARIS

Vrigny
There is a good patch of grass behind the fuel station.

Romigny ★
Small, but with some trees so quite pleasant.

Péage de Dormans *i*
Pay here.

Le Tardenois *i*
There is a covered footbridge to the facilities across the motorway, not accessible to the disabled.

La Fontenelle
A gravel track leads to tables at the back of this smallish site.

Péage de Montreuil
Pay here.

Ussy sur Marne
Bar/buffet in fuel station; pedestrian access to the woods at the back of the site.

Vaucourtois
Interesting location with nodding donkeys in the surrounding fields; oil is drilled here. Basic but OK.

Péage de Coutevroult
Pay here. Go to Carte Bleu booths to throw correct money into net; pay attendant at booths to the right.

Ferrières
4 Pentes grill and caféteria.

Wild boar and roe deer roam in the forests of oak, beech and chestnut of the **Parc Régional de la Montagne de Reims**. The **Route de Champagne** takes the driver through pretty villages and the impressive sight of hectares of vineyards on the north, east and south facing slopes of the mountain. These are also visible from the motorway. Champagne is stored in 'galleries', carved out of chalk, some of which date from Roman times.

'**Ville sacre**' is a reference to the fact that Kings of France were traditionally crowned at **Reims**.

A town principally associated with champagne, **Epernay** is a good centre for exploring the Montagne de Reims vineyards.

There are several **memorials** along the A4, **war cemetaries** and other reminders of battles in this century and the last in eastern France. The Monument Notre Dame de la Marne, erected in the autumn of 1914 to celebrate, not so much a victory as a halting of invasion, is north of Meaux; north of the motorway just before the Aire de la Talmouse there is an American memorial to those who died taking Hill 204, in July 1918.

The Champagne vineyards extend to **Chateau Thierry**, and there is a champagne cooperative. The great writer of fables, La Fontaine, was born here,

The **Marne** is a green, chalky river, in a landscape of rolling wheat fields, sugar beet, small woods and occasional orchards.

There has been a women's abbey at **Jouarre** since the 7th century; the crypt dates from then and is one of the oldest religious monuments in France.

A Gothic cathedral, a 13th century tithe barn, the Archbishop's palace and superb gardens designed by Le Notre are worth discovering in **Meaux**.

The **Grand Morin** river winds its way up from the Brie region through a wooded valley with meadows and orchards to join the Marne near Coupvray where you can visit Louis Braille's childhood home.

It might amuse you to know that the colours at **Disneyland** have been painted brighter here than in the Florida and California versions to compensate for dull European skies. No way of disguising the cold of European winters has been discovered, though. It is boasted that the 'cast members'are always smiling!

The red rose of **Provins** was adopted by supporters of the Lancastrian cause during the War of the Roses; the Duke of Lancaster was married to the widow of a Count of Champagne and introduced it to his troops.

To the south of the motorway lies the Forest of **Ferrières** and, on its northern edge, the chateau. Designed for James de Rothschild in the 1830s by the architect of London's Crystal Palace, Joseph Paxton, it is an extraordinary building blending Renaissance style and modern materials and techniques. **Guermantes,** a mainly 17th century chateau, can be seen to the north of the motorway, just east of the Aire de Ferrières.

PARIS (N6)

The A5 begins at the outer Paris ring road, the A104 La Francilienne. There will eventually be a second point of entry further west along the A104 to provide closer access to the A6.

Aire de Service

There is a McDonalds fast food restaurant here, one of only two as far as I know on the French motorway system.

Péage de Montereau

Take a ticket.

Les Jonchets - La Grande Paroisse

A large fuel station here, and an excellent shop in a separate spacious building. Facilities include Fax and Minitel machines; for lorry drivers there is cable TV and a laundry! The wooded site is not large, fitted in between the motorway and the TGV line, but an exercise track is planned. With a roundabout at each end of the site, you can drive back to the services if you wish.

Les Rasets ★

There are echoes of the First World War in the sculpture and design of this medium-sized aire, and of the one on the opposite side of the motorway. Even the WCs and the telephone are camouflaged, the former a stainless steel block inside a white-tiled pillbox! There is a point relaxe, and an exercise track is planned.

Montard

Villeneuve-l'Archeveque

Tommelles

St Pouange

AIRES PARIS ~ TROYES

	km	from Paris (periphérique)
		Réau
TGV	38	
Aire de Service	=	**Aire de Service**
TGV		*Vaux le Vicomte*
		St Germain Laxis
Melun		
Montereau Fault Yonne		*Blandy*
		Chatillon
		Donnemarie Dontilly
Moret sur Loing		
Les Jonchets-La Grande Paroisse	64	**Les Jonchets-Les Recompenses**
		Forges
Fontainebleau		
La Bassée et le Montois		*La Motte Tilly*
		Marolles Sur Seine
Les Rasets	81	**Gravon**
Vallée de l'Yonne		
Sens		
Aqueduc de la Vanne		
		A160
Montard	102	**Montaphilant**
Villeneuve-l'Archeveque	118	**Villeneuve–Vauluisant**
		Vulaines
Tommelles	141	**Fontvannes**
		Torvillers
St Pouange	155	**La Coloterie**

TROYES

Aire de Service

Péage de Montereau
Pay here.

Les Jonchets - Les Recompenses
★

Set in birch woods, an aire with lots of parking and leisure space. The pleasing design of the fuel station includes a sunken courtyard outside, colonnades and tasteful planting of shrubs. You can return to the fuel station from the end of the site.

Gravon ★ ★

Lovely view over the Seine valley from the back of this spacious, well-designed aire which has the same theme as the Aire des Rasets. Drive round to the back to escape TGV noise which is quite intrusive despite being on the far side of the motorway! Exercise facilities are planned.

Montaphilant

Villeneuve-Vauluisant

Fontvannes

La Coloterie

The Melun - Sens section of the A5 follows the line of the **TGV**. Two lines actually meet close to the St Germain Laxis exit. The trains are visually attractive, frequent, fast - and noisy, as warning signs point out. This could be quite distracting for drivers and affects picnic areas on the south side of the motorway in particular.

The large industrial complex to the north of the motorway near the intersection of the A5a and A5b is **SNECMA**, the French manufacturer of military aircraft.

The interior of the chateau of **Vaux le Vicomte**, built by Le Vau for a 17th century Minister of Finance, is sumptuous. The formal gardens, designed by Le Notre, and the coach room, are renowned.

The attractive town of **Blandy** in the Brie region was built around an imposing pentagonal fortress.

To the east of **Melun** is the region which gives its name to surely the best known French cheese, Brie; it is indeed made in the town. To the west is the beautiful Forest of Fontainebleau

The town of **Montereau Fault Yonn**e is situated where the Yonne flows (old French 'fault') into the Seine. Historically it has always had strategic importance, being at the point where Ile de France, Champagne and Burgundy meet.

Moret sur Loing is where English painter Sisley spent the last few years of his life. The narrow main street has, at each end, a fine medieval gate, much of the wall remains, and the old streets near the keep buzz with restoration work.

A hunting lodge in the 12th century, added to, extended and restored over the years, the chateau of **Fontainebleau** holds memories of such diverse characters as Thomas Becket, Louis XIII, XIV and XV, Napoleon and General Patton! Its variety of historical and architectural interest, together with its delicate interior, make it as worthy of a visit as Versailles. Among the oak, beech, hornbeam, birch and Scots pine in the surrounding forest are sandy clearings, rocky outcrops, caves and gorges.

When you see the sign for **La Bassée et Le Montoi**s the motorway is close to the viaduct over the Seine; La Bassée is the flood plain of this stretch of the great river and Le Montois the wooded slopes which rise from it to the Brie plateau. Hidden in a fold in these hills is the town of **Donnemarie Dontilly** and a little further to the east in La Bassée is the 18th century chateau of **La Motte Tilly**.

The **Yonne** is navigable at this point, and to beyond Auxerre, an important means of communication and trade for Burgundy through the ages.

One of the great Gothic cathedrals of France is at **Sens**, a reminder of the former importance of that town, rather than Paris, as a centre of Christendom in France.

The Roman **Aqueduc de la Vanne** can be glimpsed to the south of the motorway at the junction with the A160; a better view of it is obtained from that road.

Troyes Fresnoy ★ ★

There are very good facilities here; a Relais cafeteria, cafe/bar and boutique. The roundabout at the entrance to the aire means that you can return to the fuel station from the extensive picnic area. Oak woods and a pleasant grassy area with point relaxe exercises.

Mondeville ★

A rather exposed but pleasant site, with a good view of the vineyards. The circular design allows you to return to the centre and to the WC block from your picnic spot. There are point relaxe exercises.

Chateauvillain Val Marnay

Quite an attractive picnic area then a tunnel for cars to get to the facilities on the far side of the motorway.

Le Bois Moyen

Heavily wooded at the back, there are steps up to a small picnic area among the trees.

AIRES TROYES ~ A31 (LANGRES)

TROYES

	km	from Paris
		St Thibault
		A26
La Seine		*Lac de la Foret de l'Orient*
Troyes Fresnoy ←	168	→ **Troyes le Plessis**
		Vitraux de l'Aube
		Magnant
		Bar sur Aube
		Cristal d'art de Bayel
Mondeville	203	**Champignol**
		Foret de Clairvaux
Chatillon-sur-Seine		
		Ville-sous-la-Ferté
L'Aube		
		Colombey les deux Eglises
Chateauvillain Marnay←	228	→ **Chateauvillain Orges**
Foret de Chateauvillain		
		Chaumont-Semoutiers
		Nogent en Bassigny
Le Bois Moyen	247	**Le Champ à la Croix**
		Vallée de la Marne
		Langres

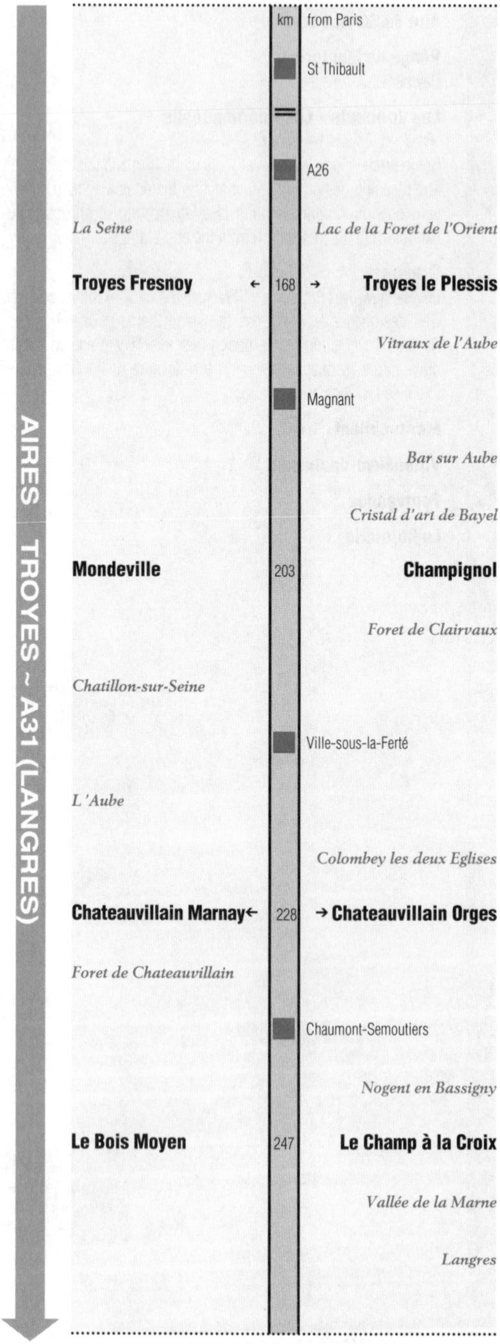

A31 (LANGRES)

In a children's play area

The start of an exercise track

RELAIS W

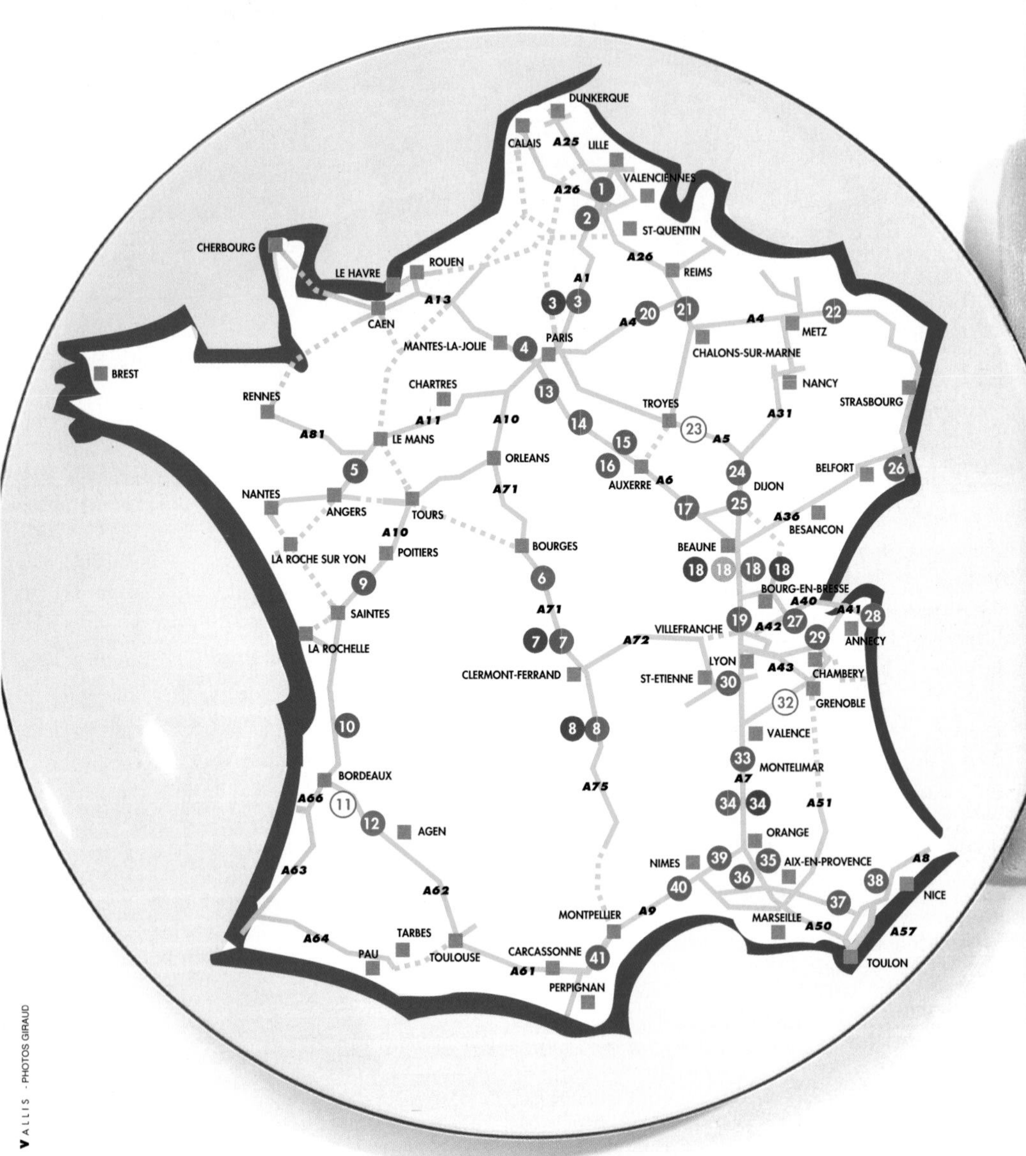

FRANCE CONSEIL VALLIS - PHOTOS GIRAUD

ere you find quality

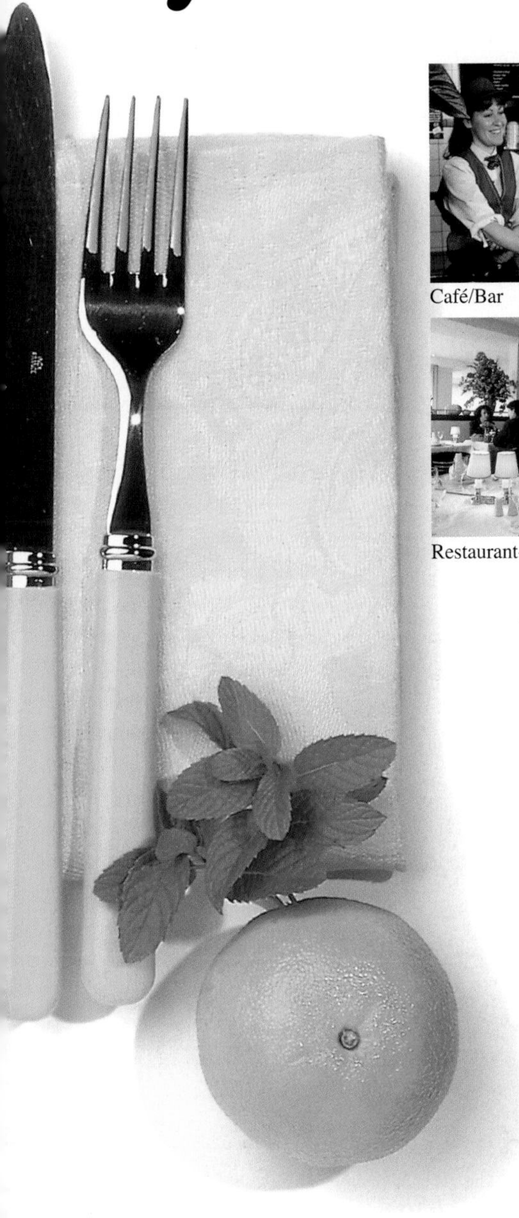

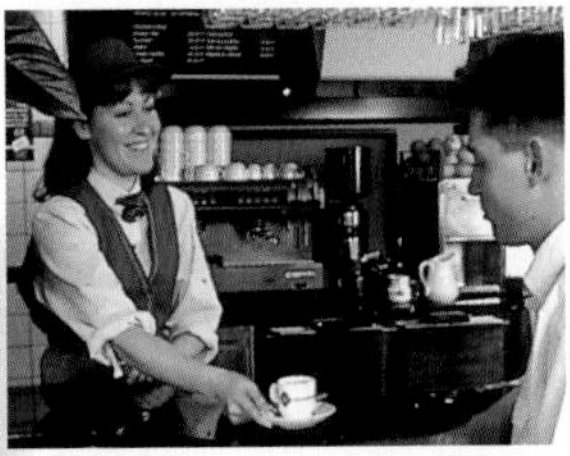

Café/Bar

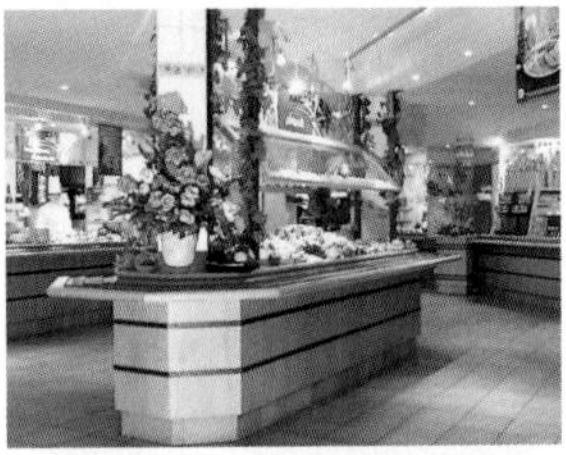

Cafeteria

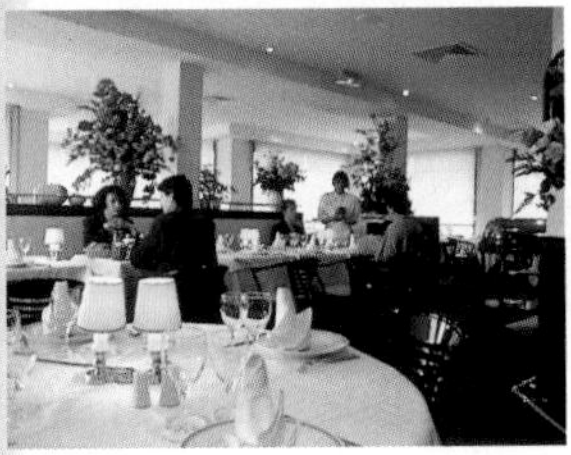

Restaurant-Brasserie

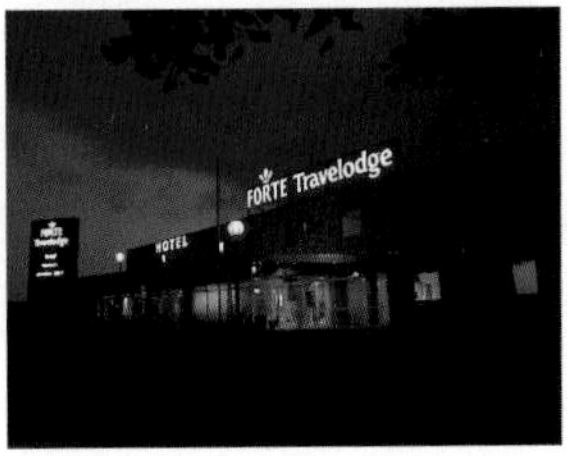

Hotel

Under the sign of RELAIS, discover on France's motorways a whole range of catering formulas, for all tastes and budgets : Bar/Cafés, Cafeterias, high-speed Catering and «waiter service» Restaurants-Brasseries. There is the same quality of attention in each of these : meticulous welcome and service, balanced and varied regional cuisine.

Relais

FORTE

me

The memorial at the Aire de Curney, A6

The vineyards of Beaune seen from the Aire de Savigny, A6

Troyes le Plessis ★

A lovely wooded picnic area, well back from the road, and pedestrian access to the Relais facilities on the other side of the motorway.

Champignol ★

What a view of the slopes of southern Champagne you get as you reach this aire; you can almost touch the vines. A rather exposed but pleasant site, with point relaxe exercises.

Chateauvillain Orges ★

La Crocade bar/buffet (24 hours) in the fuel station shop, and a separate Caferoute. The picnic area is well planted and has very good shade.

Le Champ à la Croix

A pleasant picnic area.

The motorway crosses the river **Seine**, swelled by the waters of the **Aube**, south of Troyes. That river gives its name to the region, renowned for its stained glass windows, (**vitraux**).

The **Lac de la Foret d'Orient** is a centre for leisure and outdoor pursuits not, as the name suggests, in the east but near a former garrison of the Knights Templar. There is a wild life reserve at the northern end, with an observation post.

The motorway runs through the southern part of **Champagne**; you will see plenty of vineyards to remind you where you are!

The site of a Roman fortified town, but with no trace left of that, **Bar sur Aube** has some nice medieval houses.

Chatillon sur Seine is an old feudal town in a pleasant situation by the river.

Fine glassware has been produced in **Bayel** since the 17th century.

The famous Abbaye de **Clairvaux** was founded by St Bernard in the forest of the same name.

President/General de Gaulle is buried in the cemetery at **Colombey les Deux Eglises**, where he had a much loved country home.

The **Foret de Chateauvillain et d'Arc** is part of the large forested region west of Langres.

At the western approach to **Chaumont** is an imposing railway viaduct.

Surgical instruments and cutlery are made at **Nogent en Bassigny.**

Langres is at the south western edge of the Champagne Ardennes region, a gateway into Burgundy from the east, its medieval ramparts looking out over the plain reminding one of its former strategic importance.

PARIS

Les Lisses ★
Relais de l'Essonne caféteria; no picnic facilities.

Nainville ★
Pleasant wooded site with motorway information point in summer.

Péage de Fleury *i*
Take a ticket. Travelling through in August we were handed a bag of freebies including iced cans of drink; very welcome. The tourist information office is just before the toll booths, tyre pressure check after.

Achères la Foret *i*

Villiers ★ ★
An imaginative play area - send the children to look for the ox and cart - and a lovely view. There is an interesting sculpture ensemble in bronze among the Mediterranean Pines, and well-displayed samples of soil from the Forest of Fontainebleau. Point relaxe, too.

Nemours *i*
Lots of facilities, including Relais Bébé. Relais de Nemours grill and caféteria (open 24 hours) on the bridge. Snack bar at ground level in summer. Tunnel for car access to Altea hotel on far side of motorway.

Sonville ★

Liard ★ ★
Take the unmade track beyond the main tarmac one, and you will be far away from the road for comfort. The excellent play area, where there is entertainment for children in summer, has a lunar theme. Point relaxe exercises.

Le Parc Thierry ★ ★
A more spacious wooded site, with plenty of tracks for cars leading back into the trees. Point relaxe exercises.

Les Chataigniers ★ ★
Space to walk in the woods here. Drive down the track to the back to be well away from the road, but access to the disabled facilities is from the front of the aire only.

La Réserve
Relais de l'Auxerrois grill and caféteria.

La Racheuse ★
Small; take the gravel track to tables back in woods.

La Biche ★ ★
Space to walk in the woods here; well off the road, and popular.

AIRES PARIS ~ AUXERRE

	km	from Paris
		Rungis Orly
		Evry
	■	N104 La Francilienne
Les Lisses	22	**Villabé**
Valleé de l'Essonne		*Vaux le Vicomte*
Nainville	35	**St Sauveur**
	■	Cely
		Barbizon
Péage de Fleury ←	=	→ **Péage de Fleury**
	52	**Arbonne**
Milly la Foret		*Foret de Fontainebleau*
Achères la Forêt	58	**Achères**
	■	Ury
		Fontainebleau
		Moret sur Loing
Villiers	65	*Nemours*
	■	Fontainebleau
Larchant		
Nemours ←	74	→ **Darvault**
Sonville	86	**Floée**
Liard	91	**Egreville**
Le Parc Thierry	103	**La Roche**
Chateau St Fargeau		*Sens*
	■	Courtenay
Les Chataigniers	115	**Les Chênes**
La Réserve	123	**La Couline**
		Joigny
	■	Joigny
La Racheuse	132	**La Loupière**
	145	**Les Patures**
La Biche	150	
	■	Auxerre Nord

AUXERRE

Villabé
Excellent fuel station shop; well-stocked, good coffee area, good-sized WCs. Beyond the fuel station is a Burger King.

St Sauveur
Hardly more than a lay-by, no picnic facilities.

Péage de Fleury *i*
Pay here. Footbridge over the toll booths to the facilities on the other side of the motorway,

Arbonne ★
Limited parking; the facilities are across a little stream, in the woods.

Achères

Darvault *i*
As you drive into this aire, you pass the Hotel Altea. La Ferme restaurant and other facilities are on the covered bridge, or, as in the case of the Relais Bébé, on the other side of the motorway. The fuel station is at the end of the aire.

Floée
Small site.

Egreville ★
Point relaxe again here.

La Roche ★ ★
A large, wooded site; good climbing apparatus for children; very pleasant.

Les Chenes ★
If you want a break before tackling the Paris conurbation, stop here, or at one of the next two aires. Limited parking apart from in the woods, but caravans, as well as cars, are allowed to drive into the wooded area here.

La Couline
The Relais de l'Yonne caféteria and shop are quite small; avoid it if there are coaches in the car park!

La Loupière ★ ★
More spacious than the two previous aires.

Les Patures ★

As at Covent Garden in London, the main fruit and vegetable market, Les Halles, has moved out of the capital, to **Rungis**.

The older of the two main airports of Paris is **Orly**, the other being Charles de Gaulle at Roissy.

Evry, the administrative centre of the Essonne, was one of 5 new towns designated by the French authorities in the mid 1960s to channel urban growth away from the centre of Paris. What the French did not foresee was the attraction of the new town to immigrants, mainly young and working class, from other depressed areas of France. The interior of the chateau of **Vaux le Vicomte**, built by Le Vau for a 17th century Minister of Finance, is sumptuous. The formal gardens, designed by Le Notre, and the coach room merit a visit too.

On the western outskirts of the Forest of Fontainebleau, there is a picturesque wooden market hall at **Milly la Foret**, and the ruins of a 12th century chateau. Jean Cocteau, film-maker, lived here.

Every other house in the centre of **Barbizon** seems to have been the home of one or other of the painters- Rousseau, Millet, Seurat, Sisley, for example - who made it's name famous.

A hunting lodge in the 12th century, added to, extended and restored over the centuries, the chateau of **Fontainebleau** houses memories of such diverse characters as Thomas Becket, Louis X111, X1V and XV, Napoleon and General Patton! Its variety of historical and architectural interest, together with its delightful interior, makes it as worthy of a visit as Versailles.

The scale and beauty of the magnificent **Forest of Fontainebleau** can only be guessed at from the A6 which runs through it's western edge. Among the oak, beech, hornbeam, birch and Scots pine are to be found sandy clearings, rocky outcrops, caves and gorges.Coming out of the Aire de Villiers, the road descends steeply; **Larchant** lies in the valley ahead. It's church **St Mathurin** was a place of pilgrimage for French kings from the 12th to the 17th century.

The sculpture at the Aire de Villiers, an attractive group of lovers, is **Mignonne Allons Voir.**

The pretty Loing joins the Seine just north of **Moret sur Loing**, where the English painter Sisley spent the last few years of his life. The narrow main street has, at each end, a fine medieval gate, much of the wall remains, and the old streets near the keep buzz with restoration work.

Just up the Loing from Moret lies **Nemours**, the ancient capital of Gatinais.One of the great Gothic cathedrals of France is at **Sens**, a reminder of the former importance of that town, rather than Paris, as a centre of Christendom in France.

The imposing 13th century **Chateau St Fargeau** has an interesting connection to Versailles, for it was to here that the Sun King, Louis XIV, exiled his cousin, La Grande Mademoiselle, after she had incurred his displeasure.

Joigny is on the northern edge of Burgundy.

Les Bois Imperiaux ★
A grand name for a fairly small site! Point relaxe exercises.

Venoy Grosse Pierre
Good facilities on both sides of the road, accessible by covered footbridge. On this side, Arche caféteria (open 24 hours) and Caféroute, both with terrace, and newsagents. In summer there is entertainment for children. Nice view.

La Grosse Tour ★
Rather close to the road.

La Couée ★★
Walk in the woods in this large aire; the 'Magic Roundabout' theme in the play area, and the summer entertainment, would be good for small children. Point relaxe.

Montmorency ★
Take the gravel track back into the woods, which are quite extensive. As you leave, look towards the south-west to see a splendid view over Northern Burgundy.

La Chaponne
Aubepain snack bar; no picnic area.

Epoisses ★
This is a fairly new site, set well back from the road. A 'must' for railway enthusiasts; as you leave the motorway, you drive under the TGV line to Lyon, and the track then runs alongside the aire.

Ruffey

Fermenot ★★
Set back in the woods, with plenty of space. Point relaxe.

Le Chien Blanc ★★
Relais de l'Auxois grill and caféteria. Not only has this aire good services, but they are spaced well apart on a pleasant wooded site in the middle of a beautiful area of France.

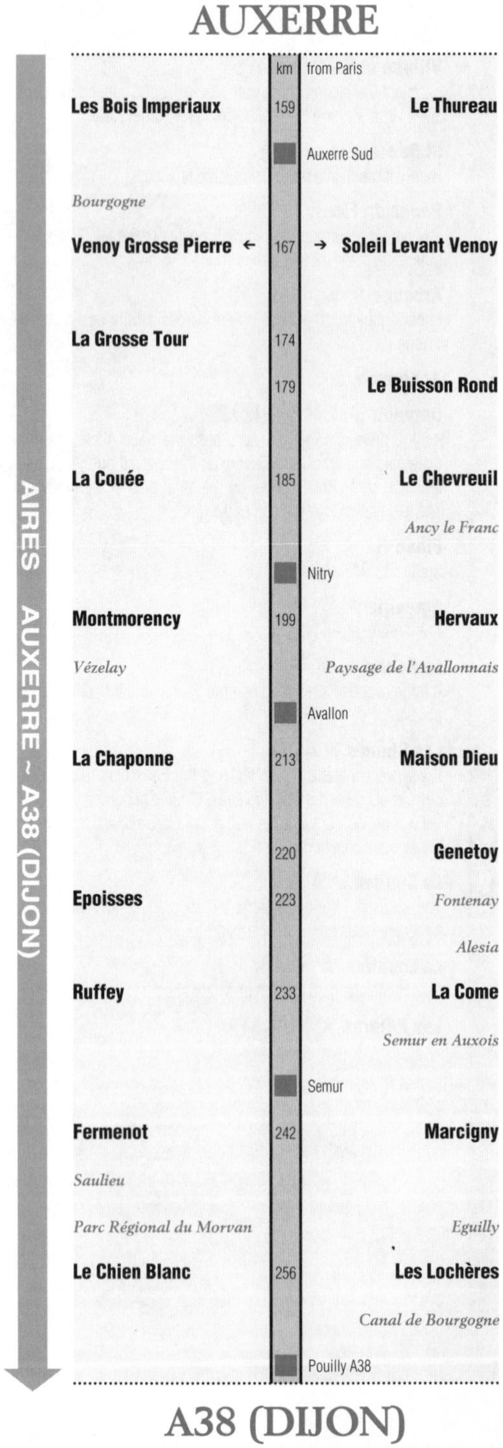

AIRES AUXERRE – A38 (DIJON)

AUXERRE

	km	from Paris
Les Bois Imperiaux	159	**Le Thureau**
		Auxerre Sud
Bourgogne		
Venoy Grosse Pierre ←	167	→ **Soleil Levant Venoy**
La Grosse Tour	174	
	179	**Le Buisson Rond**
La Couée	185	**Le Chevreuil**
		Ancy le Franc
		Nitry
Montmorency	199	**Hervaux**
Vézelay		*Paysage de l'Avallonnais*
		Avallon
La Chaponne	213	**Maison Dieu**
	220	**Genetoy**
Epoisses	223	*Fontenay*
		Alesia
Ruffey	233	**La Come**
		Semur en Auxois
		Semur
Fermenot	242	**Marcigny**
Saulieu		
Parc Régional du Morvan		*Eguilly*
Le Chien Blanc	256	**Les Lochères**
		Canal de Bourgogne
		Pouilly A38

A38 (DIJON)

AIRES A38 (DIJON) ~ AUXERRE

Le Thureau ★
Pleasant, but not much parking space.

Venoy Soleil Levant
Arche grill, caféteria (open 24 hours) and snack bar, with terrace. I have eaten in the grill here; high quality of food and service. Cash dispenser. The Hotel Ibis is at the end of the site.

Le Buisson Rond ★
Not sure of the reference to a round bush! A slightly smaller wooded site, but still a lot of parking among the trees; I spotted a table tennis table towards the end of the site.

Le Chevreuil ★ ★
Some unusual children's games, and space to go for a walk, in this pleasant site.

Hervaux ★ ★
Two lovely wooded areas, both accessible by car, the second from the lorry park. There is entertainment for children in summer in the play area.

Maison Dieu
Arche caféteria (open 24 hours), with terrace, and outside snack bar (summer only).

Genetoy
A small, neat aire, sandwiched between the motorway and a village.

La Come
Very basic, no picnic facilities.

Marcigny ★ ★
Large, wooded site, with access into the woods for cars. Space for a stroll, and point relaxe.

Les Lochères
Drive in front of the fuel station to reach the Relais de l'Auxois caféteria (open 24 hours) and snack bar, both with a terrace. To reach the picnic area at the end of the site, drive behind the fuel station, and follow the signs.

Vous etes en Bourgogne; you are in Burgundy, a vast area of disparate regions , renowned for its churches and monasteries in the Romanesque and Gothic style, its chateaux and its wines. Despite tree-clearing by medieval monks, much of the forests remain. The Yonne and the Cure were logging rivers from the 16th to the early 20th century, and wood distilling, charcoal-making, sawmills and tree nurseries all contribute to the industrial life of the region. Another traditional source of wealth lies in quarrying. **Auxerre**, pronounced 'Ossair', is in the centre of vineyards, **Les Vignobles de l'Auxerrois**, of which Chablis is probably the best-known name.

Described on the panel as 'La Colline Eternelle', **Vézelay** grew up around the abbey church of La Madeleine. When, in the 13th century, it was decided that Mary Magdalene's remains were elsewhere, this little town's prosperity declined! The church, was restored in the 19th century by Viollet le Duc, after 400 years of neglect and decay. Efforts have been made to retain the medieval character of the town itself; like the pilgrims of old, visitors walk up the hill, to be rewarded with a magnificent view from the top.

The Chateau d'**Ancy le Franc** is said to be one of the most beautiful Renaissance houses in Burgundy.

Look out for mistletoe in the trees in the **Paysage de l'Avallonnais** and for buzzards along the verges.

The philosophy behind the **Parc Naturel Régional du Morvan**, and similar French regional parks is the protection of the environment and local culture, the economic growth of the area and the education of those who live there and who visit the area. This particular park, south of Avallon, is a happy mix of forests, lakes, pretty villages with houses made of the local granite, and a varied agriculture.

Familiar to readers of Asterix books, the **Site historique d'Alésia** is reputed to be the place where Caesar's armies laid seige to, and finally defeated, Vertingetorix, leader of the Gauls, in 52 BC. The defeated chief was taken to Rome where he was murdered 6 years later.

A picturesque town, former regional capital, **Semur en Auxois** became part of Burgundy during the 11th century. From its ancient ramparts, there is a fine view.The Cistercian Abbey of **Fontenay** was founded by Evrard, Bishop of Norwich who, on his retirement from work in England, came to end his days here. The abbey, used as a paper mill during the 19th century, has been restored to its former splendour in recent years.

You can't miss the partly-restored **Chateau d'Eguilly**, sadly separated from its pretty village by the motorway. 17th century travellers from Paris to Lyon would stay a night at **Saulieu**; its reputation for good food dates from then.

The A38, A31 and Burgundy canal all lead towards **Dijon**, the largest town in Burgundy. It is the centre of the Burgundy wine trade, also famous for mustard, creme de cassis and gingerbread.

Chaignot ★
Small, wooded, well off the road.

La Garenne ★
As you approach this aire, the road sweeps down across a viaduct to offer you marvellous views. The aire is long and narrow, not large, but it has a covered picnic area for use in wet weather. The WCs are at the far end of the site.

La Foret ★ ★ *i*
After the fuel station, the road winds round to a good sized parking area. Best to walk along the gravel path into the woods, behind the fuel station, where there are tables among the trees. A good picnic area, not immediately noticeable as you drive in.

Le Rossignol ★ ★
Well back from the road, with taped ancient music in summer and a work of art, or maybe I should say nine, entitled Nine Glass Columns. Beyond the picnic area, through gaps in the hedge, there is a large area of unspoilt natural beauty where you can stroll. In the Spring, you may hear the nightingale sing - hence the name - and find many varieties of wild flowers, and butterflies galore. It's a surprising place to find, just yards from the A6. This is the last aire before the descent into the Saone valley, and the heavier traffic you will meet as the A31 joins the A6.

Beaune Tailly *i*
This is a super aire with lots of facilities in lots of space. Among the Relais facilities there is a variety of places where you can eat including two cafeterias (one is open 24 hours) and a restaurant-brasserie, La Bourguignotte. The well-stocked shop sells food as well as newspapers, maps etc. There is a cash dispenser, a Relais Bébé and a regional products shop. It is a well-landscaped site, with several grassy areas where you could picnic if you prefer. If you have time visit the recently-enlarged and refurbished **Archeodrome**. In its **Espace Bourgogne** you can see the splendours of Burgundy on a panoramic screen; in the **Chronoscope** you will experience the creation of the universe in a display of images, sound and special effects; the **Espace Museographe** covers human life from prehistoric times up to the year 1000; the life-size **Reconstructions Park** includes a Gallic farm, a neolithic hut and the fortifications of Alesia. All pretty impressive and great fun.

Curney ★ ★ ★
Another large and pleasant aire. At the far end of the site is a second picnic area among the trees which is unlikely to be crowded. Walk in the woods, or try the point relaxe. The Mémorial pour l' Avenir commemorates the victims of all road traffic accidents, but in particular the French schoolchildren killed in a coach crash on this motorway near Beaune on 31 July 1982. You may not care for the actual memorial, but, in its sentiments, I am reminded of the Mémorial pour la Resistance at Caen in Normandy, which also looks to the future in order to make more bearable some awful event of the past.

A38 (DIJON)

AIRES A38 (DIJON) ~ CHALON

	km	from Paris
Chaignot	269	**La Repotte**
		Commarin
		Chateauneuf
		Dijon
		Viaduc de Pont d'Ouche
La Garenne	279	
Foret de Bligny		
La Foret	285	**Le Creux Moreau**
		Col de Bessey en Chaume
	294	**Le Bois des Corbeaux**
Le Rossignol	298	**Savigny**
		Vignobles de Beaune
		A31
		Beaune
Autun		
Beaune		
Beaune Tailly ←	311	→ **Beaune Merceuil**
		La Saone
Curney	323	**La Loyère**
		Chalon Nord *Chalon*
		Chalon Sud

CHALON

La Repotte ★ ★

The ceramic walls, Murs Mire, are not only nice to look at and touch, but also give different perspectives on Chateauneuf, to be surveyed through its spy holes. The view towards the castle includes a most pleasant rural scene of cattle grazing in unimproved pastures. It's a delightful aire. Turn right just before the WC block for extra parking, picnic space and point relaxe, among the trees or in a field.

Le Creux Moreau ★ ★

Past the fuel station, drive down the gravelled path into the woods, to find a picnic spot. Limited WC block in the picnic area; the ones in the fuel station are excellent, and you could walk back there if needed.

Le Bois des Corbeaux ★

Not large, but a pleasant, wooded site with point relaxe.

Savigny

This was the place, halfway between Lille and Lyon, where President Pompidou opened the link between these two cities in 1970, and a plaque on the rocks beside the road commemorates this feat of engineering. Have a look at La Vigne et le Vin, a colourful, attractive set of ceramics of the wine-making process at the far end of the site, where the only shade is to be found. In summer, the heat of the sun will encourage you to move on, but do stop for the amazing view of the vineyards.

Beaune Merceuil

Apart from the fuel station and a snack bar, all the facilities are on the other side, reached by a footbridge.

La Loyère ★

Point relaxe exercises.

The present day **Chateau de Commarin**, to the north of the motorway, dates from the 17th century, and has two 14th century towers.

The road south has been following the **Canal de Bourgogne** for the last 15 kms or so. Completed in 1832, and 242 kms long, the canal links the rivers Yonne and Saone, following the valleys of the Armancon and the Ouche. Its most exciting feature is the tunnel under the ridge separating the Seine and the Rhone basins, below the junction of the A6 and the A38.

Travelling south, look up to the east, and you will see the village of **Chateauneuf** perched high on a hill. The ruins date from the 12th to the 15th century; hardly new! Travelling north, your first glimpse of the castle will be just after crossing the spectacular **Pont d'Ouche viaduct** which separates the Burgundian pastures from the forests to the south.

A magnificent section of the motorway, the road climbs through the dense **Foret Domanial de Bligny sur Ouche** in the central uplands of France, populated by boar, fox and deer.

From the **Col du Bessey en Chaume**, the road south descends to meet the A31 in the Saone valley. Enjoy the vistas which open up before you, and in particular the expanse of vineyards on the south-facing slopes of Beaune which never fail to impress, however often you see them. Travelling north, it descends to the Pont d'Ouche viaduct and the gentler landscape of the Burgundy Canal.

Although there are many excellent red wines from the **Cotes de Beaune**, the region is especially noted for its fine white wines, among them Montrachet, Meursault and Puligny. Great attractions in and around the town of Beaune itself in November are the traditional wine auctions, tastings and other ceremonies at which the character of that year's vintage is publicly assessed. Further panels advise of the proximity of the great Maconnais and Beaujolais vineyards.

There are a number of Roman remains, and a fine cathedral, in **Autun**, an interesting walled town on the slopes of the Signal de Montjeu hill.

Not only does it have the attraction of being surrounded by vineyards, **Beaune** is a charming town, with ancient walls, and a medieval town centre whose steeply pitched roofs, coloured tiles and gilded vanes are much photographed. There is an interesting wine museum in the Hotel des Ducs, and a fine Romanesque church.

'The cradle of photography' is how **Chalon sur Saone** is described. Nicephore Niepce, an amateur scientist born here in 1755, was the first person to adapt the 17th century camera obscura for photographic purposes by substituting silver chloride paper for the ground glass on which the image was formed in 1816. Daguerre (with whom Niepce was to collaborate) and Fox-Talbot, whose names are maybe better known in this country, did their pioneering work 15 or so years later.

La Ferté
Arche caféteria(open 24 hours) with a terrace, and a summer-only snack bar. There are two picnic areas, both rather exposed to the road.

Jugy ★★★
For the past 10 miles this aire has been heralded by large colourful toadstools, mushrooms and cheery, waving figures along the side of the motorway. If you are travelling with children, it would be a pity to miss this aire, an extraordinary fungal kingdom; not only the childrens' play area but the tables, seats, bins, everything imaginable follows the toadstool theme. You will find clowns here in summer. It is all great fun, and informative too, with clear and accurate diagrams of edible and not so edible fungi. Inadequate WC block in children's play area; use the one in the main aire. The site is sizeable, and there is a wooded area at the back.

Farges
Small, near the road.

Macon St Albain *i*
Large and busy aire; lots of parking and plenty of space for a picnic. There is a covered picnic area near the main facilities, a cash machine and a Caféroute. Among the facilities on the bridge, reached by escalator, are a Relais H shop, Boeuf Jardinier grill, Arche caféteria (open 24 hours), tourist information desk and a fountain! The caféteria is a bit cramped; apart from that, the facilities are excellent. The Mercure Hotel is at the far end of the site.

Les Creches ★★
A pleasant, wooded site with a view and space for a stroll.

Dracé
Long and narrow site, quite a good view; the Caféteria du Beaujolais, with terrace, is at the end.

Patural
Rather exposed to the road.

Péage de Villefranche Limas *i*
Pay here.

A46, Lyon by-pass, forks off just after the péage.

Les Chères
A good sized picnic area after the fuel station.

Dardilly
On the outskirts of the Lyon conurbation.

CHALON

AIRES CHALON ~ LYON

	km	from Paris
La Ferté	342	**St Ambreuil**
Jugy	352	**Boyer**
		Tournus
		Tournus
Brancion		
Taizé		
Farges	365	**Uchizy**
Monts du Maconnais		
Macon St Albain ←	379	→ **Macon La Salle**
		Macon Nord A40
Paray le Monial		
Macon		
Solutré		*Bourg en Bresse*
		Macon Sud
Les Creches	397	**Les Sablons**
Monts du Beaujolais		
Dracé	408	**Taponas**
Mt Brouilly		
		Belleville
Patural	419	**Boitray**
Péage de Villefranche	=	**Péage de Villefranche**
		A46
		Anse
Les Chères	436	**Les Chères**
		Limonest
Dardilly	447	**Les Bruyères Paisy**
Mont du Lyonnais		

LYON

St Ambreuil
Arche caféteria (open 24 hours) with a terrace; outside snack bar in summer only.

Boyer

Uchizy

Macon La Salle
A large site, with Caféroute at ground level. Separate snack bar outside in summer. Quite a lot of space for a picnic, and a little shade at the end of the site. Towards the end of the site is the budget-priced Hotel Formule 1, and a phone booth to use to book in to the Hotel Mercure on the other side of the motorway.

Les Sablons ★
An attractive site, rather close to the motorway. Have a look at the story of the ancient history of this region of France in cartoon form, La Préhistoire de Solutré, which is amusing. You can see the hill of Solutré from the aire. There are point relaxe exercises here.

Taponas
Relais de Beaujolais caféteria with terrace (open 24 hours), and a separate summer snack bar outside.

Boitray ★ ★
After the heavy traffic of the Lyon conurbation it's a pleasant surprise to reach this aire, and you will probably not be the only people there! However there should be room for everyone, even on a busy August day, for the road winds around to the banks of a lake in both directions, with picnic tables, points relaxes, room to stroll about and facilities over a wide area including several WC blocks. There is a Musical Promenade for children to try at summer weekends. Near the entrance to the aire, overlooking the lake, is a Relais regional restaurant, a Petit Cafe snack bar, a fast food outlet and a shop. So a good choice for a meal break, especially if you are planning a picnic, for you would need to drive a further 100 kms to the hills beyond Beaune to find a comparable picnic spot.

Péage de Villefranche Limas Est *i*
Take a ticket. Motorway information point and tyre pressure check after the barriers.

Les Chères
Point relaxe exercises in picnic area.

Les Bruyères Paisy
Snacks only available.

Between Chalon and Lyon, the motorway runs along the **Saone valley**. The river is navigable for 3/4 of its length, meeting the Rhone at Lyon.

Old market village with a tiny medieval hall, a partly restored castle and several well-restored old houses; the special charm of **Brancion** is its mountain setting.

Catholics, Protestants and Orthodox clerics joined together in 1940 at **Taizé** to form an ecumenical centre devoted to peace and offering hospitality to young people from all over the world. Over 800 brothers from 20 countries live there now, receiving hundreds of visitors annually.

The view of **Tournus**, an interesting old riverside town, from the motorway is dominated by the bell-towers of the remarkable Romanesque abbey church.

Poet Lamartine was born in **Macon** in 1790 and, on his first visit to Europe, Turner painted here. The area marks the transition between north and south, with the first Mediterranean influences of flat roofs and orange pantiles.

To the west of the motorway between Tournus and Macon are the **Monts du Maconnais**; Romanesque churches, views, prehistoric sites and many links with Lamartine; his various homes, the home of his mistress, and the little octagonal house among the Maconnais vineyards where he liked to come and write.

The Benedictine **Abbaye de Cluny** was a centre of tremendous religious, political and artistic influence during the Middle Ages, with 2,000 outposts and 10,000 monks throughout Europe. Little remains of the abbey church, once the largest in all of Christendom. There is a Romanesque basilica at **Paray le Monial**.

On a hill to the west is **Solutré**, a rock familiar to the French, not least because Francois Mitterand is said to have climbed it every year! An archaeological 'dig' at the foot of the rock has turned up much evidence of early human habitation.

A busy road and rail junction, **Bourg en Bresse** has a nice tale concerning the church in its suburb Brou, which is a symbol of married love to the French (see A40).

At the top of Mount Brouilly, the Chapelle de **Brouilly en Beaujolais** is a place of pilgrimage for local wine growers. The **Monts du Beaujolais** form the western edge of the Saone valley between Villefranche and Macon. On its slopes are the villages which give their names to the great wines of Beaujolais; Julienas, Brouilly, Chenas, Fleurie.

The third largest city in France, **Lyon** is a natural crossroads linking north and south, east and west, to be avoided by the motorway driver! Traffic is heavy, often blocked during the rush hour, especially in the Tunnel de Fourvière, and finding one's route not easy. However, bypassing Lyon is now possible, at least to link up with east/west routes, freeing both the driver and the city.

Solaize
Relais caféteria; no picnic area.

Péage de Vienne Reventin
Take a ticket. Gendarmerie and motorway information point.

Vienne
100 metres after the péage; no picnic area.

Auberives ★★
Large, well laid out, and busy, wooded site. Drive to the very back where there is a little river, beside what must have been an old road and is now part of the aire.

St Rambert d'Albon *i*
A large aire with facilities on both sides of the motorway. On this side, Relais Bébé and the Isardrome hotel. Also a restaurant, La Grillandine, open May-September, which has a terrace overlooking a pretty lake with fountains and ducks. Inside the main building are a variety of facilities including a cash dispenser and newsagents. Go up to the stairs to another restaurant, Le Pressoir, a large regional products shop and the bridge to the other side.

Blacheronde
Small, but OK.

Le Bornaron ★★
Follow the road round to the back where there is a lot of space.

Pont de l'Isère
Maybe your children will be delighted to find a McDonalds on a French motorway! It's a nice building, with a lovely terrace, and the eating style and content look familiar. It's sparkling clean (I even noticed someone scrubbing a manhole cover outside), and very popular.

AIRES LYON ~ VALENCE

LYON

	km	from Lyon ring road, A46
Solaize	15	**Serrezin**
		A46, A47
		Chasse Sud
		Vienne Nord
		Vienne Sud
Péage Vienne Reventin ←	=	→**Péage Vienne Reventin**
Vienne	5	
Auberives	13	**Grande Borne**
Massif du Pilat		
		Auberives
		Chanas
St Rambert d'Albon ←	29	→ **St Rambert d'Albon**
Blacheronde	39	**Combe Tourmente**
Le Bornaron	45	**La Galaure**
Les Cévennes		*Romans*
	54	**La Bouterne**
		Tain L'Hermitage
Pont de l'Isère	65	**Latitude 45**
Cotes du Rhone		*Le Vercors*
		Valence Nord

Serrezin
Bar/buffet in fuel station shop, and 4Pentes restaurant.

Péage de Vienne Reventin *i*
Pay here. Beyond the toll barriers, enter the aire at the far end, and exit by the Gendarmerie. An ASF (Autoroutes du Sud de la France) exhibition and information gallery is underground, with pedestrian access from the aire on each side.

Grande Borne ★
This is a long and narrow site; rather close to the motorway, but pleasant.

St Rambert d'Albon ★ ★ *i*
The eye-catching modern Isardrome which houses most of the facilities, is definitely worth a visit. Enter by the automatic doors; surprising luxury on a motorway. A boutique first; then a snack bar, La Croquemandise, and a caféteria, both with terrace. Use the lift or stairs to reach the facilities on the south side of the motorway, which include a hotel.

Combe Tourmente ★ ★
Well screened from road, with a large grassy hollow between it and the aire. The access road winds up a hill, away from the motorway, to a parking area. Park here and walk up the slope further to picnic higher where there is a lot of space and a parcours de santé at the very back. Lovely view.

La Galaure
Not much room to park here, but well screened from the road.

La Bouterne ★ ★
From parking area, go down some steps or down the slope towards the back of the aire, and there is a further lovely picnic area at the far end of the site, nearer the road. Return to main area to get back onto the motorway.

Latitude 45
Arche caféteria.

Between the Rhone valley and the Loire basin, a watershed influenced by both the Mediterranean and the Atlantic, **Mont Pilat** is on the northern edge of the **Cévennes**. Long renowned for its flora and fauna (Jean-Jacques Rousseau came here to collect plants in 1769), it now forms part of a Parc Naturel Régional.

The traditional industry of shoe making continues today in **Romans**; the Musee de la Chaussure contains an amusing range of shoes from the ancient and the modern world.

The rivers of the **Vercors** carve their way through gorges from the great limestone plateau to join the Isere. From the motorway one is impressed by the seemingly solid walls of rock which enclose the region, a natural fortress. Little wonder that it became a stronghold of the Resistance during 1943 and 1944. After D-Day, with passions running high and liberation apparently imminent, a republic was proclaimed. This was too much for the Germans, and parachutists and troops specially trained in mountain warfare were sent in to restore order. By the end of August 1944 hundreds of resisters and local inhabitants, from old folk to babies, had been killed. Their deaths are recorded throughout the region on poignant memorials.

The river **Ardèche** rises in the Cevennes, at 1467 metres, and flows into the Rhone 119 kilometres later at Pont-St-Esprit, north of Orange. On its way it cuts the Vivarais plateau in two by its deep course; the gorges so formed are spectacular. It gives its name to the Département and to the wines of the region.

The **Pré-Alpes du Sud** are the Vercors and the Devoluy ranges.

Whether or not it was the Ancient Greeks who introduced the vine to the **Cotes du Rhone** area, this was the first part of France where wine was made, so successfully that a Roman emperor ordered half the vines in Gaul to be pulled up, ostensibly to encourage wheat growing, in reality to protect Roman vine growers from competition. You may notice a rose bush at the end of a row in some vineyards; once used as a protection from the dreaded phylloxera, which was supposed to attack the rose first and give the wine grower a chance to combat it, all the vines in France are now grafted from American stock, which is resistant to the disease. Where it remains, the rose bush is an ornamental tradition rather than a necessity.

Portes les Valence ★
Cafeteria Le Petit Café on the right after the fuel station. Good picnic area at the end of the site, but a bit close to the motorway.

Bellevue
Close to road, and small; there is no view, despite its name!

Bras de Zil ★
The mountains of the Ardeche form the backdrop for this small but pleasant aire. There is a further picnic area at the end of the site.

La Coucourde ★ ★ ★
More like a park than an aire, my personal choice for a picnic on this motorway, if I didn't need a shop, and if a play area wasn't a priority. Drive past the viewpoint/monument and then round to the right; it's a very large aire, and there are lots of places to park, in the Mediterranean forest, or on the grass.

Savasse ★
A neat, pleasant aire in a pretty setting, with a striking sculpture, 'Porte du Soleil'.

Montelimar ★ ★ ★
(Such a large wooded area, so many picnic spots, you can't imagine this highly recommended aire ever getting full; there are play areas to suit all ages, table tennis tables (take your rackets with you) and a 'parcours de santé' at the back. You can try out the climbing wall; at summer weekends there is tuition. Horse riding, shooting and fencing are also promised. The Relais de Montelimar has a restaurant, cafeteria (both with lovely terraces) and fast food counter and there is a well stocked shop. Another shop sells nougat - fun, but not cheap. The Relais Bébé is near the covered footbridge leading to the Forte Travelodge Hotel on the other side of the motorway. The fuel station is at the far end of the site.

Pierrelatte ★
There is an extra picnic area at the back of the site; walk down here, to the little brook.

Mornas Village ★ ★
The 4 Pentes, at the entrance to the aire, has a snack bar on the lower floor, under the restaurant. The Arche caféteria, (open 24 hours) which I prefer, is beyond the fuel station. Try archery at the weekend, or take a walk to Mornas; follow the sign 'Circuit Pedestre'.

Orange le Grès ★ ★
The road winds through the Mediterranean forest in this pretty aire.

VALENCE

AIRES VALENCE ~ ORANGE

	km	from Lyon ring road, A46
		Valence Sud
Portes les Valence	78	**Portes les Valence**
Bellevue	88	**Livron**
		Loriol
Montagnes de l'Ardèche		
Bras de Zil	96	**Saulce**
		Montelimar Nord
La Coucourde	104	**Le Logis Neuf**
Savasse	111	**Roubion**
Les Cévennes		*Chateaux de la Drome*
Montelimar ←	120	→ **Montelimar**
		Montelimar Sud
Le Vivarais		*La Garde Adhémar*
		Les Baronnies
	128	**Donzère**
Pierrelatte		
Gorges de l'Ardeche		
	142	**Tricastin**
		Bollene
		Vaison la Romaine
		Forteresse de Mornas
	156	**Mornas les Adrets**
Mornas Village		
		Orange Nord
		Le Mont Ventoux
		Dentelles de Montmirail
		Orange, A9
Orange le Grès	172	**Le Coudoulet**
		Orange Sud

ORANGE

Portes les Valence
Le Petit Café cafeteria with terrace.

Livron

Saulce ★★
A lake adds to the charm of this lovely aire.

Le Logis Neuf ★★ *i*
Large, lovely site.

Roubion ★
Slightly limited parking, but a lovely aire, with a specially nice grassy area.

Montelimar ★ *i*
In the Relais de Montelimar on this side of the motorway is a cafeteria, fast food counter and a shop. There is access to the restaurant by way of the footbridge across the motorway. Nougat is popular enough for there to be a shop selling only that (but what a selection!) on both sides of the road. The Forte Travelodge Hotel is at the end of the site. I would go on to **Le Logis Neuf** if you were planning a picnic.

Donzère

Tricastin

Mornas les Adrets
On the sunny side (les adrets), but slightly run down. 4 Pentes restaurant and caféteria, also some separate snack bars in summer. Inadequate number of WCs.

Orange le Coudoulet ★★
Lots of room in this extensive area of Mediterranean forest.

A picturesque village, its church perched above it, to the east of the motorway, **La Garde Adhémar** has good views over the plain to the **Vivarais** and its high point, the Dent de Rez.

When the Ouvèze burst its banks in the autumn of 1992, the charming Provencal town of **Vaison la Romaine** and the countryside around were the scene of devastating floods. There is significant evidence here of Roman occupation, and medieval prosperity.

Extending from the Montagne Noire in the Aude to the Monts du Beaujolais and Charolais in the Loire, the **Cévennes** form the eastern edge of the Massif Central.

At the top of a hill overlooking the walled town below is the 11th century **Forteresse de Mornas**, with the tricolore flying.

Impressive Roman remains - the theatre is the best preserved in the Roman Empire, the triumphal arch sits incongruously in the middle of a traffic island - lively **Orange** is at the centre of the Cotes du Rhone wine industry, and at the crossroads of two motorways.

There is a spectacular drive along the long, windswept ridge of the **Mont Ventoux** to the observatory on the summit.

The **Rhone** is the most industrially exploited river in France; the Donzère-Mondragon Canal feeds the hydro-electric power station at Bollene and the vast nuclear complex at Tricastin.

Le Fournalet
Small, and pretty, but close to the road, with industrial buildings behind.

Morières ★ ★
Behind the fuel station is a nice wooded picnic area. The Relais d'Avignon caféteria with terrace is at the end of the site, and there is a further picnic area in the Mediterranean forest area at the back of the Relais.

Cabannes
Hardly more than a lay-by; no picnic area.

Cavaillon
Rather basic.

Sénas ★
A stream runs through the aire with footbridges across; not much shade, but quite pleasant.

Péage de Lancon
Pay here.

Lancon ★ ★ *i*
This pleasant aire is 500m after the péage. Drive past the fuel station to the bar/buffet (summer only) with terrace, and the hotel Mercure. There is a cash dispenser. On the bridge over the motorway are the regional products shop, a newsagents, Porte de Provence restaurant and Arche caféteria (open 24 hours); a Caféroute with terrace is at ground level. Organised sport includes archery and speedball, and there are table tennis tables. The WC block at the end of the site, near the parcours de santé, is the best.

Vitrolles

AIRES ORANGE ~ MARSEILLE

ORANGE

	km	
		from Lyon ring road, A46
Le Rhone		*Chateauneuf du Pape*
Le Fournalet	184	**Sorgues**
		Avignon Nord
Uzés		
Morières	195	
		Fontaine de Vaucluse
		Chartreuse de Bonpas
		Avignon Sud
Cabannes	200	**Noves**
		Le Lubéron
Cavaillon	209	**Cavaillon**
		Cavaillon
N. D. de Beauregard		
		La Durance
St Rémy de Provence		
Sénas	219	**Sénas**
		Sénas
		Fruits de Provence
	228	**Lamanon**
Les Baux de Provence		
		Salon Nord
Mémorial Jean Moulin		
Arles		
		Salon Sud
		A54
Péage de Lancon	=	**Péage de Lancon**
Lancon ←	242	→ **Lancon**
		Coudoux, A8
		Berre
Vitrolles	260	**Vitrolles**
La Camargue		
		A55, A51

MARSEILLE

Sorgues ★ ⛽ ✕ ♿ /⊓\ ♤

Small but pleasant Relais du Ventoux with terrace and shop. Wooded, medium-sized, picnic area.

Noves ♿

Very basic.

Cavaillon Plan d'Orgon ♿

A small and basic aire, but it does overlook a pretty lake.

Sénas ♿ ♤

Small aire with marvellous views.

Lamanon ★ ★ ★ ♿ /⊓\ ♤ 🚿 📞

Large, attractive aire, in two sections; forested first, then a more open, recently planted area with good views, with groups of tables under canopies and cylindrical artwork to puzzle over.

Péage de Lancon

Take a ticket. Tyre pressure check and Gendarmerie.

Lancon ⛽ 🔧 ✕ ♿ /⊓\ 🚿 *i*

Drive between fuel station and road to reach other facilities. Separate snack bar, summer only, kiosk selling local produce, such as garlic, also summer only. There is a Caféroute at ground level. The picnic area on this side is rather close to the motorway.

Vitrolles ⛽ ✕ ♿

La Pyramide restaurant; no picnic area.

The remains of one of the summer residences of the Pope are at **Chateauneuf du Pape**, as are the renowned vineyards. The Tour Fenestrelle at **Uzés** is a unique cylindrical belfry. The **Fontaine de Vaucluse** is one of the most powerful springs in the world; a magnificent spectacle.

Park beside the Rhone and walk through one of the gates into **Avignon**, **Cité des Papes**, a lively, elegant Provencal city. The Palace of the Popes, the Cathedral and the gardens, which offer superb views, are situated on a fortress site on a bluff overlooking the Rhone; a more energetic entrance would be by way of the steps near 'that bridge'. Melons from Cavaillon, cherries from Remoulins and peaches, pears and apricots from the valley of the Rhone; some of the **Fruits de Provence**.

In a commanding position overlooking the Rhone delta, the fortunes of **Arles** as a Roman capital owed much to having chosen the right general to support when it provided Caesar with ships for his campaign against Pompey's Marseille in 49 BC. The Roman amphitheatre, is used to this day for bull-fighting, a traditional Camargue sport. Van Gogh lived here for a short time towards the end of his life.

The **Camargue** is the delta of the Rhone; an immense alluvial plain with salt marshes, lagoons and islands, visited for its bird life, bulls and horses, and its wild, natural beauty.

The village of **Les Baux de Provence** has a spectacular setting, on a bare spur of rock with vertical ravines on either side. Bauxite, the basis for aluminium, was discovered here in 1822.

Cavaillon could be the starting point for exploring **Le Lubéron** - a forested mountain region with fortresses and villages perched on rocky promontories and spurs. In the squares of **St-Rémy de Provence** are the plane trees and fountains typical of towns of the region. In the ancient town of Glanum, there are buildings dating from the Greek colonisation of the 2nd century BC on the Plateau des Antiquites.

Notre Dame de Beauregard has a splendid setting on the top of the hill, with a castle below it at road level. Cliffs below descend to the river Durance, which the motorway follows for 15kms. Petrarch's Laura, in memory of whom he wrote his sonnets, lived in **Noves**. The **Alpilles** are one of the east-to-west mountain ranges of Provence.

Charteuse de Bonpas is a church and monastery near the motorway bridge over the **Durance** at Noves.

The fine **Mémorial de Jean Moulin**, a celebrated hero of the French Resistance, is situated close to the motorway on the N538 north of **Salon de Provence.** On a beautiful stretch of the old Salon to Aix road stands the restored, partly 12th century, **Chateau de la Barben**. In Roman times there was a port, now submerged, at **Fos sur Mer** , and there is still a medieval fort, contrasting strangely with the hectares of oil refinery and industrial zone which surround the town.

A8

Ventabren Sud t

Péage de la Barque *i*
Take a ticket. Facilities are 200 metres after the toll barrier.

L'Arc
The view of Mont Ste-Victoire is stunning, but don't stop here unless you need fuel, provisions (the shop is a good size), or a bite to eat in Le Petit Café caféteria (open in summer only). On the day we visited, the car park was pretty full of cars and lorries, and we drove on to picnic at the next aire.

Barcelone ★★★
You will appreciate the shaded parking area when you return to the car. Climb up the terraced hillside, through olive groves, to the old mill; sit in the shade of a gnarled tree, watch the butterflies, and look over to the expanse of vineyards on the Var plain, the picturesque villages and the surrounding mountains. Look down, too, on this lovely aire; clean, neat and spacious, it has been carefully landscaped and planted. There are picnic tables under thatched roofs, a stream and a pond, lots of grass, and super children's games. If you picnic up near the mill, you will probably be alone; afterwards, discover how olives were turned to oil here, for this is a Moulin à Huile. Near the WC block at the front of the aire is 'Reflections Gothiques', a panel showing some of the Gothic treasures of the region.

Cambarette ★★★ *i*
Another incredible view, this time over pine trees to the Montagne de la Loube. Drive through to the well-landscaped Aire de Détente, situated on land between the two carriageways, approached by car from both sides through a tunnel. I don't think I have ever seen a longer slide than the one here! It is an exceptionally spacious site, with lots of room for cars and caravans, and, on the August day we visited, it was almost empty. The nice Relais Cote d'Azur has a caféteria, shop and newsagents. The tourist office is open in summer only. Overnight caravan park.

Roudai ★★
The road winds back among the trees in this spacious aire.

Vidauban Sud
The bar/buffet in the fuel station is not recommended; apart from the loud canned music, its terrace is very close to the fuel pumps. There is a large picnic area at the end of the site.

Le Jas Pellicot ★
A pleasant, wooded site.

Péage du Puget

L'Estérel
Disappointing that, in such a lovely position, there is only a minimal Aire de Détente at the far end of the site.

AIRES SALON DE PROVENCE ~ CANNES

SALON DE PROVENCE

	km	from Salon
Ventabren	8	**Ventabren**
	■	Aix Ouest
	■	A51
	■	Aix Est
	■	Le Canet
Aix		*Le paysege de Cézanne*
Péage de la Barque	=	**Péage de la Barque**
	■	A52
		Mont. Ste Victoire
L'Arc	38	**Rousset**
	■	Trets Pourieres
St Maximin		
Mont Aurélien		
Barcelone	53	**St Hilaire**
	■	St Maximin
Cambarette ←	120	→ **Cambarette**
	■	Brignoles
La Ste Baume		*Ferme des Templiers*
Mont. de la Loube		*Palais des Comtes de Pr.*
Roudai	85	**Candumy**
Les Maures		*Abbaye du Thoronnet*
	■	Le Luc, A57
		Le Vieux Cannet
		Ste Brigitte
Vidauban	106	**Vidauban**
	■	Draguignan
St Tropez		*Les Arcs*
Rochers de Roquebrune		*Gorges du Verdon*
Fréjus		
Le Jas Pellicot	128	**Le Canaver**
	■	Pujet sur Argens
Péage du Puget	=	**Péage du Puget**
	■	Fréjus
L'Estérel	143	
	■	Les Adrets
Massif de l'Estérel		*Grasse*
Corniche de l'Estérel		
Pic de l'Ours		
	■	Mandelieu

CANNES

Ventabren Nord
A pleasant, medium-sized aire but close to the road so rather noisy.

Péage de la Barque *i*
Minimal WC block.

Rousset
Le Petit Café is not open in winter.

Saint Hilaire ★
Pleasant picnic area and a sculpture of a grasshopper!

Cambarette ★★★
The Relais Cote d'Or has a caféteria and newsagents; the Aire de Détente is between the two carriageways.

Candumy ★★
This is an attractive, terraced aire.

Vidauban Nord

Le Canaver ★
Not one but two works of art here; the splendid, glittering Dragon de Draguignan and a mural on the service station wall. Use the fuel station shop for provisions; the one in the Relais caféteria building only sells tourist goods and regional products. Separate snack bar in summer.

Péage du Puget
Take a ticket.

The ancient capital of Provence, **Aix** was a city in decline as Marseille developed in the 19th century. This century, however, it has expanded considerably and is now a popular cultural, tourist and industrial centre.

Cézanne came from Aix-en-Provence. He painted the **Montagne Ste Victoire** many times, never satisfied with his results. The mountain dazzles white in the sun. From parts of the motorway the hills in the foreground appear as a skirt to the main ridge; there is, in fact, a valley between the two ranges.

To the south of the motorway, behind the Aire de Barcelone, **Mont Aurélien** rises to 875m.

Travelling west, you will see the **Ferme des Templiers** just below the motorway to the north.

La Ste Baume; legend has it that Mary Magdalene spent the last years of her life here. She had been set adrift in a boat from the Holy Land with St Maximinus, the first Bishop of Aix, and others 13 years after the Crucifixion; they landed at Stes Marie de la Mer and evangelised until Mary decided to move to the cave. When her relics were stolen and taken to Vézelay in the 11th century, it was a catastrophe for Ste Baume; the pronouncement 200 years later that they had been in a nearby abbey all along led to the decline of Vézelay's fortunes!

The **Montagne de la Loube**, 830m, lies south-west of Brignoles. **Brignoles**, once a home of the counts of Provence, is a centre for the wine trade of the Var, and for fruit and olives. With bauxite in the surrounding hills, there is an aluminium industry.

The **Abbaye du Thoronnet** is one of the most interesting in Provence. Close to the motorway, **Le Vieux Cannet** is a typical Provencal village.

Two million years ago the continent that covered what is now the Mediterranean Sea broke up, leaving Corsica, Sardinia and the Maures and Esterel mountains; these then are the most ancient lands in Provence. '**Maures**' might refer to Spanish pirates, or come from a Provencal word for 'wooded'.

The pretty church near the motorway, south of Vidauban, is **Ste Brigitte**. A good place to begin a tour of the vineyards of the Var would be **Les Arcs**.

In the hills to the north the great gorge carved by the river **Verdon** through the high limestone plateau, has produced exciting scenery. There are roads with viewing points along the top and it is possible, though arduous, to walk down into the gorge using the Sentier Martel footpath.

St Tropez is a fashionable resort, with a picturesque harbour in a beautiful bay.

At the north-eastern edge of the Massif des Maures, the **Rochers de Roquebrune** is the rock face close to the motorway. A staging post for Julius Caesar on his expedition to Spain, **Fréjus** became a thriving Roman, then medieval town.

The **Massif de l'Estérel** is spectacular from the motorway, and offers to those who can make a diversion some marvellous drives and walks. The hills are as old as the Maures but not as high.

Belvedere Piccolaret ★ ♿ ☎
Very neat, well planted, aire overlooking the bay of Cannes. The nicest part is at the far end, near the Table d'Orientation; park there.

Les Bréguières
The terraced picnic area at the top of this site is pleasant; there is pedestrian access to the north side of the motorway.

Péage d'Antibes
Pay here; automatic to left.

Péage de St-Isodore
Pay here. Gendarmerie and motorway information office.

Péage de la Turbie *i*
Pay here.

Beausoleil ★
Either on entering the aire, or at the far end, drive down the slope behind the fuel station to reach terraced parking areas with good views of Monaco, Monte Carlo and the Mediterranean Sea. It is pleasant; there are picnic tables, a WC block and a Table d'Orientation. The fuel station, shop and (separate) bureau de change may well be crowded, but most people appear to stay at that higher level.

AIRES CANNES ~ ITALIAN BORDER

CANNES

	km		
		from Salon	
		Cannes Ouest	
Cannes			*Route Napoléon*
		Mougins	
Piccolaret	161		
Les Bréguières ←	168	→	**Les Bréguières**
Iles de Lérins			*Alpes Maritimes*
Vallauris			*Biot*
		Antibes Ouest	
Péage d'Antibes	=		**Péage d'Antibes**
		Antibes Est	
		Bouches du Loup	
		Villeneuve Loubet	
			Le Vieux Cagnes
		Cagnes sur Mer	
		St Laurent du Var	
		Nice Promenade des Anglais	
		Nice St Augustin	
Péage de St Isidore	=		**Péage de St Isidore**
Viaduc du St Isidore			
		Nice St Isidore	
		Nice Nord	
Nice Cimiez			*Massif du Mercantour*
		Nice Est	
Eze			*Les Alpes*
		A800	
Péage de la Turbie	=		**Péage de la Turbie**
		La Turbie	
Trophée des Alpes			
	210		**La Scoperta**
Beausoleil	212		
Monaco Monte Carlo			
Roquebrune			
		Roquebrune	
L'Annonciade			*Ste Agnès*
Menton			*Sospel*
		Menton	

ITALIAN BORDER

Les Bréguières

All services except the fuel station are at the far end of the site; aim for Parking 2. The Relais de l'Automobiliste has a restaurant and sandwich bar. The setting is pleasant but there are not many places for a picnic. Cross the little bridge to reach the attractive modern building housing the motor museum which is open all year and has 100 cars on display, as well as special exhibits. You may well decide not to visit it unless you have a lot of time to spare , for it is expensive for a motorway museum.

Péage d'Antibes

Pay here.

Péage de St Isidore

Pay here.

Péage de la Turbie

Pay here.

La Scoperta *i*

The tourist office is open in summer only.

The 19th century habit of the English aristocracy to spend the winter in **Cannes** contributed to its rapid growth from a small fishing port to a fashionable resort. It is in a fine position on the beautiful bay of Napoule and has three exits from the A8.

When Napoléon escaped from Elba in 1815 and returned to the mainland, landing at Golfe Juan with a thousand or so men, and camping in an olive grove, he could not have foreseen the rapturous welcome he was to receive as he made his way to Grenoble. The journey, which took no more than a week, fired the imagination of the French; today the **Route Napoléon** is commemorated in every town or village where he stopped.

Two pretty islands, the **Iles de Lérins,** are in the bay, both accessible by boat from Cannes. Ste Marguerite is the larger; the other, owned by a monastery, is St Honorat.

Antibes was built on the site of the Greek city Antipolis, a trading centre in the 4th century BC. You will notice from the motorway the number of greenhouses on the slopes around the back of the town, for this is a centre for the growing of flowers for cutting. Mimosa, the yellow flower synonymous with Provence, is cultivated in **Biot and Vallauris**.

The picturesque walled **Vieux Cagnes** is to the north of the motorway.

Constructing the eastern end of the A8 involved impressive feats of engineering. The section behind Nice, in particular, consists largely of a series of **viaducts**, including **St Isadore**, and **tunnels**.

There is a statue of Queen Victoria at the end of the Boulevard de Cimiez, the most expensive area of **Nice** to live in. **Cimiez** is also the site of the Roman town.

The **Massif du Mercantour** is a national park in the foothills of the Alps north of Nice. There are ski resorts within easy reach of the Mediterranean, in the Mercantour region of **Les Alpes**.

A typical ancient fortified village, **Eze** is particularly attractive in its site overlooking the sea.

You can see the restored white stone **La Turbie Trophée des Alpes**, built to celebrate the conquests of the Roman Emperor Augustus in the area.

The **Principauté de Monaco**, a sovereign state ruled by the Grimaldis, consists of the old town of Monaco, jutting out to sea to the west; Monte Carlo, recogisable by its casino; and, linking the two, the Condamine. When the casino was first built in **Monte Carlo** in the 19th century, to restore the fortunes of the Grimaldis, no one wanted a house anywhere near.

The remarkable feudal village of **Roquebrune**, perched above Cap St Martin, contains the ruins of a medieval castle. The last town before the Italian border is **Menton**, where oranges and lemons grow in profusion and palm trees abound. The **Annonciade** is a chapel in the hills to the north. From picturesque **Ste Agnès**, high above, there is quite a view, including the motorway. A tortuous road leads to **Sospel**, a town in the Alps.

Roquemaure ★
Lovely views of vineyards with hills in background. Well presented, informative motorway exhibition in an extra-terrestrial building.

Tavel ★★★ *i*
Drive round the back of the fuel station to get to the Aubepain snack bar which includes a drive-in, shop and Interval restaurant. If you prefer the Relais restaurant on the far side, walk through, because the tunnel is one-way only for traffic! The small hotel, which is reasonably-priced, is primarily for lorry drivers, but can also be used by other travellers. At the very end of the site, the road leads up into a super picnic area in the hills.

Estezargues ★★
You are venturing into the Garrigue at this enormous aire. Drive through to the far end, then follow the road as it winds through the scrubland, with views from the high point, and lots of shade and space lower down.

Ledenon
A small aire.

Marguerittes
You come first to the 4 Pentes restaurant, caféteria and snack bar, then to the fuel station. There is no separate WC block in the small picnic area at the end of the site.

Milhaud
The road at last rises out of the plain around Nimes. A very small aire, with a little shade at the end of the site.

Vergèze ★★
Turn right immediately you enter the aire, and the road winds up to a large area of woodland which mixes tall trees and the shorter ones of the Mediterranean forest. There is a good play area in this nice, but busy, aire.

Péage de Montpellier 1
Pay here.

Ambrussum (Via Domitia) *i*
Travelling south, you would have to turn off at the next exit and drive back to Lunel, 2kms south of the motorway, to actually stand on part of the Via Domitia, the helpful staff at the tourist information office assure me. There is a nice but small Relais d'Oc cafeteria and shop, and a Bouquet restaurant and cafeteria. The whole place is well laid out, but it is a busy aire, and there really isn't much space.

Nabrigas ★★
A lovely, wooded site, a bit close to the road, but the noise of the cicadas here almost drowned the sound of traffic!

St Aunès
Small and basic.

AIRES ORANGE ~ MONTPELLIER

ORANGE

	km	
		from A7
Le Rhone		
Roquemaure	10	**Roquemaure**
	■	Roquemaure
Tavel ←	18	→ **Tavel**
Uzès		*Villeneuve les Avignon*
La Garrigue		
Estezargues	25	**Estezargues**
	■	Remoulins
Pont du Gard		*Le Rhone*
Ledenon	36	**Ledenon**
Marguerittes	45	**Marguerittes**
	■	Nimes Est
Abbatiale de St Gilles		*Nimes*
		La Camargue
	■	Nimes Ouest, A54
Milhaud	59	**Milhaud**
Vergèze	67	**Vergèze**
		Aigues Mortes
	■	Gallargues
Péage de Montpellier 1	=	**Péage de Montpellier 1**
Ambrussum	77	**Ambrussum**
Nabrigas	83	
	88	**Mas du Roux**
		Castries
	■	Vendargues
St Aunès	95	**St Aunès**
	■	Montpellier Est

MONTPELLIER

Roquemaure

Tavel ★ ★

The Relais, after the fuel station, has a caféteria with terrace and regional products shop; picnic area and parcours de santé at the far end of the site.

Estezargues ★ ★

Extensive picnic area in a splendid setting, with wonderful views over the Garrigue.

Ledenon

Marguerittes

4 Pentes grill.

Milhaud

Vergèze ★ ★

Distant view of the Mediterranean as you approach this large, nicely landscaped aire. Park in an olive grove, or in the shade of a pine tree. The best in the area unless you want children's games.

Péage de Montpellier 1.

Take a ticket.

Ambrussum (Via Domitia)

Fenced play area behind fuel station, and archery at summer weekends. There is a Relais d'Oc caféteria with a regional products area. The A9 follows fairly closely the probable route of the Roman road from the Rhone to the Pyrenees, the Via Domitia. Entire portions of the road are visible today, as are milestones and traces of camps and villas along the way. Several aires reflect this link with the past, including Ambrussum, site of a pre-Roman settlement used by the Romans as a staging post. If you would like to visit Ambrussum and part of the Via Domitia, 1km to the south, ask at the tourist office for the service gate out of the aire to be opened for you.

Mas du Roux ★ ★

Very large, wooded site; good parcours de santé around edge of aire.

St Aunès

Magnificent crossing the **Rhone**, with the hills of the Gard to the west. You will notice a chateau built on a superb site overlooking the river.

On the opposite bank of the Rhone, **Villeneuve les Avignon** is the best place for viewing its illustrious neighbour! It is also worth visiting those marvellous buildings you see when you look over from Avignon, the tower of Philippe le Bel and the Fort St Andre.

The Tour Fenestrelle at **Uzès** is a unique cylindrical belfry.

A desolate but beautiful expanse of rocky limestone moors north of Nimes, the sparse vegetation of the **Garrigue** consists largely of gorse, thistles and stunted oak trees.

The **Pont du Gard** is one of the highest and finest of Roman aquaducts.

Settlements surely existed on this plain, at the foot of the hills, for thousands of years before the Romans built a road, the Via Domitia linking Rome with the south of Spain, through it in 118 BC. It was under Augustus, who came here in 31 BC, that **Nimes** had its heyday, and many of the splendid remains were built at that time. By the fourth century, Arles had gained ascendancy and Nimes never really recovered its power, but its history contains several other periods of cultural and economic growth. Its textile industry, which flourished in the 18th century, has given us the word 'denim', a fabric 'de Nimes'.

The **Abbatiale de St Gilles** is unexceptional 17th century Gothic, except for its medieval west front.

La Camargue is the delta of the Rhone; an immense alluvial plain with salt marshes, lagoons and islands. Designated a Parc Naturel Régional, it is visited for its bird life, bulls and horses, and its wild natural beauty.

Not dead at all! The medieval ramparts of **Aigues Mortes** rise out of the marshland which gave the town its name.

There is an imposing chateau at **Castries**, with an aquaduct in its grounds.

Péage de Montpellier 2
Take a ticket.

Montpellier Fabrègues
On this side of the road is a snack bar, Relais Bébé and sports facilities; climbing wall in summer. Cross the footbridge or go through the tunnel to the large Arche complex on far side.

Gigean ★
View from the back of this aire to the pretty town of Gigean.

Mèze ★

Florensac
A small site.

Béziers Montblanc
Le Buffet Languedocien caféteria, with terrace, in a pleasantly laid out site.

Lespignan

Narbonne Vinassan ★ ★
A lively site; lots of facilities, lots of people, too! The Relais de Languedoc fast food and caféteria are a good size, and have a terrace. There is weekend instruction in golf, gymnastics, fencing and archery, to name but four; good children's games, and table tennis, too. The Aude hotel, at the back of the aire, looks very nice, certainly has a lovely view over the valley of the Aude. Find the shady goldfish pond, down some steps towards the back of the site, and picnic near there; very pleasant. Or drive on to the further picnic area behind the fuel station.

MONTPELLIER

AIRES MONTPELLIER ~ NARBONNE

		km		
			from A7	
Grotte des Demoiselles				*Lattes*
Gorges de l'Hérault				
		■	Montpellier Sud	
		■	St Jean de Védas	
	Péage de Montpellier 2	=	**Péage de Montpellier 2**	
Grotte de Clamouse				
	Montpellier Fab. ←	111	→ **Montpellier Fab.**	
Lac du Salagou				
	Gigean	120	**Gigean**	
		■	Sète	
Abbaye de Valmagne				*Frontignan*
Vallée de l'Hérault				*Sète*
	Mèze	130	**Loupian**	
Pézenas				*Mont St Clair*
				Bassin de Thau
	Florensac	143	**Florensac**	
		■	Agde Pézenas	
Parc du Haut Langueboc				*Agde*
	Béziers Montblanc	154	**Béziers Montblanc**	
		■	Béziers Est	
Oppidum d'Ensérune				*Canal du Midi*
Béziers				*Vallée de l'Aude*
		■	Béziers Ouest	
	Lespignan	173	**Lespignan**	
	Narbonne Vinassan	182	**Narbonne Vinassan**	
		■	Narbonne Est	
Narbonne				*Narbonne Plage*
		■	Narbonne Sud	
		■	A61	

NARBONNE

Péage de Montpellier 2
Pay here.

Montpellier Fabrègues
Drive past fuel station and wooded picnic areas, to reach facilities. Excellent Arche here, with caféteria (open 24 hours), grill, sandwicherie and terraces; Relais H, tourist information area and bureau de change. The Hotel Ibis is at the end of the site. Relais Bébé, sports and games are on the far side, over the footbridge. To reach the picnic area, follow the signs to park before the Arche building; no access after, although you can get back to fuel station.

Gigean
Steps up to the WCs and picnic area. Overlooked by a castle.

Loupian ★ ★
Drive round to the back of this attractive, spacious, rocky site with a hill; views over Sète from the top.

Florensac
Small site, among vineyards.

Béziers Montblanc
Pleasant shaded seating around a fountain beside the summer-only bar-buffet. There is a separate Relais caféteria. Apart from the facilities there and in the fuel station, the only WC block is a minimal one in the main parking area. A quite delightful botanical walk, Decouvrez la Flore Méditerranéenne, has been laid out in a shady oak wood, with heather, broom, juniper and small shrubs, and paths meandering on into the Garrigue scrubland beyond.

Lespignan
Proper shower; some shade at the end of this small site.

Narbonne Vinassan ★ ★ ★
Nice Relais du Languedoc caféteria, shop and snack bar at the entrance to the aire. Gymnastics, fencing and children's motor-biking are the weekend sports on offer. Splendid, wooded picnic area to drive into, but cars are not allowed right up to the large parcours de santé at the top of the site. We are reminded that this is a 'Foret Fragile'.

A Roman port is being excavated at **Lattes**, south of Montpellier.

The shape of the stalagmites in the **Grotte des Demoiselles** gave rise to the name of this cave in the southern Cevennes. The **Hérault** cuts through **gorges**, and passes the **Grotte de Clamouse** , in the foothills. The **Lac de Salagou** is in an attractive mountain setting.

A bit of a come down for a Cistercian abbey; the church of the **Abbaye de Valmagne** is now used as a wine store.

You will probably notice the ruins of the ancient abbey of **St Felix de Montceau** on a hillside opposite the Aire de Gigean (travelling towards Spain).

Frontignan is the home of a delicious Muscatel wine often served chilled as an aperitif in France.

A commercial and fishing port, **Sète** is at the foot of the Mont St Clair, at the end of the bar separating the **Bassin de Thau**, the largest of the salt water lagoons west of the Camargue, from the sea.

An important town in the 17th century, **Pézenas** is proud of the fact that Molière came here several times to perform his plays, and based some of his characters on the customers at the barber's shop where he lodged.

The chief interest of **Agde** lies in its antiquity; the town was founded during the 6th century BC. The river Herault and the **Canal du Midi** reach the sea here. It was the vision of Paul Riquet in the 17th century to link the river Garonne, which flows into the Atlantic Ocean, to the Mediterranean by means of a canal. 240kms long, it was an amazing feat of engineering.

The bird on the sign for the **Parc Naturel du Haut Languedoc** is a bee-eater.

Béziers, a centre of the Aude and Herault wine trade, has an extraordinary rugby stadium in the shape of a giant tortoise, close to the motorway.

There is evidence of a hill fort in use from the 6th century BC to early Christian times at **Oppidum d'Ensérune**.

A flourishing port in Roman times, **Narbonne** was prosperous through the Middle Ages, and work began on a cathedral so huge that, had more than the choir been finished, it would have been magnificent! It nevertheless looks impressive from the motorway. To the east of the town the motorway is La Languedocienne; to the west La Catalane.

There is a small mountain range to negotiate in order to get to the seaside! The shorter route is also the most picturesque. When you arrive, **Narbonne Plage** does appear to be on the beach, and every year it seems to spread a little further away from land.

Prat de Cest ★
Pleasant aire on a slope, with steps up to different levels. View of the foothills of the Pyrenees ahead as you leave the aire.

Les Gasparets ★
The road winds up to a viewpoint, and then down again. Another aire on a slope, with steps up to picnic tables on different levels.

Lapalme

Fitou
Small, quite pleasant, in a lovely setting.

Chateau de Salses *i*
You will want to walk through the underpass to see the castle better; this is an attractive, well-kept aire, and the covered parking is effective.

Rivesaltes
Small, but pleasant. Gendarmerie here.

Les Pavillons
Small, but pleasant. Good view of the Pyrenees.

Le Village Catalan
Drive past the fuel station; the road winds up, across the motorway and into the large aire on the other side. Rather tempting to spend a night in the hotel here, which is reasonably-priced, and has a pool with quite an outlook!

Péage du Perthus
Pay here.

AIRES NARBONNE ~ SPANISH BORDER

NARBONNE

		km		
			from A7	
Abbaye de Fontfroide				
Prat de Cest		198		**Bages**
Languedoc				*Etang de Bages*
		■	Sigean	
Les Gasparets		209		**Sigean**
Les Corbières				
Lapalme		218		**Lapalme**
		■	Leucate	
cru Fitou				*Etang de Leucate*
Fitou		227		**Fitou**
Roussillon				*Les Etangs*
Chat. de Salses	←	235	→	**Chat. de Salses**
		■	Perpignan Nord	
Tautavel				
Rivesaltes				
Rivesaltes	←	245	→	**Pia**
		■	Perpignan Sud	
Les Pyrénées				*Perpignan*
Les Pavillons		257		**Les Pavillons**
Le Village Catalan	←	265	→	**Le Village Catalan**
				La Cote Vermeille
Péage du Perthus		=		**Péage du Perthus**
		■	Le Boulou	
Le Canigou				*Thermalisme*

SPANISH BORDER

AIRES SPANISH BORDER ~ NARBONNE

Bages ★
Small, but very pleasant aire.

Sigean ★
The old stone walls around fields have been left here to create attractive picnic areas among the trees.

Lapalme ★★
A beautiful, well-designed aire. The Calypso caféteria is spacious and tastefully decorated; not only does it have a terrace, it has a swimming pool, for the use of customers only, with views over to the Mediterranean. At the back of the site the road descends towards vineyards and the sea to a pleasant picnic area, though if you want shade, stay in the higher area.

Fitou ★★
Having just had the best views of the Mediterranean on the A9, you come into this lovely aire. With wonderful views over the Etang de Leucate towards Port Barcarès, you can walk out of the aire towards the south to picnic in the shade of Mediterranean pines.

Chateau de Salses ★★ *i*
If the tourist office isn't open (summer only), there is the Table d'Orientation which explains the view over to the coast; the Chateau de Salses is in the foreground. There is a delightful 400m walk down to the castle; allow half an hour to get there and back. Take the pebble path out of the aire, through a turnstile, then the track through the vineyards, probably deserted apart from yourself - and the cicadas. In an absurd situation, marooned between railway and motorway, this attractive, but over-restored relic of the past has been made surreal with giant rigid balloons swaying over the roof; great fun, and definitely worth the visit, although I'm not sure I would pay to actually go in. Besides, we are on a journey, so back to the car in the covered parking area.

Pia ★
There is a tunnel for cars to the Gendarmerie on the other side of the road.

Les Pavillons ★
An attractive, well-kept aire, with a variety of Mediterranean trees, but not a large site .

Le Village Catalan
★★★ *i*
Oleander and cacti frame the ensemble of modern buildings which are built around a courtyard in the Catalan style; very pleasant. Canned music, which I don't remember hearing in any other aire, spoils the caféteria; there is a restaurant, Le Mas Catalan, and an Aubepain snack bar. Inadequate WC block in the courtyard. The craft workshops are interesting, the staff in the tourist office very helpful. Climb the tower to the Table d'Orientation; sit in the courtyard and watch the world go by if you have time; look for the statue of the motorway worker, and look at the view. However crowded this part of the aire might get, the picnic area is enormous, and you will certainly find space there. The 'Etape Sportive' is in a more open area than usual, with baseball, archery, fencing and gymnastics to try at summer weekends. It's a lovely aire.

The well-restored **Abbaye de Fontfroide** is in a secluded valley in the **Corbières**; a region of chateaux, abbeys and vineyards which, stretching from Narbonne nearly to Carcassonne, and south towards Roussillon, produces a full-bodied wine. The village of **Fitou**, where the wine of the same name is produced, lies among vineyards not far to the north of the motorway.

Two languages, both deriving from Latin, were spoken in France at the end of the Roman occupation, langue d'oil in the north and **langue d'oc** in the south. ('oil' and 'oc' were the respective words for 'yes') That the former became more important was due to the developing political power of the north, but much medieval literature had been written in langue d'oc, and so although not spoken today, efforts are made to preserve it as a language of culture.

The remarkable red-brick **Chateau de Salses** was one of the earliest forts built specifically to resist artillery.

With the feel of a frontier town, **Perpignan** is the ancient capital of Roussillon which became part of France in 1639; the influence of Catalonia is still noticeable in its dialect. Along this coast are salt water lagoons, **étangs**, where flamingoes breed.

The oldest human skull in Europe, said to be 450,000 years old, was found at **Tautavel** in 1971.

Rivesaltes is known for its dessert wine.

Driving towards Spain, the mountain chain **Les Pyrénées**, looms ahead; the Pic de Canigou, to the west, is 2784m high.

There are a number of resorts, mainly old fishing villages, on **La Cote Vermeille**, the bright red coast of Roussillon; the road is very pretty, the resorts picturesque, but the area is very crowded in summer. The purpose-built resort of Argeles Plage is no easier for cars; one balmy (weekday) evening last summer I sat in a traffic jam for a couple of hours as thousands of car drivers jostled to find one of the very few remaining parking spaces so that they could walk along the promenade, shop or eat.

The motorway péage is at Le Boulou which is a spa town, a centre of **thermalisme**.

A10

Limours Janvry
Pleasant Caféteria, its terrace rather close to the road; no picnic area.

Péage de St Arnoult
Take a ticket. There is a cool drinks machine and a free tyre pressure check after the barrier.

Boutroux ★ ★
Medium sized wooded aire, with picnic tables well back from the road, and a good childrens play area.

Francheville
24-hour bar/buffet in fuel station. No picnic area.

Le Heron Cendré ★ ★ ★
As you enter this aire, you will see a 20 foot high steel sculpture of a grey heron, glistening in the sun if it's a fine day. It's by the same artist who sculpted Sur la Trace des Vikings on the A13 near Rouen. You will pass a small lake as you enter this large, well-laid-out site with several very good childrens' play areas and lots of picnic tables among the trees.

Orléans Saran *i*
Excellent facilities in the Total shop. Then have a look at the nice spiky sculpture outside the entrance to the Arche facilities on the bridge over the motorway (caféteria open 24 hours, grill, sandwicherie, newsagents, etc). Caféroute at ground level; no picnic area.

Bellevue
Despite its name, there is no view!

Meung sur Loire

Les Fougères ★
This small aire is quite well shielded from the road by a screen of trees.

Blois Villerbon *i*
Nice Arche Caféteria with a terrace; no picnic area. There is a covered footbridge over the road to the Pizzeria.

La Chatière ★ ★
A large, well-maintained wooded area well off the motorway, with paths back among the trees for cars and a very good childrens' play area which includes a marvellous stegosaurus. Cold drinks machine.

La Courte Epée ★ ★
Having just driven under the modern TGV bridge which crosses the motorway,you drive across a very different little bridge to enter the aire. A large and pretty site, spoilt by the basic WC block.

Péage de Monnaie *i*
Pay here; free motorway around Tours.

PARIS

AIRES PARIS ~ TOURS

	km	from Paris, A6
	■	A104 La Francilienne
Limours Janvry	5	**Limours Briis sous Forges**
	■	Dourdan
Dourdan		
Péage de St Arnoult	=	**Péage de St Arnoult**
La Beauce	■	A11
	■	Allainville
Boutroux	43	**Les Marnières**
Francheville	57	**Val Neuvy**
	■	Allaines
Le Heron Cendré	75	**La Dauneuse**
		La Sologne
	■	Artenay
Orléans Saran ←	90	→ **Orléans Gidy**
		Orleans
	■	A71
Bellevue	105	
	109	**Les Chauvry**
	■	Meung
Meung sur Loire	117	**Beaugency Messas**
Les Fougères	127	**Brusolle**
	■	Mer
Val de Loire		*Chambord*
Blois Villerbon ←	143	→ **Blois Menars**
	■	Blois
		Blois Cheverny
		Chaumont
La Chatière	166	**Les Bruéres**
		Chenonceaux
		Amboise
	■	Amboise
La Courte Epée	181	**La Picardière**
Péage de Monnaie	=	**Péage de Monnaie**

TOURS

Limours Briis sous Forges
Le Boeuf Jardinier grill and Caféroute. No picnic area.

Péage de St Arnoult *i*
Pay here.

Les Marnières
Small, close to the road.

Val Neuvy
Buffet/bar in the service station, separate snack bar as well, serving very basic snacks. There are pay phones in both. No picnic area.

La Dauneuse ★ ★ ★
Well back from the road, this is a rather smart, new aire; very large with lots of trees and shrubs, and good childrens games. Something unusual for this motorway: a childrens play enclosure with sandpit.

Orléans Gidy
Separate snackbar in summer only.

Les Chauvry ★
A small aire, but quite OK.

Beaugency Messas
No picnic area.

Brusolle
Basic, and close to the road. As you leave, look out for a nice dovecote among the farm buildings to the right.

Blois Menars
Pizzeria del Arte on this side; pizzas and pasta are the only food served, and they are pretty good! The price, which is reasonable, includes a salad and bread. Service is speedy and cheerful. There is a 'take-away' service, too. No picnic area.

Les Bruères ★ ★
Look out for the sundial as you enter this good-sized aire; a further pleasant wooded area, closed in winter, at the back of the site.

La Picardière ★ ★
A medium sized wooded site, with a good screen of trees between it and the road and a nice play area. There is a cold drinks machine.

Péage de Monnaie
Gendarmerie just before péage; take a ticket.

The keep, restored in the 13th century, is all that remains of the castle at **Dourdan**.

Partridges, corn, and wheat are illustrated on the brown sign; La **Beauce** is known as 'the granary of France'. Just south of the Aire de Val Neuvy are some **menhirs** beside the motorway.

There are ducks and deer on the sign for **La Sologne**. Once a desolate waste, tree planting and canal building in the 19th century changed it into an attractive area of heathland, forests and pools.

An ancient trading centre, **Orléans** is famous for its connection with Joan of Arc, who delivered the town out of the hands of the English in 1429. The town was heavily bombed during the Second World War.

The **Val de Loire** is known as the garden of France; a gentle and peaceful landscape, a wealth of chateaux with reminders of life in pre-revolutionary France, a variety of fruit and vegetable cultivation, and vineyards. Some of this can be glimpsed from the motorway. New industry is also evident, especially on the outskirts of the larger towns, and there is a sizeable nuclear industry along the banks of the Loire.

King Francois I had several great chateaux constructed; **Chambord** was the first, built in 1519, the largest, and maybe the finest. It has a magnificent double staircase, and the only roof terrace of its kind.

Cheverny is a lovely, classical chateau; less grand architecturally than some, but richly decorated and furnished.

Overlooking the town, **Blois** is a vast and imposing chateau built in various stages and in many styles.Its most famous feature is probably the splendid spiral staircase built on a facade in the inner courtyard by Francois I; those who have visited Blois will remember the dramatic story of the murder of the Duc de Guise in the chateau in 1588.

On the banks of the Loire, **Chaumont** overlooks the town and is set in a fine park.

Only a small part of the old chateau of **Amboise** remains intact, since much of it was razed to the ground in the 17th century; what remains dominates the town and its bridge over the Loire.

On the site of an ancient mill, the beautiful chateau of **Chenonceaux** stretches across the River Cher in a most picturesque setting. Richly decorated and furnished, it is one of the most visited of the Chateaux of the Loire.

Tours La Longue Vue
Grill and sandwicherie on this side of the road; access to the 24-hour Arche caféteria by a footbridge. Newsagents. No picnic area.

Le Village Brulé ★ ★
Set well back from the road, a pleasant but not large wooded site.

Péage de Sorigny
Take a ticket. Tyre pressure check after the barrier.

Ste Maure de Touraine
Caféroute (24 hours in summer). No picnic area.

Maillé ★ ★ ★
Well back from the road in a lovely setting of Scots pines, a spacious and modern picnic area. On the 15 August 1944, most of the inhabitants of the village of Maillé were executed by the Germans in a reprisal raid, and the event is recorded on a striking stone memorial at the aire.

Chatellerault Antran *i*
Arche caféteria (24 hour) with terrace and a summer-only snack bar. No picnic area. There is a footbridge over the motorway.

Les Meuniers ★ ★
Above the road, set back in a pleasant, medium-sized wooded site.

Poitiers Jaunay Clan
Caféroute (24 hours in summer). No picnic area.

Les Cent Septiers ★
The setting, beside a car dump, spoils it somewhat!

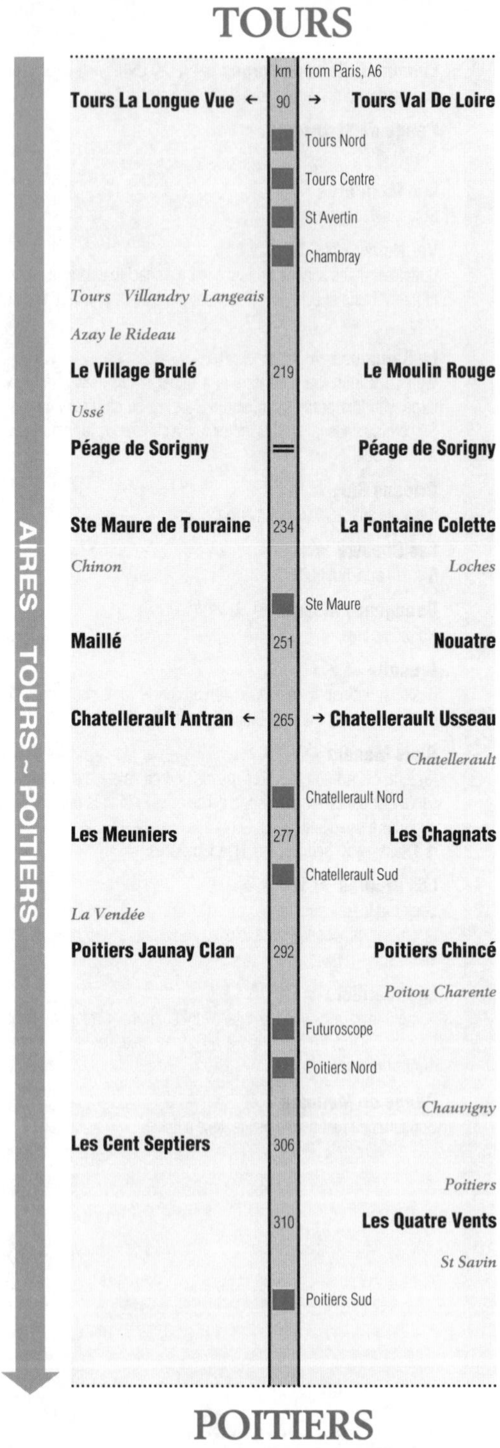

AIRES TOURS ~ POITIERS

TOURS

	km	from Paris, A6
Tours La Longue Vue ←	90	→ **Tours Val De Loire**
	■	Tours Nord
	■	Tours Centre
	■	St Avertin
	■	Chambray
Tours Villandry Langeais		
Azay le Rideau		
Le Village Brulé	219	**Le Moulin Rouge**
Ussé		
Péage de Sorigny	=	**Péage de Sorigny**
Ste Maure de Touraine	234	**La Fontaine Colette**
Chinon		*Loches*
	■	Ste Maure
Maillé	251	**Nouatre**
Chatellerault Antran ←	265	→ **Chatellerault Usseau**
		Chatellerault
	■	Chatellerault Nord
Les Meuniers	277	**Les Chagnats**
	■	Chatellerault Sud
La Vendée		
Poitiers Jaunay Clan	292	**Poitiers Chincé**
		Poitou Charente
	■	Futuroscope
	■	Poitiers Nord
		Chauvigny
Les Cent Septiers	306	
		Poitiers
	310	**Les Quatre Vents**
		St Savin
	■	Poitiers Sud

POITIERS

AIRES POITIERS ~ TOURS

Tours Val de Loire
Arche caféteria (open 24 hours in summer). Pedestrian bridge to grill on other side.

Le Moulin Rouge ★ ★
Quite extensive, with very good childrens games.

Péage de Sorigny
Pay here; the motorway around Tours is free.

La Fontaine Colette
Caféroute. (open 24 hours in summer).

Nouatre ★ ★
Wooded area and games at the back of the site; the whole recently upgraded and modernised.

Chatellerault Usseau
Arche caféteria in pleasant building; in summer a snack bar outside as well. Minimal picnic area.

Les Chagnats ★ ★
Pines and oak trees, well back from the road. Plenty of space, plenty of shade, but not much parking space.

Poitiers Chincé
A few picnic tables and even less trees; Le Boeuf Jardinier restaurant, and a Caféroute snackbar (24 hours in summer).

Les Quatre Vents ★
Well above the road, with a good screen of trees, a small aire with its picnic area on a higher level than the car parking, but not far to walk.

There is an interesting skyscape as the motorway sweeps across the Loire at **Tours**; the outlines of ancient buildings contrasting with, and rather outnumbered by, modern blocks of flats. Even more beautiful at this point is the River Cher, which the road crosses soon after. Tours is a fine example of French enthusiasm for the restoration of old buildings.

Langeais never underwent the extensions and alterations which make most ancient monuments examples of a variety of styles, and its refurbishment this century in the style of the 15th century makes it an interesting place to visit. Its keep is the oldest in France.

Was **Ussé** the inspiration for the setting of 'The Sleeping Beauty'? A lovely setting on the edge of the Forest of Chinon, backing onto a cliff and looking down over the River Indre.

There are no terrassed gardens in France to compare with those at **Villandry;** quite outstanding, in the Italian style. The elegant fortified chateau of **Azay le Rideau** is strategically placed on an island on the Indre, where the river is crossed by the road from Tours to Chinon.

Chinon is where Joan of Arc picked out the Dauphin, disguised among his courtiers, and from where she and her soldiers set out to save France.

There has been a fortress on the bluff above the River Vienne at **Loches** for 1000 years; the chateau, the old town and the keep are situated there to this day.

The **Chatellerault** sign shows the bridge over the Vienne. It is a lovely old town, with an interesting Motor Museum.

La Vendée is one of the ancient provinces of France. There are numerous Romanesque churches in **Poitou Charente**, many of them humbly proportioned but unique works of art because of the richness of their decoration; the region also has its cognac; its canals and rivers with charming names; its forests and marshes.

With its five forts and its Romanesque church, **Chauvigny** dominates the Vienne valley.

The **Futuroscope** is a sizeable and impressive leisure park, its buildings futuristic in design. It is said that the windows are cleaned by mountaineers; you will understand why when you look around. Open from April to October; quite pricy; a number of different exhibition halls to visit. Leave the motorway at Junction 18. Take the second exit at the roundabout, past the Hotel Ibis,and at the next roundabout take the third, and the Futuroscope is ahead of you.

On the **Poitiers** sign are the baptistry of St Jean, the oldest religious building in France (4th century)(centre), the Romanesque Tower of St Radegonde(right) and the spire of the Church of Montierneuf. The Maubourget Tower, where Joan of Arc was tried, is also here.

There are remarkable 10th - 13th century frescos in **Saint Savin's** Romanesque church.

Coulombiers ★ ★
Set well back from the road, with a large grassy slope and trees which need time to mature. There is a good selection of climbing frames.

Rouillé Pamproux ★ ★ ★
Drive past the fuel station where there is a bar/buffet in summer and you will come to the picnic area which has a good 'parcours de sante'; with a shower afterwards, just the thing to keep the driver alert! Or try gymnastics on a summer weekend. There are grassy ares, pine trees and a pond. Very nice.

Ste Eanne ★ ★
Above the level of the road, with a good screen of pine trees.

Ste Neomaye ★ ★
A small site, but with quite a lot of grass, swings and climbing logs for the children. The trees need time to mature, but it is a pleasant aire.

Les Ruralies *i*
As you approach this large aire you will not fail to notice a tall wooden structure with giant rings of red, yellow and blue strung along poles on either side; a striking introduction to an aire which contains a cluster of modern buildings which echo traditional architecture in their rounded corners and sloping tiled roofs. Drive up past the fuel station to the large parking area. There is an excellent regional products shop with a small exhibition of farm machinery alongside. Then a splendid building housing the tourist information office and exhibition centre. Beyond the courtyard is the Museum of Agricultural Machinery, which you have to pay to go into. There is rather a smart restaurant and a nice Relais cafeteria, fast food snack bar and shop. Practise fencing, golf or shooting on a summer weekend. It is possible to return towards Paris from here; ask for a 'jeton' at the hotel to open the barrier.

Gript ★
This is quite a new site with ponds and good planting of trees.

Doeuil sur le Mignon ★
A small aire, but there is a nice grassy bank and some good climbing apparatus for children. We are far enough south now for there to be a shady seating area around the drinking fountain in the WC block.

Lozay ★ ★
A really nice aire, quite sizeable with plenty of grass and a good number of picnic tables. Some of the WC blocks on this motorway are very attractive!

Fenioux ★ ★
After the fuel station there are steps up to a large picnic area on a higher level with a good children's play area among the trees.

POITIERS

AIRES POITIERS ~ SAINTES

	km	from Paris A6
Coulombiers	324	**Coulombiers**
Sanxay		*Seuil de Poitou*
Rouillé Pamproux	338	**Rouillé Pamproux**
Sèvre Niotaise		
	■	St Maixent Lusignan
Sainte Eanne	347	**Sainte Eanne**
St Maixent l'Ecole		
Sainte Neomaye	361	**Sainte Neomaye**
Le Marais Poitevin		
		Pays Mellois
	■	Niort Nord
Les Ruralies ←	372	→ **Les Ruralies**
Niort		
	■	La Rochelle Niort Sud
Gript	382	**Gript**
La Vendée		
L'Ile de Ré		*Forét de Chizé*
Doeuil sur le Mignon	397	**Doeuil sur le Mignon**
La Rochelle Surgères		
Lozay	406	**La Benate**
Rochefort		
La Boutonne		
Ile d'Oléren Marennes		
La Charente		
	■	St Jean d'Angely
Fenioux	422	**Fenioux**
La Saintonge		

SAINTES

Coulombiers ★

Quite a lot of trees with a grassy area at the back; good climbing frames for children; not many tables.

Rouillé Pamproux ★ ★

A pleasant site, backing onto fields with woods in the background. Imaginative climbing apparatus for children.

Ste Eanne ★

Small, but pleasant, with the play area on a grassy mound at the back of the site.

Ste Neomaye

A small aire, with a bank between it and the road, but not many trees.

Les Ruralies

Drive past the service station, and through the tunnel under the motorway. It is possible to return towards Bordeaux from here.

Gript ★

Surrounded by fields, this is quite an open site, but a lot of young trees have been planted.

Doeuil sur le Mignon ★

A small, grassy area.

La Benate ★ ★

The site extends well back into the trees; plenty of space.

Fenioux ★ ★

A well-laid-out picnic area beyond the fuel station.

Roman remains, pointing more to the existence of a villa, rather than a military settlement, were found at **Sanxay** in the early 19th century.

Between Niort and the sea the wide, lazy **Sèvre Niortaise** river is the source of the canalisation and land reclamation that is the Marais.

On the threshold of Poitou, the **Seuil de Poitou**; Romanesque churches and abbeys; canals, rivers and marshes, greenness. Every village seems to have its Romanesque church, almost as if those 10th and 11th century craftsmen were motivated not only by piety but also the desire to encourage pilgrims bound for Santiago de Compostela to stop in their village rather than in the next!

The ancient abbey at **St Maixent l'Ecole**, ruled by St Maxentius, was destroyed by the Huguenots.

Melle's three Romanesque churches indicate its former importance as the seat of a mint, there being lead mines in the **Pays Mellois** area, rather than the enthusiasm of its craftsmen.

Niort is renowned for its angelica, which used to be produced by monks. Napoleon spent his last night in France here before being shipped off to St Helena in 1815.

The largest area of woodland in the region, the **Foret de Chizé** is to the east of the motorway,bounded by the Boutonne.

All its public buildings in **Surgères** are within the 16th century walls, scattered among beautiful gardens and parkland.

The **Marais Poitevin** is an extensive area of fen-like country north of La Rochelle, reclaimed from the sea in the 17th century.

Children using a Tricolore textbook in their French lessons know quite a lot about **La Rochelle**. M. Dhome and his family really do exist and, at least when the book was first published, enjoyed being recognised by English visitors! A 17th century stronghold of Protestantism, its inhabitants were among the first in Europe to trade with America.

L'Ile de Ré is a flat, sandy island reached by a regular car ferry service.

The region around Saintes is, of course, **Saintonge**, with a wealth of fine churches.

Rochefort's brown sign says it all; a military port and arsenal, designed and built to a regular plan by Colbert in 1666. Novelist Pierre Loti was born here. A charming little town, once a stronghold of Protestantism, **St Jean d'Angely's** abbey was destroyed by the Huguenots. There are half timbered houses in narrow streets, one spanned by an ancient bell tower, a Renaissance fountain and a Romanesque church to see.

We pass through the **Vallée de la Boutonne**; what a quaint name for a river, the Button!

La Charente flows into the sea at **Rochefort**. In a low-lying, marshy area, **Marennes** is famed for its oysters.

The largest of the islands off this coast of France, **L'Ile d'Oléron** is linked to Marennes by a viaduct.

Port d'Envaux ★ ★
Well back from the road, another large site. There is a strange concrete structure in the woods, but enough trees around for it not to be an eye sore.

Chermignac ★ ★
This is small, but quite pleasant, its picnic area on a higher level.

St Leger ★ ★ ★ *i*
An excellent, large site. Beyond the fuel station and the Arche caféteria, there are plenty of tables among the trees, concrete reclining chairs, lots of footpaths to further picnic spots, a nice grassy area and a good parcours de santé. Have a go at fencing, golf or archery on a summer weekend.

St Palais de Phiolin ★ ★
Surrounded by the vineyards of Cognac, this site extends a little further to the south than you might realise at first.

St Ciers du Taillon ★ ★
A nice, wooded site, with a good play area.

St Caprais de Blaye ★ ★
Well off the road; not large, but pretty, with tables among the tall Mediterranean pines.

Saugon ★ ★ ★ *i*
Beyond the Boeuf Jardinier grill and Caféroute (open 24 hours in summer), there is a lovely, spacious picnic area among the pine woods with good climbing frames.

St Christoly ★ ★

Péage de Virsac
Pay here.

L'Estalot
No more than a lorry park, really. No picnic area.

BORDEAUX RING ROAD
Avoid this if you can, especially in the rush hour, as it is mainly 2-lane. However, there are services if needed, as described below.

Le Lac
As you travel west, this is beside the lake which has the Exhibition Centre on its far side. Fuel station with mini-caféteria inside the shop, but little parking.

The second fuel station on the ring road is just before the Merignac turn off.

There is a third fuel station soon after the A63 turn off.

AIRES SAINTES - BORDEAUX

SAINTES

	km	from Paris A6
Port d'Envaux	434	**Port d'Envaux**
		Saintes
Le Verdon		Saintes
Royan		
Chermignac	445	**Chermignac**
		Vignobles de Cognac
Saint Leger ←	456	→ **Saint Leger**
		Pons
		Pons
St Palais de Phiolin	467	**St Palais de Phiolin**
St Ciers du Taillon	476	**St Ciers du Taillon**
Estuaire de la Gironde		
		Mirambeau
St Caprais	493	**Bois Redon**
		Blaye Montendre
Saugon	506	**Saugon**
Vignobles de Bordelais		
St Christoly	515	
	520	**Cezac**
		L'Isle
Péage de Virsac	=	**Péage de Virsac**
		Libourne
		St Andre de Cubzac
La Dordogne		
L'Estalot	530	**Meillac**

BORDEAUX

Aire de Venoy Grosse Pierre, A6

Aire de Narbonne-Vinassan, A9

Monte Carlo seen from the Aire de Beausoleil, A8

Aire de Caissargues, A54. © Autoroutes du Sud de la France, J. Chatin

Les colonnes de Suchères at the Aire de Suchères, A72

Aire d'Hastingues, A64. © Autoroutes du Sud de la France, Y. Collet

Autoroutes du Sud de la France

The largest motorways company in France

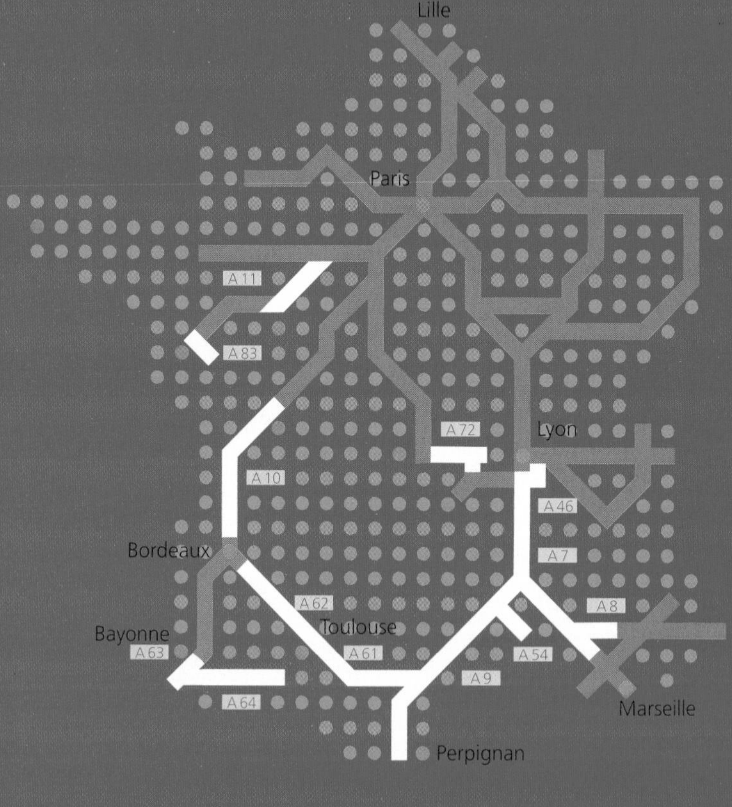

1044 miles in service
85 rest areas, 166 service areas,
53 restaurants, 10 hotels

AIRES BORDEAUX ~ SAINTES

Port d'Envaux ★ ★

Rather small, but OK.

Chermignac ★

This is a small site.

St Leger ★ ★ *i*

Some of the picnic tables are remarkably close to the road. Drive past the fuel station, the large lorry park and yet more tables by the road, and you can park near the pedestrian tunnel which leads to the Arche caféteria and grill on the other side of the motorway. It's a great tunnel, light and airy, with trees and shrubs growing in it and posters of local tourist spots on the sides. The picnic area on the far side is better if you have children because of the games and the organised activities in summer; this involves a trek through the tunnel, though, so stay this side if games are not what you want; there is quite an extensive area of woodland here, too.

St Palais de Phiolin ★ ★

Quite well screened; a very well laid out, wooded site.

St Ciers du Taillon ★ ★

Again, well screened from the road, with a lot of tables among the trees and a good grassy area.

Boisredon ★ ★

A good screen of trees between it and the road; a large grassy area with woods beyond.

Saugon ★ ★ ★ *i*

Drive past the front of the service station and you come to a Relais de Bordeaux caféteria. Petit Café snack bar in summer. Beyond these is the picnic area and parcours de santé among the trees. It is a really good aire; lots of tables and space in a nice setting.

Cezac ★ ★

A high wooded bank between this spacious aire and the road, and paths for cars to drive back into the woods.

Péage de Virsac

Take a ticket. Tyre pressure check and traffic information after the barrier.

Meillac

An Aubepain drive-in snack bar serving from two windows direct to your car; seating area inside as well. No picnic area.

The northernmost point of the Medoc peninsula is La Pointe de Grave, where a memorial marks the landing of U.S. troops in 1917; sheltered by it is **Le Verdon**, an industrial town linked to **Royan** on the north bank of the Gironde estuary by a car ferry from La Pointe.

With its great sandy bay, pine woods and cliff walks, **Royan** is a popular resort. Out to sea can be seen the old lighthouse, Le Phare de Cordouan.

The brown sign for **Saintes** reflects its Gallo-Roman past; there is also a beautiful Romanesque abbey and medieval quarter.

The countryside of the **Estuaire de la Gironde** would lack character if it were not for the world famous vineyards; the great names of Medoc to the west, the Cotes de Bourg and de Blaye to the east. There are pretty fishing villages on the coast south of Royan, and the suberb 12th century church of Ste Radegonde at Talmont worthy of a special visit.

Pons is a picturesque town with a feudal castle.

The **Vignobles de Cognac** are at the centre of the Charente brandy trade.

The two great rivers of the region, the **Isle** and the **Dordogne,** meet at Libourne, then flow out as the Dordogne into the Gironde estuary. The view from the motorway as it crosses it south of St Andre de Cubsac is very fine.

Bordeaux - the very name conjures up wine - is surrounded by the **Vignobles du Bordelais**, vineyards which have thrived here since Roman times. Among the world famous names are Graves, Entre Deux Mers (from between the Garonne and the Dordogne), St Emilion and Fronsac.

Bordeaux; 'at the edge of the water' with a busy port, the export of wine is its most important trade. With its long history of links with England, it is an interesting town to visit; it is also a lively modern centre with a university, and post-war industrial development in its suburbs which makes it a less-than-ideal place to drive through!

Limours Janvry
Pleasant Caféteria, its terrace rather close to the road.

Péage de St Arnoult
Take a ticket. There is a cool drinks machine and tyre pressure check after the barriers.

Gourville ★
A pretty location, surrounded by fields, a village in the distance. Take the track to the back of aire to reach picnic tables among trees, good childrens games.

Chartres Gasville
Arche caféteria, (open 24 hours) with a good terrace. There is a separate snack bar with terrace. The fuel station is further on. No picnic area.

Souchet

La Poele Percée ★ ★
Good screen from the road in this large, wooded aire; there is a further picnic, WC and play area at far end of site.

La Charonnerie ★
Well back from road, good grassy area at back for games.

Brou Frazé
After the fuel station there is a separate snack bar, Le Perche, with terrace. No picnic area.

Les Charmes ★
Well sheltered from the road, a heavily wooded site extending back among the trees. A good choice on a hot day.

Théligny ★
Set well back, medium sized, with a large grassy area.

La Ferté Bernard
Good-sized bar/buffet in fuel station, Arche caféteria and Relais Bébé tent beyond. Separate snack bar with terrace; no picnic area. Footbridge to other side of the motorway.

Parnouette ★
Well sheltered from road, heavily wooded.

Haras de Maulepaire
Small, but OK.

Le Mans La Pivardière
There is a footbridge to the facilities on the other side of the motorway.

AIRES PARIS – NANTES

PARIS

	km	from Paris A6
Limours Janvry (A10)	5	**Limours Briis sous Forges (A10)**
		Dourdan
		Dourdan
Péage de St Arnoult (A10)	=	**Péage de St Arnoult (A10)**
		A10
		Ablis
Gourville	35	**Les Chaudonnes**
		La Beauce
Chartres Gasville ←	52	→ **Chartres Bois Paris**
		Chartres
Chartres		
Le Souchet	64	**Les Moineaux**
		Thivars
La Poele Percée	76	**Les Dix Sept Setiers**
		Chateaudun
La Charonnerie	88	**La Leu**
Brou Frazé	99	**Brou Dampierre**
		Luigny
Les Charmes	110	**La Petite Jardinière**
Le Perche		
Théligny	123	**Montmirail**
		La Ferte Bernard
La Ferté Bernard ←	136	→ **Villaines la Gonais**
Parnouette	150	**La Charpenterie**
Haras de Maulepaire	160	**La Martinière**
		Le Mans Est
		Abbaye de l'Epau
La Pivardière	166	**Sarge Le Mans**
		Le Mans Nord
		Le Mans
		A81
		Le Mans Centre

LE MANS

AIRES NANTES ~ PARIS

Limours Briis sous Forges
Le Boeuf Jardinier grill restaurant and Caféroute.

Péage de St Arnoult *i*
Pay here.

Les Chaudonnes
Picnic before you reach Chartres, if possible; this small aire, the last before Paris, gets rather crowded.

Chartres Bois Paris
Arche caféteria (open 24 hours) and separate bar/buffet after the fuel station. No picnic area. There is a footbridge over the motorway.

Les Moineaux

Les Dix-Sept Setiers ★ ★
The road winds around inside the aire to several parking places and good play areas. There is a second parking area beyond the main one, with its own WC block, and exercise circuit.

La Leu ★
There are steps up at the back of the aire to the picnic area.

Brou Dampierre
Separate bar-buffet, with terrace, beyond the service station. No picnic area.

La Petite Jardinière ★
Includes a good area of grass; very pleasant.

Montmirail ★

Villaines la Gonais
Courte-Paille Grill, serving simple but good meals, and snack bar (summer only) on this side; footbridge to the far side of the road. No picnic area.

La Charpenterie

La Martinière
Not a lot of space, but pleasant.

Sarge Le Mans *i*
Good facilities in the Arche building include a caféteria, regional products shop and a small car museum. Separate snack bar with terrace. No picnic area.

La Beauce is the granary of France; a gently undulating, arid plain with hamlets and occasional clumps of trees surrounded by neat fields of corn in which game birds abound. It was from the Beauce that pilgrims, travelling on foot to Chartres from Paris, would see the Cathedral, well before any of the surrounding town became visible, giving the illusion of isolation, and a similar splendid view can be seen from the motorway.

Chartres Cathedral, a masterpiece of 13th century architecture, with stained glass of a blue never quite copied elsewhere, the old town along the banks of the river Eure, charmingly restored in recent years and the lively shopping centre are all worth a visit.

Picturesque **Chateaudun** has a well-preserved and atmospheric fortified castle.

Le Perche is a charming and peaceful part of France, wooded and hilly, the region is noted for its horse rearing, its cider and its cooking. The best black pudding I have yet tasted was in Mortagne sur Perche, served in the local fashion with a puree of Normandy apples.

The restored 13th century **Abbaye de l'Epau** near Le Mans is where Berengaria, the widow of Richard the Lionheart, spent her last days and is buried .

The ramparts of **Le Mans** date from Gallo-Roman times, the old town itself, overlooking the Sarthe, is medieval. It had close links with England through the House of Plantagenet in the Middle Ages. Today, of course, we link the town with the 24 hour motor race, and the motorway traveller will be reminded of this by direction signs to the circuit and by the museum at the Aire de Sarge Le Mans.

A11

Pruillé le Chétif ★
Very good play area, but close to road.

Pirmil ★
Lots of grass; a pleasant situation.

Parce sur Sarthe ★ ★ ★
Drive past the fuel station to the extensive wooded picnic site where you can try archery or shooting on summer weekends. It is very pleasant. At the Relais de la Sarthe there is a cafeteria, snack bar and shop.

La Chapelle St Laud ★ ★ ★
Drive past the main aire and take the gravelled path which leads to the best picnic site so far, a large wooded area with plenty of individual parking places. There is a good parcours de santé at the very back.

Péage de Corzé
Pay here; Gendarmerie after the barriers.

Baune ★ ★
Take the gravelled path into the large wooded area where there are tables among the trees.

Les Portes d'Angers
There is a vehicular bridge over the motorway to reach the facilities other than the fuel station.

Les Montilets ★

Varades le Genetais *i*
Bar-buffet with terrace at the fuel station shop. Minimal picnic area.

Péage d'Ancenis *i*
No tickets; pay the one rate Angers-Nantes.

Le Cellier ★
Thick woods, but not a large site.

AIRES LE MANS ~ NANTES

LE MANS

	km	
		from Paris, A6
		Le Mans Ouest
Pruillé le Chétif	181	**Pruillé le Chétif**
		Le Mans Sud
Pirmil	197	**Pirmil**
Parcé sur Sarthe ←	211	→ **Parcé sur Sarthe**
		Sable la Fleche
		Durtal
		Chateau de la Fleche
		Chateau du Lude
La Chapelle St Laud	234	**La Chapelle St Laud**
		Seche Sur le Loir
Péage de Corzé	=	**Péage de Corzé**
Baune	248	**Baune**
		Pelloualles les Vignes
Les Portes d'Angers	258	**Les Portes d'Angers**
		Angers Est
		N23
		Angers
		St Jean de Lignieres
Les Montilets	277	**Reveillon**
Varades les Genetais	296	**Varades la Bedoire**
		Ancenis
Péage d'Ancenis	=	**Péage d'Ancenis**
Le Cellier	326	**Launay**
		Carquefou

NANTES

Pruillé le Chétif ★ ♿ /Π\ ☎
Quite a lot of space; good games for small children.

Pirmil ★ ♿ /Π\ ☎
Pretty view of 12th century church from the aire.

Parcé sur Sarthe ★ ⛽ 🔧 ✕ ♿ /Π\
The picnic area is beyond the fuel station and snack bar; it will be very nice when trees mature. There is quite an amazing entrance to the pedestrian tunnel to the Relais de la Sarthe and sports facilities on the other side of the road.

La Chapelle St Laud ★ ♿ /Π\ ☎
A pleasant, well laid out aire, but choose to go here when it's not sunny.

Péage de Corzé ♿
Take a ticket. Tyre pressure check after the barrier.

Baune ★ ★ ♿ /Π\ 🌳 ☎
Drive back along the gravel path into the trees; there is a good play area.

Les Portes d'Angers ⛽ 🔧 ✕ ♿
Boeuf Jardinier grill, Caféroute snack bar.

Reveillon ☎
Plan not to arrive here at lunchtime; it is very small, and the next picnic site is beyond Angers, a good half-hour away.

Varades la Bedoire ⛽ ♿ 🌳
Quite a crowded aire, without much space.

Péage d'Ancenis
Pay here for Nantes - Angers section. Gendarmerie after the barrier.

Launay ★ 🌳
A pleasant, thickly wooded site.

The fine **Chateau du Lude** has a huge tower at each of its four corners.

There has been a military college at **La Fleche** since 1604. The old **Chateau** des Carmes houses the town hall.

There is no motorway by-pass of **Angers**, but the drive along the 10kms or so of dual-carriageway through the town, is straightforward and usually without hold-ups. There are fine views of the old town, too.

Despite not being on the sea, **Nantes** is a busy commercial port and industrial town with a cathedral and castle. The local wines are the white Muscadet and Gros Plant.

No tickets on this motorway. Throwing the correct change into a net at one of the left hand booths is the most rapid means of paying; if you have no change, go to one of the booths on the right hand side, where there is an attendant.

Giberville

There are a few tables among the trees at the end of the aire.

Péage de Dozulé

Pay here.

Beaumont ★ ★

Quite spacious, nice woods at back, pleasant.

Beuzeville

Despite having a snack bar sign (cup), the Elf shop shuts at 20h00; automatic drinks machines only open after this. Dont rely on the shop staying open even though fuel stations are open 24 hrs.

Péage de Beuzeville

Pay here.

Le Moulin ★

Screen of a few trees; a road winds its way around this small but pleasant site to picnic tables, one of which is covered. There is a horizontal bar for adult exercise.

AIRES CAEN ~ PONT-AUDEMER

CAEN

	km	from Paris	
Caen			*Mémorial pour la Paix*
			Sidérurgie
		Mondeville	
Giberville	220		**Giberville**
		Troarn	
			Normandie
			Cabourg
			Houlgate
		Dozulé	
Péage de Dozulé	=		**Péage de Dozulé**
Le Pays d'Auge			
	195		**Annebault**
Beaumont	191		
		La Haie Tondue	
			Deauville
			Trouville
		A932	
Lisieux			*LaCote Fleurie*
St Germain de Livet			
			Honfleur
Beuzeville	171		**Beuzeville**
Péage de Beuzeville	=		**Péage de Beuzeville**
		Beuzeville	
Le Moulin	148		**Josapha**
		A131, Le Havre	

PONT-AUDEMER

Giberville

Péage de Dozulé
Pay here.

Annebault ★ ★

A good sized aire, set well back, and screened by a bank of trees. The tables are among the trees and on a grassy bank at the back which stretches up into woods.

Beuzeville

Péage de Beuzeville
Pay here.

Josapha

Just after the bifurcation to Le Havre.

The two splendid abbeys of William the Conqueror, and of his queen Matilda, survived the bombing of June 1944 which destroyed three-quarters of **Caen**. Make time to visit the **Mémorial pour la Paix** one day; hope for the future manages to emerge from the horror of the deportations of the Second World War. A sloping path descends from the end of the First War to the hell of the Second. A most moving experience, and an excellent film of the Normandy landings to see at the end, which, for me, depicted the horror rather than the glory of that occasion.

The iron and steel industry, **La Sidérurgie**, of Normandy is based at Mondeville where an industrial zone has been developed alongside the blast furnaces and steel works. The Caen canal is its link with the sea.

Cabourg is a seaside resort with wonderful sandy beaches where Marcel Proust stayed and wrote. **Houlgate,** its neighbour has equally fine beaches.

The hinterland of the Cote Fleurie is the **Pays d'Auge**; a region of woods, pastures, orchards, half-timbered manor houses, farmhouses and thatched cottages. Local goodies include cider, calvados, cream and cheeses.

The largest of the resorts on this coast is **Deauville**, on the west side of the river Touques where it joins the sea. Its promenade of wooden planks, Les Planches, is famous as a gathering place for holidaymakers.

At the mouth of the Touques, on the east side, and with its own Planches, **Trouville** is the town which launched the Cote Fleurie in 1852.

La Cote Fleurie is that part of the coast from Honfleur round to Cabourg which has been popular for seaside holidays since the mid 19th century, and was immortalised in the paintings of the Impressionists who came to its beaches and rivers, attracted by the light and the beauty of the scenery.

St Germain de Livet is a charming stone and brick chateau, typical of the Auge region.

The basilica of St Theresa dominates **Lisieux**, the town where she lived as a Carmelite nun.

A delightful, picturesque and crowded fishing port at the mouth of the Seine, **Honfleur** was much loved by the Impressionists, one of whom, Boudin, was born and lived here. Eric Satie, the composer, was also born here and has a square named after him.

Dubious fame of having been Europe's worst damaged port in the Second World War, **Le Havre** is the point of entry into France for many travellers from the UK and Ireland. It is a relatively easy town for the motorist to leave, clearly signposted to the Pont de Tanquerville, the motorway to Caen or Paris and to other roads. Having left the city centre, keep in the left hand, outer lane and use the three subways to avoid crossroads with lights. Try to remember to do the same on entering the town, even though traffic for ferries is signalled to take the inner lane.

Eturqueraye

Bosgouet
Not a well cared for site; there are a few tables, very close to the road. The Maison de Normandie is on this side of the road, and a footbridge provides access from the other side. A modestly-priced menu is served, as well as snacks. Quite pleasant, quick service. The building is a copy of a Norman barn. There is a ramp up to the entrance, but not up to the shop/WC level, which is on the first floor. At the far end of the site is a test-your-reflexes driving centre (Centre Centaure).

Bord ★ ★
Situated in beechwoods on the brow of a hill and screened from the road by a grassy bank, this is a super spot.

Vironvay
Cross the covered footbridge to the Arche facilities.

Péage de Heudebouville
Pay here.

Beauchene
A pleasant site; not large, but you can walk in the woods.

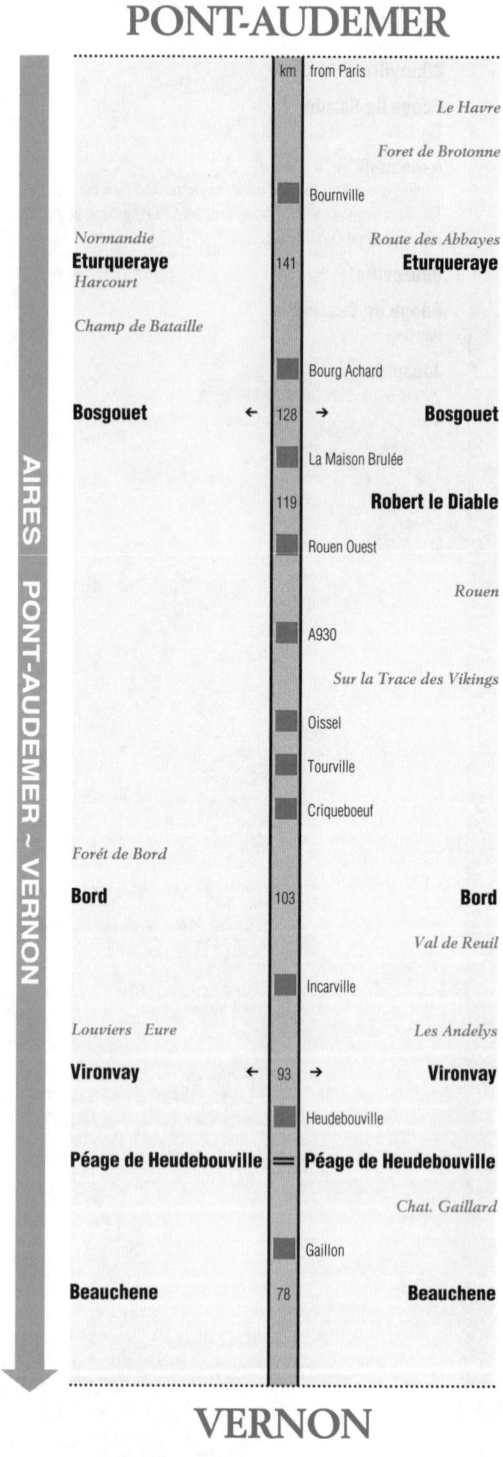

AIRES PONT-AUDEMER ~ VERNON

PONT-AUDEMER

	km	from Paris
		Le Havre
		Foret de Brotonne
	■	Bournville
Normandie		*Route des Abbayes*
Eturqueraye	141	**Eturqueraye**
Harcourt		
Champ de Bataille		
	■	Bourg Achard
Bosgouet ←	128	→ **Bosgouet**
	■	La Maison Brulée
	119	**Robert le Diable**
	■	Rouen Ouest
		Rouen
	■	A930
		Sur la Trace des Vikings
	■	Oissel
	■	Tourville
	■	Criqueboeuf
Forét de Bord		
Bord	103	**Bord**
		Val de Reuil
	■	Incarville
Louviers Eure		*Les Andelys*
Vironvay ←	93	→ **Vironvay**
	■	Heudebouville
Péage de Heudebouville	=	**Péage de Heudebouville**
		Chat. Gaillard
	■	Gaillon
Beauchene	78	**Beauchene**

VERNON

AIRES VERNON ~ PONT-AUDEMER

Eturqueraye

Bosgouet

Covered footbridge to Maison de Normandie on far side of the road. No picnic area.

Robert le Diable

Small, attractive and well planned, with a good view over the Seine valley.

Bord ★★

Medium sized aire in beech woods.

Vironvay

Arche facilities include a caféteria, open 24 hours. There is an outside snack bar, open in summer only, and a cash dispenser. No picnic area.

Péage de Heudebouville

Pay here. Tyre pressure check after the barrier.

Beauchene ★ *i*

A covered picnic area; could be useful! The best aire since Paris.

Christianity reached the region in the third century, and monasteries developed as centres of learning, religious and intellectual life from the 6th century. Relative peace and stability followed the foundation of the Dukedom of **Normandy**, and monastic life flourished, leading to renewed building and restoration of abbeys and churches. The **Route des Abbayes** guides the tourist to some of the finest of these.

Now a regional nature reserve, the **Foret de Brotonne** comprises oak, beech and Scots pine, and provides a natural check to urban development in the giant loop in the Seine as it approaches it's estuary.

Not the site of a battle, **Champ de Bataille** is the name of a 17th century mansion near Le Neubourg.

Harcourt is a fortified medieval castle, surrounded by a 66ft wide moat, and set in a fine park with an arboretum.

The **Chateau**, supposedly built by the mythical **Robert le Diable**, a figure inspired by the father of William the Conqueror, the ruins house a Viking museum, and have a good view down to the Seine.

On the site of the first Roman settlement on the Seine, and with a rich and varied history, there is a lot to see in the port of **Rouen**; the old streets, the Great Clock, the churches. The cathedral with memories of Monet; so often did he paint it that it is familiar even on a first visit. But don't miss the modern church dedicated to Joan of Arc in the old market place. And, for devotees, there is a stuffed parrot in the house where Flaubert was born!

'**Sur la Trace des Vikings**', Georges Saulterre's stainless steel structure, can be seen for three kilometres due to its splendid site on a col between the two banks of the Seine near Pont de l'Arche. It was at Pont de l'Arche that a wooden bridge was built in 873 to defend the area from the 'men from the north', but to no avail; the Viking raiders passed, and eventually reached Paris and from there the valleys of the Marne and the Yonne. Years of terror ended when the Viking Rollo was created the first Duke of Normandy by the French king, Charles the Simple, in 911. **Sur la trace des Vikings** points forward and to the interior of France, so relating not only to the Viking invasion but to the A13 motorway itself and to the varied destinations of those travelling along it.

The **Eure** joins the Seine at Pont de l'Arche, and gives its name to the Département you are driving through. The motorway runs through the beechwood **Foret de Bord**. On a loop in the Seine, 100kms from Paris, the new town of **Val de Reuil**, built in the 1970s, is well placed for water sports and other leisure activities.

A paradise for fishermen, **Louviers** is in the centre of the valleys of the Seine, the Iton and the Eure, whose many branches criss-cross the town. The traditional woollen mills have made way for the light industry of a modern industrial estate. There are several half-timbered houses to see near the church.

Douains
Small, in an area of open fields.

Villeneuve en Chevrie ♿
Fairly basic; small wooded area at back.

Rosny sur Seine ⛽ ✕ ♿
Le Bistro restaurant. No picnic area.

Péage de Buchelay
Pay here. There is a motorway information office after the booths.

Epone
Small, basic site, with woods at back.

Morainvilliers ⛽ 🔧 ✕ ♿
This aire really looks in need of a facelift. The cafeteria and newsagents are on the bridge over the motorway; there is a lift but to reach that you have to go up some steps, so no access for the disabled. There is, however, one WC for the disabled behind the fuel station. We were personally not impressed by the coffee served over the counter in the cafeteria. The best coffee at French motorway services generally comes out of serve-yourself espresso machines and we have not seen one in this cafeteria yet. However we noticed later that there was a Zanussi machine behind the counter; we should have asked for that. There is a shower in the men's WC block. No picnic area.

If your destination is beyond Paris and you are heading for the A10, A11, A6 or A5 avoid the Paris ring road, the Peripherique, which is almost always very busy, by turning off the A13 at the **Triangle de Rocquencourt**, signposted to **St Quentin des Yvelines**, not to Versailles as you might expect. Then follow the **Evry/Lyon** signs; do not rely on road numbers which are not used as often in France as one would like.

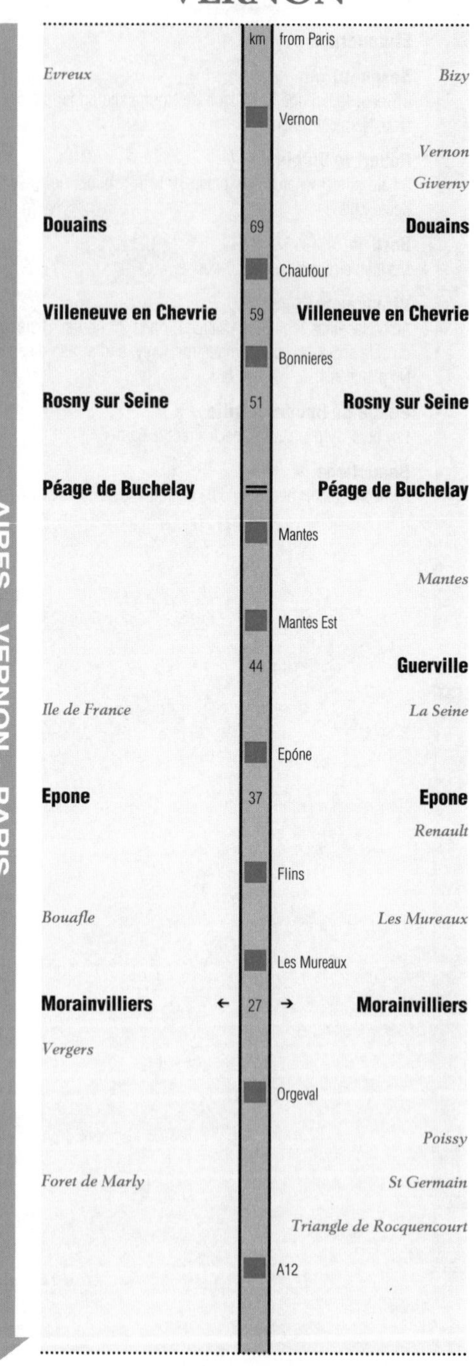

AIRES PARIS ~ VERNON

Douains
Small and basic. No access to woods at back.

Villeneuve en Chevrie ★
Small and wooded, but pretty basic.

Rosny sur Seine
No picnic area, but quite a large parking area beyond the fuel station. The only WCs are through the fuel station shop, past the Espace Communications which includes a FAX machine.

Péage de Buchelay
Pay here.

Guerville
A very basic aire, no WC or picnic area, but a good view over the Seine.

Epone
Less than basic; no picnic area.

Morainvilliers
Facilities are on the bridge over the motorway–see A13 south. No picnic area.

A pretty walk along the banks of the Iton below its ancient ramparts belies **Evreux**' history of violence, from its sacking by vandals in the 5th century to the German and Allied air raids of the Second World War.

In a magnificent setting deep in one of the loops of the Seine, the ruins of **Chateau Gaillard** overlook the town of **Les Andelys**, but cannot be seen from the motorway. There is a medieval **farmhouse** to the north of the motorway, near Louviers, just after crossing the Eure, travelling towards Paris.

Vernon on the Seine is close to **Giverny** and **Bizy**, where there is an 18th century chateau. Monet lived and painted at Giverny for over 40 years; his house and garden are open to the public, thanks largely to an American benefactor, and is one of the most popular tourist attractions in France. It is quite delightful. Not open in winter, nor on Mondays; try going at lunchtime to avoid the queues.

The region around Paris is known as the **Ile de France**; steeped in history, with palaces, chateaux and religious buildings, forests, rivers and gardens, and new towns built in the 1960s to relieve population pressure on the capital.

The building of the beautiful church at **Mantes**, as fine as many a cathedral, was partly funded by William the Conqueror. As the motorway runs through the town, its residents are protected to some extent from the noise by attractive perspex, concrete and wooden panels in 1930s style.

Driving towards Paris, there is a good view of the river **Seine**, on your left, and a glorious one of the Porcheville EDF power station, all 2400 megawatts! Near Aubergenville, there is a huge **Renault** complex beside the Seine. Look out for the extra-terrestrial power lines, just after. **Les Mureaux** is the home of the French aerospace industry. South of the motorway, just west of Flins, is a small group of medieval farm buildings and the village of **Bouafle**.

A royal residence from early times, a religious centre and then a market town, **Poissy** is now the home of Talbot cars. It also boasts a Romanesque church, the **Collégiale**, where St Louis was christened in 1214. Since then the faithful have scraped the dust from the stone walls to dissolve in water and drink as a remedy for fever.

There has been a fortified stronghold at **St Germain** since the 12th century. The present chateau, dating from the 16th century, was the childhood home of Mary Queen of Scots. It has a lovely 17th century terrace, one of Le Notre's finest achievements. In the midst of this industrial area, is the unexpected sight of orchards, the **Vergers de Chambourcy et d'Orgeval**, apparently thriving despite having been cut in two by the motorway, close to a medieval village and ruined castle.

Where once Louis XIV hunted, wild boar and deer still roam, though you are unlikely to see them! If you are caught in a traffic jam in the **Foret de Marly**, and at certain times this is likely, you can at least admire the impressive shaved walls of beech and oak, 15m high, on either side of the road.

A23

This section of the motorway system is non-toll; it is, therefore, quite busy, and facilities are not as good as you would find on motorways where you pay. It is best avoided in the morning and evening rush hours, especially the approaches to Lille.

Genech ⛽ 🍴 ♿
Good bar/buffet in shop
No picnic area.

Millonfosse
Large lay-by; no WC, no picnic area

Petite Foret ⛽ 🔧
No picnic area

AIRES LILLE ~ VALENCIENNES

LILLE

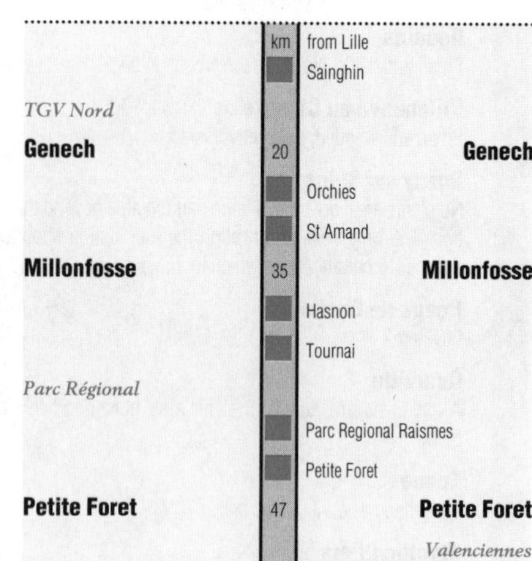

VALENCIENNES

St Eloy ⛽ 🔧 🍴 ♿ £
Separate Caféteria de Steenevoorde with shop beyond fuel.
No picnic area.

Steenwerk
Basic, close to road, untidy.
No WC block.

AIRES DUNKERQUE ~ LILLE

DUNKERQUE

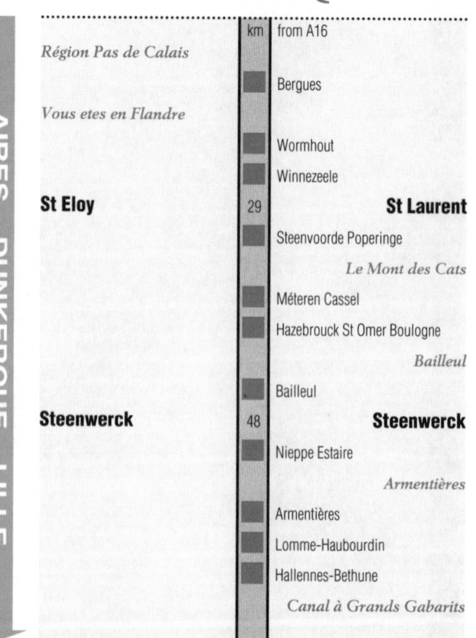

LILLE

LILLE ~ VALENCIENNES A23

AIRES VALENCIENNES ~ LILLE

Genech
Bar/buffet in shop. No picnic area.

Millonfosse
Large lay-by; no WC,no picnic area.

Petite Foret
No picnic area

Just south of Junction 1, the TGV Nord line, the high speed train linking the Channel Tunnel with Paris, crosses the motorway

The **Parc Naturel Régional de Raismes** was the first regional park created in France; there are footpaths, bridleways, picnic spots and a sailing centre. At the Mare à Goriaux is an ornithological reserve.

Valenciennes is an industrial town on the Escaut; a major industry is refining sugar beet.

DUNKERQUE ~ LILLE

AIRES LILLE ~ DUNKERQUE

St-Laurent
Separate Caféteria de Steenevoorde with shop beyond fuel station. No picnic area

Steenwerk
Basic, close to road, untidy
No WC block

Vous etes en Flandre, the history of this plain has been bound up with that of several nations. Flanders was controlled at various times by England, Burgundy, Spain and Austria, and was at the centre of frequent squabbles before the Treaty of Utrecht confirmed it as part of France in 1713. Few visible scars remain to remind the traveller of the prolonged fighting of the First World War. The scenery is rather dull, but you are soon into more undulating countryside.

On the top of the **Mont des Cats**, the view from the motorway rather spoilt by a radio mast, is a Trappist monastery, rebuilt after 1918. The lace-making town of **Bailleul** is not the place which gave its name to two Scottish kings and the Oxford college of Balliol; that was another town, coincidentally also in northern France. For three and a half years during the First World War, **Armentières** was only 3 kms behind the British trenches; it was virtually destroyed, and rebuilt.

Canal à Grands Gabarits means it carries wide loads. **Lille** began on an island, 'L'Isle', the first reference being in the same year as the Battle of Hastings, and it has had a battle-scarred history. Today it is the economic and cultural capital of the north-east, a lively centre with lots to see and do. The A25 through it can also be lively, with five junctions in quick succession; avoid it during the rush hour if you can!

Zutkerque ♿
Small, neat, well-planted picnic area.

Péage de Setques *i*
Take a ticket.

Grand Riez ★ ♿ /Π\ 🌳
Nice planting; steps at the back lead down to a second small, sheltered picnic area. There is a large grassy area at the end of the site.

Rely ⛽ ♿ *i*
The tourist information is on a board. The picnic area has no separate WC block.

Le Reveillon ★ 🌳
In a wooded area, well shielded from the road, the site slopes up into a lightly wooded area, very pleasant, with a grassy area at the end of the site.

Souchez ⛽
Vimy Ridge, which the Canadians held in the Second World War, is nearby. There is a nice field at a lower level at the end of this pleasant aire.

Les Trois Cretes 🌳
Well screened from the road; there is quite a pleasant shaded area at the end of the lorry park.

AIRES CALAIS~ A1 JUNCTION

CALAIS

	km	from Calais	
	■	A16	
Burghers of Calais			*Pas de Calais*
Camp du Drap d'Or 1520			
Zutkerque	13		**Nortkerque**
	■	Nordausques	
			St Omer Musée Sandelin
Péage de Setques	=		**Péage de Setques**
	■	Saint Omer	
Vallée de l'Aa			*Arques*
			Aire sur la Lys
	■	Therouanne	
Vallée de la Lys			
Grand Riez	46		**Villefleur**
Rely	55		**Saint-Hilaire Cottes**
	■	Lillers	
Le Reveillon	68		**La Grande Bucaille**
			Béthune
	■	Béthune	
			Les Terriles
Colline de N. D. de Lorette			
			Lens
	■	A21	
Mont St Eloi			
Souchez	90		**Angres**
			Vimy-Canadian memorial
	■	Arras	
Arras			
Les Trois Cretes	100		**La Cressonière**
	■	A1	

A1 JUNCTION

AIRES A1 JUNCTION ~ CALAIS

Nortkerque ♿
A small aire, with nice planting.

Péage de Setques
Pay here.

Villefleur ♿
Small but pleasant.

St Hilaire Cottes ⛽ ♿
A grassy field at the end of the site.

La Grande Bucaille
This aire would be fine, but it is spoilt by having a scrapyard all along the back.

Angres ⛽ ♿
There is a nice grassy area after the fuel station .

La Cressonnière
An attractive screen of willows between this small aire and the road.

When Edward III of England seized **Calais**, the story goes, six burghers offered themselves as hostages in order to save the other townsfolk; Rodin's sculpture depicting the event is outside the town hall.

The **Camp du Drap d'Or**, the Field of the Cloth of Gold, was the scene of an extraordinary meeting in 1520 between Henry VIII of England and Francois I of France, supposedly to patch up their quarrels and even form an alliance, but in the event a chance for each to show off his wealth and the splendour of his court to the other. Maybe it was the mortification of taking a tumble in the joust that led Henry to sign a treaty with Francois' main enemy soon after returning to England!

The 18th century Hotel **Sandelin** is now the museum of **St Omer**.

The brown sign for **Arques** refers to the glass-works. Nearby is an interesting hydraulic lift, the Ascenseur de Fontinettes which, from 1888 until 1967, performed the work of 5 locks.

The river **Aa** is canalised. Indeed the whole region is a labyrinth of canals among the marshes, the land reclaimed used primarily for market gardening.

Aire sur la Lys is the site of an ancient fortress.

The first Artesian wells were dug at **Lillers**.

Much damaged in 1918, **Béthune** is an industrial town on the edge of the mining belt.

A famous French battle was fought on the hill of **Notre Dame de Lorette** in 1915; there is a memorial and French war cemetery here.

Approaching **Lens**, you will notice the contrast of the slag heaps in otherwise flat terrain. Some of the heaps, **Les Terriles**, must be 100m high; grass grows on some, a few trees have appeared, they have been there so long. But most are starkly grey, in a grey landscape.

There has been an abbey on **Mont St Eloi** since the 7th century.

Vimy Ridge is now wooded. It was taken by Canadian troops in 1917, and there is a **Canadian Memorial** here.

Largely rebuilt after damage in both wars, the Grand Place and Petit Place of **Arras** have been nicely restored.

Bois d'Huez ★ ♿ 🌳
A well kept aire, with lots of shrubs and space. Walk up some steps to a picnic area.

Baralle ★ ⛽ ✕ ♿
There is a small caféteria at one end of the fuel station shop, and a tarmac road into the extensive, grassy area beyond. No separate WC block in the picnic area.

La Vacquerie ★ ♿ 🌳
Down below road, and with a lot of shrubs and trees, there is a second picnic area at the end of the site.

L'Omignon ★ ♿ /Π\
The picnic area is between the car and lorry park.

Urvillers
Cross the bridge to the other side of the motorway to this very large aire; after the fuel station are the Arche facilities which include a caféteria, with terrace, and a regional display. There is an interesting gazebo structure near the Arche building, concrete and steel arches with plants creeping up them. There is a lot of picnicing space.

St Brice ♿

La Croisette ♿

Mont de Nizy ⛽ ✕
The bar-buffet is in the fuel station shop.

Cauroy Hermonville

Péage de Courcy
Pay here.

Join A4 and drive through Reims

AIRES A1 JUNCTION ~ A4

A1 JUNCTION

	km	from Calais
Bois d'Huez	112	**Les Bonnettes**
		Etangs de la Sensée
Baralle	122	**Rumaucourt**
Canal du Nord		
	■	Cambrai Ouest
	■	A2
La Vacquerie	140	**Le Plateau**
		Abbaye de Vaucelles
	■	Cambrai Sud
		Touage souterrain
L'Omignon	160	**La Haute Bruyère**
	■	St Quentin Centre
Viaduc de la Somme		*St Quentin*
	■	St Quentin Gauchy
Urvillers ←	199	→ **Urvillers**
Canal de la Sambre		
	■	La Fére
St Brice	209	**Broyon**
Foret de St Gobain		
	■	Laon
Laon		
La Croisette	219	**Les Pelerins**
Soissons		
Mont de Nizy	239	**Le Champ Roland**
	■	La Vallee de l'Aisne
Cauroy	250	**Loivre**
Péage de Courcy	=	**Péage de Courcy**
Montagne de Reims		*Reims cité des sacres*
	■	Reims la Neuvillette
	■	A4

A4

Les Bonnettes ♿
Small but OK.

Rumaucourt ⛽
The fuel station is entirely automatic. The picnic area is fine but to get to the WCs you have to walk back back to the fuel station.

Le Plateau ♿
A small aire, but OK.

La Haute Bruyère ★ ★ ♿
A neat, well planned aire, with a nice wooded dell going back between the car and lorry park.

Urvillers ★ ⛽ ♿ *i*
see south.

Broyon ♿
There is a pleasant grassy slope with tables at the end of the site.

Les Pelerins ♿
A large grassy site with very little landscaping; basic but OK.

Le Champ Roland ⛽ ♿
The fenced play area and picnic tables are situated between the rows of car parking spaces, but it is quite a pleasant aire because of all the planting.

Loivre ♿
Good planting of shrubs; small but OK.

Péage de Courcy ♿
Take a ticket.

There is a pretty stretch of the river Sensée between the A26 and the A2 where ponds , the **Etangs de la Sensée**, have formed; a popular place to walk or picnic.

Industrial **Cambrai** was devastated in both world wars.

The **Abbaye de Vaucelles** is a ruined Cistercian abbey.

One of the many brilliant ideas of Napoleon 1 was a tunnel to link the Somme and the Escaut, the **Touage Souterrain de Riqueval**. Barges are towed through by a boat using an underwater winch and chain.

St Quentin became an early place of pilgrimage after a Christian was beheaded here. Portrait painter Quentin de la Tour lived here; you will see his head on the brown sign. The town was behind German lines for most of the First World War. Within the ramparts of the castle at nearby **Péronne** is a remarkable modern museum L'Historial de la Grande Guerre.

The **Foret de St Gobain** is beautiful, but its name is best known as that of the factory, founded in 1692, which developed the process whereby large panes of glass could be made.

Built along a ridge commanding the whole plain, the seven towers of the ancient cathedral of **Laon** are an amazing sight from the motorway, and must dominate the town.

When, in the 16th century, the daughters of Louis XV visited friends at the Chateau de Bove, south of Laon, they travelled from the royal palace at Compiegne along the **Chemin des Dames**, a road constructed specially for them. The part of it near Soissons was the scene of a French attempt to break through the German lines in 1917 which resulted in a morale-damaging defeat with heavy loss of life.

Another town rebuilt after the ravages of 1918, **Soissons** has two ancient abbeys, and one of the finest cathedrals in France.

At the interchange with the A4, two concrete balls on either side in a cutting, form a sort of gateway to Reims.Their covering of netting is to encourage ivy to grow up them.

Reims Cité des Sacres a reference to the fact that the Kings of France were traditionally crowned at Reims.

Wild boar and roe deer roam in the forests of oak, beech and chestnut on the **Montagne de Reims** ; there are footpaths up from several villages. The Route de Champagne takes the driver through pretty, well-cared-for villages and the impressive sight of hectares of vineyards on the north, east and south-facing slopes of the mountain. These are also visible from the motorway.

A26

La Garenne ★ ♿
A small to medium sheltered site with concrete tables, a lot of grass and good tree planting. On this motorway the WC blocks have a shared WC for women and disabled people; stainless steel and modern, its door handle is a lever which turns to show red or green rather than a lock, which I found a bit disconcerting.

Sommesous
Go off at the exit to Vitry-le-Francois and cross the motorway; the aire is straight ahead; keep left, the right hand lane is the exit.

Champ Carreau ♿
Well up above road, a pleasantly landscaped, but somewhat exposed site; with lots of grass. Sandwiched between the motorway and another busy road, it is a bit noisy.

Charmont ⛽ ♿
On the exit road, this side of the motorway only, but serving both sides. Take the left hand lane for aire, which has a small automatic set of fuel pumps for emergency use only. (French credit cards, or banknotes). Then on into the small but pleasant aire, colourful with flowers, a change from shrubs!

Villechetif ★ ♿
Drive up behind an unusually high tree-covered bank, well above road, to this attractive aire which is landscaped using concrete balls. Even more striking is the circular WC block, the roof of which is covered by a triangular steel frame. The roundabouts at the beginning and end of the aire enable you to get back in if you want to.

A4

AIRES A4 – TROYES

	km		
	km	from Calais	
		A4	
	305		**Les Grands Traquiers**
Epernay			*Vallée de la Marne*
		Chalons Ouest	
La Garenne	311		
			N. D. de l'Epine
			N. D. en Vaux
		Chalons Sud	
	316		**La Bardolle**
			La Cathédrale
Sommesous ←	336	→	**Sommesous**
		Sommesous	
Plaine de Champagne			
Champ Carreau	347		**Champ l'Epée**
L'Aube			
		Vallee de l'Aube	
			Lacs de Champagne
			Der Chantecoq
Charmont	382		**Charmont**
		Charmont	
La Seine			*La Foret d'Orient*
		Troyes Nord	
Villechetif	393		**Les Crocs de la Terre**
Troyes			
		Thennelieres	
		St Thibault, A5	

TROYES

Join A4 through Reims

Les Grands Traquiers ★

A lovely neat aire, going back quite a long way with good planting, and lots of space in an undulating, grassy site. Access to the disabled WC would be difficult; the pavement has not been lowered enough for a wheelchair.

La Bardolle ★ ♿

A smallish, nicely planted site.

Sommesous ⛽ 🍴 ♿

The fuel station comes first; the interesting buildings you could see from the motorway are a Gendarmerie and a Centre d'Entretien storing grit and snow ploughs! Drive on to the attractive Mirabellier building, all modern, light and airy, where you will find an amazing range of facilities including the expected caféteria, coffee bar and well-stocked shop, but also a TV lounge, business services, washing machines, showers and saunas. Two criticisms: I took a while to find the WCs because I couldn't work out what the signs, all pictorial, meant, and once there I was surprised at how few there were, for a large aire serving both sides of the motorway. There is a large, rather exposed, picnic area behind with lots of new planting.

Champ l'Epée ★ ♿

High above the motorway, and pleasantly landscaped, this is rather an exposed site.

Charmont

Officially there is no aire for this side of the motorway,but there is access via the exit road to the aire on the other side.

Les Crocs de la Terre ★ ♿

This attractive, neat and tidy aire has been landscaped with a certain flair. It is situated behind three large mounds; trees have been planted up to the top of each on the aire side, and there are green valleys between. Looks good from the motorway, too. There is, by the way, an extraordinary selection of varied electricity pylons disappearing into the distance to the north of this aire!

Epernay claims that it has 100 kms of cellars storing Champagne.

The **Marne** is a green, chalky river, its valley a landscape of rolling wheat fields, sugar beet and occasional orchards.

A pale stone Gothic church on the scale of a cathedral, **Notre Dame de l'Epine** is unusual for the uneven height of its two spires. It has been a place of pilgrimage since the Middle Ages.

Notre Dame en Vaux is an imposing church on the southern edge of Chalons.

Chalons sur Marne is an administrative and industrial centre, with sugar, beer and champagne important products. The cathedral occupies an attractive site in the loop of the river.

Rolling fields of crops, wide strips of sugar beet, wheat and potatoes cover the **Plaine de Champagne**. Vast silos and sugar processing plants are dotted across the landscape and, depending on the time of year, you may be aware of a sickly-sweet smell drifting across the motorway from time to time. **La Cathédrale** is not quite what the name suggests; a large grain silo, in fact, beside the motorway. Look out for the way silos in this area have been painted in pastel colours to make them more attractive. It works!

The **Lac du Der Chantecoq** is the largest man-made lake in France, half as large again as Annecy. Used for a variety of leisure activities, it is also a winter home for thousands of migratory birds.

La Foret de l'Orient is a centre for leisure and outdoor pursuits, not in the east but near a former garrison of the Knights Templar. There is a wild life reserve and observation post at the northern end of the lake of the same name.

There is a charming medieval centre in **Troyes**, the town where Henry V of England married Katharine of France.

A31

St Rémy
Quite a pleasant picnic area after the fuel station.

Les Menils *i*
Pretty basic, steps up to a few picnic tables among small trees.

L'Obrion
No picnic area. Bar/buffet in fuel station shop.

Toul Dommartin
There is a view over Toul from the roof of the footbridge.(steps up!). La Nuit d'Hotel is a budget-priced hotel just behind the Mirabellier caféteria which has a large terrace. The food looks OK but lacks variety; more chips than in Arche and Relais caféterias. Newsagents and Fax machine. Quite a pleasant picnic area.

Péage de Gye *i*
Take a ticket. Motorway information point.

Faverosse ★ ★
Below the level of the road, and shielded by mature beech trees, this is one of the largest wooded aires on the A31, with tracks into the woods for cars, footpaths and a parcours de santé which starts at the main car park.

Grand Chene ★
On the edge of woods with a view over to a village on the hill across open countryside. A pleasant aire, with space for walks, but short on parking space and tables.

Lorraine Sandaucourt ★ ★ *i*
The cavalry is waiting to greet you as you drive up off the motorway, and in the parking and picnic areas of this lovely aire. A cuirassier stands guard at the viewpoint and there are wooden cannons for the children to climb on. Rubbish to dispose of? The bins are disguised as bandsmen's drums! The Arche de Sandaucourt-Vittel building has an excellent caféteria and, in the tourist information area, an innovative display of regional industry and products, from Eau de Vittel to the caps on the bottles. It's a stopping place for coaches, and the caféteria and Caféroute get pretty busy. There is a separate snack bar outside in summer. Panels displaying scenes from Napoleon's adventures line the footpaths; walk through the pleasantly wooded area to see more soldiers and their ladies and, if you do arrive at the same time as a couple of coaches, there is a big grassy area at the end of the site which is unlikely to get crowded.

Grand Repenti
A pleasant picnic area with a good view - from the top of the WC block!

Montigny le Roi
There is a bar/buffet in the fuel station shop. No picnic area.

Cote Robert ★ ★
A lovely aire with a large picnic area and footpaths extending up the hillside and into the woods.

THIONVILLE

AIRES THIONVILLE ~ LANGRES

	km	
		from Beaune, A6
		A30, Mondelange
		Talange Hagondange
		Maiziéres les Metz
		A4
St Rémy	310	**La Maxe**
		Metz - vitraux
		La Maxe
		Metz Nord
		Metz Centre
		Metz Sud
		Jouy aux Arches
		Féy
		St Avold
Les Menils	280	**Le Jure**
		Atton.
Abbaye des Prémontrés		
Butte de Mousson		
		Pont a Mousson
L'Obrion	272	**Loisy**
		Belleville
		Lustines
		Bouxieres aux Dames
		Frouard
		Nancy
Foret de Haye		*La Place Stanislaus*
		A33
	232	**Foret de Haye**
		Metz Gondreville
Toul Dommartin ←	228	→ **Toul Chaudeney**
		Toul Centre
Vaucouleurs		*La Moselle*
Péage de Gye	=	**Péage de Gye**
		Colombey les Belles
Grand village gallo rom.		
Faverosse	211	**Malvaux**
Domrémy		*Lorraine*
Grand Chene	201	**Val au Renard**
		Chatenois
Neufchateau		*Imageries d'Epinal*
Lorraine La Trelle ←	182	→ **Lorraine Les Rappes**
		Bulgnéville
Les Vosges		*Contrexeville Vittel*
Grand Repenti	162	**Bois de Chaumont**
La Meuse		
		Montigny le Roi
Montigny le Roi	138	**Val de Meuse**
		Bourbonne les Bains
		Langres Nord
Cote Robert	122	**Val de Gris**
		A5
Nogent en Bassigny		*La Marne*
Canal Marne Saone		

La Maxe
There is a bar/buffet in the fuel station shop. No picnic area.

Le Jure
Pretty basic.

Loisy
There is a bar/buffet in the fuel station shop. No picnic area.

La Foret de Haye
Very basic, no WC block, small wooded area at the back.

Toul Chaudeney
On a hill overlooking Toul; the footbridge across the motorway does not have access for the disabled.

Péage de Gye
Pay here. A star for the best WC block at a toll barrier? Not often is the approach through a tiled colonnade.

Malvaux ★
Set well back in mature beechwoods.

Val au Renard ★
Doubtless the motorway has driven the foxes out of their valley! The road weaves in and out of the trees, with tables among the beeches, and space for walks.

Lorraine Sandaucourt
A covered footbridge leads to the services on the other side of the motorway.

Bois de Chaumont ★
I wasn't at all sure why the WC block had steps up onto its roof, until I saw the view! Point relaxe exercises.

Val de Meuse *i*
A pleasant area of grass after the fuel station.

Val de Gris ★ ★
There are two picnic areas in this extensive, wooded site; the first, reached by taking the first track to the right, has tables among the trees and a play area; although nice, I recommend the further one, down the track beyond the main parking area, beside the stream and very pretty.

Metz - vitraux du 13ième au 20ième siècle - lots of fine examples of stained glass to see, in settings as diverse as the Gothic cathedral and the railway station; the medieval contrasting with the modern. The magnificent 18th century classical architecture of the centre of **Nancy** is at its finest in the **Place Stanislas**.

Bordering Nancy on its western edge, the **Foret de Haye** offers many recreational facilities for the people of the town.

At the confluence of the Moselle and the Ingressin, **Toul** was a natural place to build a fortress, and much of the town is still squeezed inside its ancient walls. You can see the cathedral from the motorway.

The source of the **Moselle** is in the Vosges; wine is produced on its banks near Metz, but its main contribution to the economy of Lorraine has been the development of industry, chiefly iron and steel, between Thionville and Nancy.

Pont à Mousson is an industrial town dominated by the fortress above. Its finest building, the **Abbaye des Prémontrés**, on the banks of the Moselle, is used as a religious cultural centre. The **Butte de Mousson** is an outcrop overlooking the town with the ruins of a castle on the top.

The view of **Neufchateau** from the motorway is of a church where a castle ought, and indeed used to be, on a fortified bluff on the edge of the town.

Grand had an amphitheatre holding 20,000 spectators in Roman times; the most significant remains, though, are the kilometres of underground sewers.

A link with Joan of Arc; at **Vaucouleurs** are the ruins of Robert de Baudricourt's castle.

The region of **Lorraine** is divided geographically into the Cotes de Moselle to the west and the Plateau Lorrain to the east. Economically, the divide is rather north-south, with the north being at its industrial heart and the south more involved in traditional rural economic life.

Joan of Arc was born at **Domrémy;** the house where she was born can be visited.

Les Imageries d'Epinal are popular 18th and 19th century prints depicting, in a naive style, traditional scenes from French life; at the Aire de Lorraine the topic is the Napoleonic Wars, and each figure will be familiar to the French. Epinal itself is a pretty town on the Moselle.

The spa towns of **Contrexeville** and **Vittel** are best known for the quantities of bottled water they produce for consumption at home and abroad.

Bourbonne les Bains is a spa town not far from the source of the Meuse.

Nogent en Bassigny is renowned for the production of cutlery, **la cotellerie**, and surgical instruments.

The source of the **Marne** is just south of Langres. The **Canal de la Marne à la Saone** crosses the Plateau de Langres to link these two great rivers, the one flowing north, the other south.

Langres Perrogney ★ ★

There is a bar/buffet in the fuel station shop. The picnic area, point relaxe and parcours de santé (translated as Take-a-break-trail) are at the end of the aire, in a very thick wood, and there is a small Relais caféteria beyond.

Fontenelle ★

Set well back, and sloping down from the motorway. Minimal play area at the entrance. Drive into the pleasant wooded area at the back. There are steps up to return to the WC block on foot, but no way back for the car.

Sainte Gertrude ★

The little chapel is on a hill close to the aire, which is very pleasant.

Dijon Brognon *i*

A large aire; cheap fuel, lots of parking space, picnic area, point relaxe, and then the Relais de Dijon Cote d'Or, which is in an attractive modern building using traditional materials and tiled roof decoration. Inside there is a caféteria, snack bar and restaurant, all with terrace, newsagents and regional products shop. We ate an excellent lunch here, speedily and courteously served in the attractive, octagonal restaurant; you will not be served here after 2pm, but the caféteria is open throughout the day. There is a small car park right beside the Relais, and the main parking area is close, too.

La Tille ★

A well-designed aire; drive past the main parking area and turn right near the end of the aire to reach the Aire de Détente. The road goes round the back, and returns to the beginning of the aire.

Gevrey Chambertin *i*

Test-your-reflexes driving centre by the entrance, and, after the fuel station, which has a 24-hour Caféroute in the shop, a large parking area with some tables from where there is a glorious view of the vineyards of the Cote d'Or.

Flagey Echezeaux ★

Just before the WC block turn right down a delightful track where there is space to park by a longer-than-usual table among the mature trees. There is a good seating area for a group of people under a large sloping roof near WC block. Point relaxe.

Serrigny ★

Take the gravelled path back among the trees to picnic.

AIRES LANGRES ~ BEAUNE

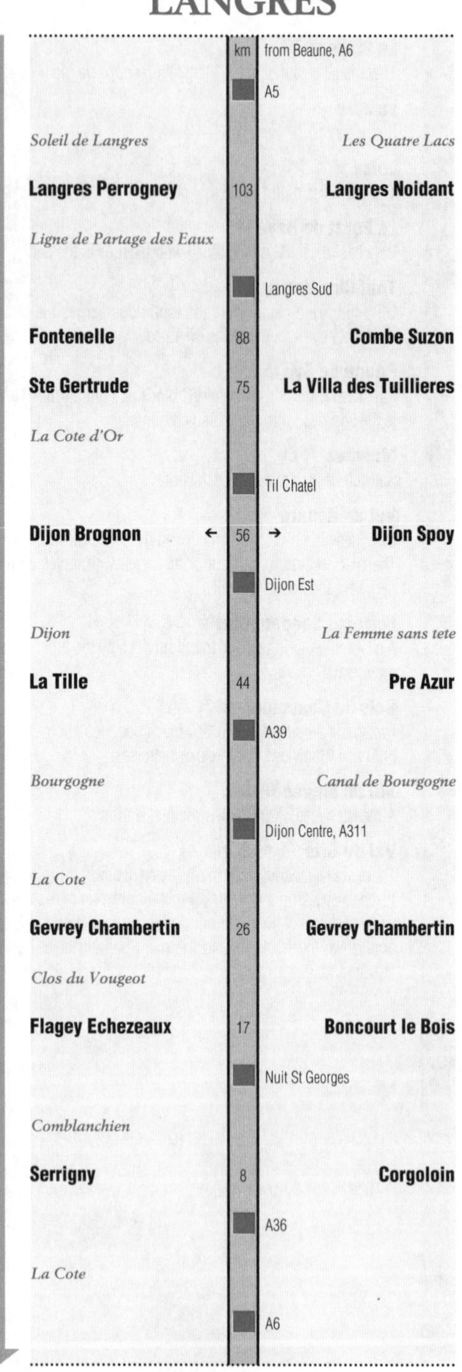

BEAUNE

Langres Noidant ★ ★

Relais Porte de Champagne caféteria, snack bar and shop selling regional products. There is a large, wooded picnic area and a parcours de santé at the end of the site; the road leads back to the Relais before leaving the aire.

Combe Suzon ★ ★

Unusually well-screened from the road; the parcours de santé (an exercise area, rather than a circuit) and point relaxe are at the back of the site with lots of parking areas and tables among the trees.

Villa des Tuillieres ★

A well-designed and nicely planted aire, on a slope down from the motorway. Drive down, past the WC block, to the Aire de Détente.

Dijon Spoy

There is vehicular access to the excellent services including the Relais de Dijon Cote d'Or on the far side of the motorway. This is the place to stop if you need fuel or to buy something from a fuel station shop for this one is run by the moderately-priced Leclerc chain. Even the coffee from the machines is cheaper than in other fuel stations.

Pre Azur ★

A circular arrangement; drive past the WC block and follow the sign to the Aire de Détente.

Gevrey Chambertin ★ *i*

Pleasant bar/buffet with terrace in the fuel station shop. The site is nicely laid out and planted.

Boncourt le Bois

Drive up into the aire and take the track immediately to the right into quite thick woods for walks and picnics.

Corgoloin ★

Take the gravelled track back among the trees.

Langres itself is at the southern corner of the **Champagne Ardennes** region which stretches up to the Belgian border in the north. A gleaming sculpture beside the motorway, denotes the sun. **Le Soleil de Langres** consists of new moons around a sort of wheel hub supported by a vertical steel structure. Langres is a gateway into Burgundy, on the main road from Lorraine to the Mediterranean even before the coming of the motorway.

The river **Meuse** rises in Bassigny, to the east of the Montigny junction.

Les **Quatre Lacs**: four lakes with water sports within easy reach of Langres.

The **Ligne de Partage des Eaux** is half-way between the Belgian coast of the North Sea, and the Mediterranean.

Both the A38 and the A31 lead to **Dijon**, the largest town in Burgundy. Situated at the confluence of the Rivers Ouche and Suzon, and the start of the Burgundy Canal, Dijon is also a major rail junction and centre of commerce and industry. It is renowned for it's gastronomic deights; our lunch in the Relais Dijon-Cote d'Or included such regional specialities as snails, pikeperch in mustard sauce, local cheeses, blackcurrant tart and local wines to accompany them.

La Femme sans Tete: the name of this little river, the woman without a head,just caught my eye.

La Bourgogne: a vast area of disparate regions united by the powerful Dukes of Bourgogne in the 14th and 15th centuries. It is renowned for its churches and monasteries in Romanesque and Gothic style, its chateaux and its wines. Despite enthusiastic tree-clearing by medieval monks much of the forests remain, and wood distilling, charcoal-making, sawmills and tree nurseries all contribute to the economic life of the region. Another traditional source of wealth lies in quarrying, and the cement, pottery and ceramic industries are all sizeable.

Completed in 1832, and 242 kms long, the **Canal de Bourgogne** links the Yonne and Saone rivers, following the Armancon and Ouche valleys.

The chateau of **Clos du Vougeot** can be visited; its vineyard, once tended by the monks of Citeaux, is one of the most famous of the Cotes de Beaune.

The **Comblanchien** quarries which are clearly visible on the Cote, produce a beautiful hard stone often used instead of marble.

The escarpment which more or less follows the course of the Saone, from Dijon to Chagny has proved exceptionally suitable for growing vines. The sight of the hectares of vineyards of the **Cote d'Or** is quite impressive.

Surrounded by vineyards, **Beaune** is a charming town with ancient walls and a medieval centre whose steeply pitched roofs, coloured tiles and gilded vanes are much photographed. There is an interesting wine museum in the Hotel des Ducs, and a fine Romanesque church.

La Porte d'Alsace
The bar/buffet is in the fuel station shop. The picnic area beyond has some shaded tables, but there is no WC block there, and no way back to the services except on foot. Good view of the Vosges.

Angeot
Small, but pleasant.

Péage de la Fontaine *i*
Pay here. Free tyre pressure check after the barrier.

Les Grands Pres
Small, and close to the road.

La Combe Ronde ★
There is a bar/buffet, with terrace, at the fuel station. The picnic area is well back from the road, with point relaxe and lots of space.

Péage de St Maurice

Galiot
Well-maintained aire in a beautiful setting. As you leave, there is a lovely view over the valley of the Doubs.

Le Boulet ★
The picnic area stretches back into the woods a little, but there is no room to park there; use the main car park. There is a fenced play area.

AIRES MULHOUSE ~ BAUME-LES-DAMES

MULHOUSE

	km	
		from Mulhouse
		Ile Napoleon
		Mulhouse Centre
		Botzwiller
		Mulhouse Ouest
		Lutterbach
Alsace		
		Burnhaupt
La Porte d'Alsace	16	**La Porte d'Alsace**
Ligne de Partage des Eaux		
Angeot	25	**Le Haut Bois**
Péage de la Fontaine	=	**Péage de la Fontaine**
Les Grands Pres	33	**La Foret**
		Belfort Nord
Les Vosges		*Territoire de Belfort*
		Belfort Centre
		Belfort Sud
	42	**Grand Bois**
Ronchamp		
		Sevenans
		Sochaux Exincourt
Montbeliard		*Eglise d'Audincourt*
		Montbeliard Centre
		Montbeliard Sud
La Combe Ronde	65	**Ecot**
		Le Doubs
Péage de St Maurice	=	**Péage de St Maurice**
		Isle le Doubs
Le Galiot	81	**Le Charme**
		Monts du Lomont
Le Boulet	89	**La Combe de Fougère**
		Baume les Dames

BAUME-LES-DAMES

La Porte d'Alsace

They are a bit pushed for space here at this busy Relais; for example the disabled WC doubles as the place to change a baby's nappy. Outside things are better; the play area to the side of the Relais is fine and the picnic area, signed Zone de Detente, is pleasant.There are shaded tables, point relaxe and play area there but no separate WC block. In summer there is a very nice regional products shop. The fuel station is at the far end of the site.

Haut Bois

Péage de la Fontaine

Pay here, no ticket needed. Gendarmerie.

La Foret

Close to the road, and small.

Grand Bois

Minimal WC block.

Ecot

The bar/buffet in the shop has a terrace; basic picnic area.

Péage de St Maurice

Pay here. A reasonable aire after the barrier, with motorway information.

Charme

No picnic area.

La Combe de Fougère ★ ★

Nicest aire on the A36 so far! Very pretty, a good variety of trees and a lovely view.

Meaning 'mill house', **Mulhouse** is a great textiles centre. The National Motor Museum is based here, in a disused mill.

Sundgau is the most southerly corner of Alsace; a typical **Ferme** will be half-timbered, and have a huge tiled roof.

Alsace reaches to the Rhine, to the border with Germany, and includes the fertile agricultural land of the plain and as well as the hills we see to the north of the motorway. Dominating the landscape is the distinctive Ballon d'Alsace in the Vosges.

The **Ligne de Partage des Eaux** is half-way between the North Sea and the Mediterranean

The heavily forested hills to the north of Belfort are the **Vosges**.

Holding **Belfort** means commanding the Belfort Gap between the Vosges and the Jura. Among the famous sieges in its history was the heroic defence of the city under Denfert-Rochereau in 1871. You will see the fort from the motorway. There is a nice lion, carved below the rock face of the citadel by Bartholdi, whose work includes the Statues of Liberty in Paris and New York.

The river at Belfort is **La Savoureuse**.

The concrete **Chapelle de Ronchamp**, designed by Le Corbusier to replace a bit of a monstrosity destroyed by artillery fire in 1944, and completed in 1955, has not lost its power to surprise. The first view shocks; walk around the outside looking at the shapes, forms and materials used; then enter; you may be taken aback by the proportions, the sense of harmony, the light, the atmosphere. It affected me, and my second tour of the outside was somehow different from the first.

Territoire de Belfort is a reminder of the area which remained in France after the German annexation of Alsace-Lorraine in 1871.

Above the road, to the east of the motorway, as you pass Montbeliard, you will see the modern **Eglise d'Audincourt**.

Montbeliard is the home of Peugeot cars and bicycles; to prevent it falling into German hands, the factory was sabotaged during the war with the permission of the owners.

The **Chateau de Belvoir** is on the southern side of the ridge of the Monts du Lomont.

The motorway follows the river **Doubs** from Dole to Montbeliard.

The long wooded ridge of the **Monts du Lomont**, visible south of the Doubs, rises to 840m.

Les Grands Brocards
Another pleasant site on the edge of woods.

Besancon Champoux
Steps up to the footbridge over to the Arche caféteria are at the end of the site; disabled access to the bridge is from the road leading out of the aire, whence a road way leads up to a lot of parking, and a good grassy area, at bridge level.

Pelousey ★
Small but pretty; a rather hazardous spot has been chosen for the play area, beside the through traffic.

Hyombre
Whoever heard of a WC block with stained glass windows? Clean, sweet-smelling and with proper WCs, too - full marks! A small, pleasantly landscaped site, which looks as if it is about to be extended; that would earn it a star. Only room for a dozen cars at the moment, and a 5ton weight limit in force.(1993)

Dole Romange ★
Summer entertainment for children which appears to involve cardboard cut-outs; 'L'Epopée Napoléonienne' reminds me of the popular prints produced at Epinal during the 19th century (see A31). There are some picnic tables and point relaxe in the woods at the end of the site.

Bois des Potets ★
Walk through to the back of the site where there are tables among the trees.

St Jean de Losne ★
Another pleasant, wooded site.

Glanon
The Grill in the fuel station, which has a terrace, looks a reasonable place to eat.

Argilly ★
Walk through the woods here; the aire is spoilt by a minimal WC block.

AIRES BAUME-LES-DAMES ~ BEAUNE

BAUME-LES-DAMES

	km	from Mulhouse	
	■	Baume les Dames	
Les Grands Brocards	107		**Chevaney**
Besancon Champoux ←	117		→ **Besancon Marchaux**
Foret de Chaillez			*Gorges de la Loue*
	■	Besancon Centre	
Pelousey	134		**Bois de Frachère**
Franche Comté			*Besancon*
	■	Besancon Ouest	
Hyombre	152		
Clochers comtois			*Saline Arc et Sénans*
Romange	166		**Audelange**
	■	Dole	
Plaine de la Saone			*Dole*
Bois des Potets	177		**Sampans**
Canal Rhone-Rhin			*Industrie Chimique*
St Jean de Losne			*Tavaux*
St Jean de Losne	190		**Les Noues**
	■	Seurre	
Abbaye de Citeaux			*La Bourgogne*
Glanon	206		**Bois Guillerot**
Argilly	214		**Villy**
Beaune			
	■	A31	

BEAUNE

AIRES BEAUNE ~ BAUME-LES-DAMES

Chevaney
Some shaded tables; a large grassy area.

Besancon Marchaux
Very good children's games, and a lovely view. At last, somewhere to eat if you haven't planned a picnic! The Arche caféteria with terrace is open 24 hours and the Ibis Hotel is at the end of the site.

Bois de Frachère ★
Disabled access to the WC block is from the lorry park. There are steps up to a wooded picnic area at the back of this pleasant site.

Dole Audelange ★
One or two shaded tables, and a point relaxe.

Sampans ★
An informative motorway map by the WC block.

Les Noues

Bois Guillerot
The bar/buffet is in the fuel station shop; there is a small picnic area beyond.

Villy le Moutier ★
Pleasant, wooded site, but minimal WC block.

What a view ahead of the **Foret de Chaillez**, as the motorway reaches the western end of the Grande Cote, a ridge of forested hills north of Besancon which the motorway follows.

Lively modern **Besancon**, a centre of micro-technology and clockmaking, has long since burst out of the horseshoe meander in the Doubs where the old town is situated. The Citadel dominates the narrowest point of the loop. The picturesque N83 south from Besancon leads to the **Gorges de la Loue** which then winds tortuously along, past Arc et Sénans, to eventually join the Doubs south of Dole.

Look out for a variety of **Clochers Comtois**, decorated, tiled and gilded belfries.

Dole, once a capital of Franche Comté, was the birthplace of Louis Pasteur. The wooded ridge north of the motorway near Dole is the **Massif de la Serre.**

A salt works, **Saline**, in an ideal town; this was the 18th century plan for the village of **Arc et Sénans**. The result is one of the architectural curiosities of France. The project was never completed, but several buildings remain.

What is known now as **Franche Comté** was once a part of Burgundy whose Count used to pay hommage to the King of Germany. When one independent-minded 12th century Count refused to do this, and remained stubborn through 10 years of conflict, the King of Germany relented and declared his adversary 'Franc Comte', free count.

Market gardening is economically important in the **Plaine de la Saone**. South of the motorway, the **Canal Rhone-Rhin** joins the Doubs at Dole. Apart from an occasional short cut, which includes tunnelling under the fort at Besancon, it follows it up to Montbeliard and then continues north-east when the river changes direction. **Tavaux**, and its **Industrie Chimique**, is on the Rhine-Rhone canal.

La Bourgogne is a vast area of disparate regions renowned for its churches and monasteries in the Romanesque and Gothic style, its chateaux and its wines. Much of its forests remain, and wood distilling, charcoal-making, sawmills and tree nurseries all contribute to the industrial life of the region. Another traditional source of wealth is quarrying.

St Jean de Losne is an industrial town on that stretch of the Saone where it is crossed by the Rhine-Rhone canal.

St Bernard settled at the **Abbaye des Citeaux** in 1114; from here, thanks to his enthusiasm, the Cistercian Order spread throughout France. The community, suppressed at the time of the Revolution, was re-established on the edge of the forest at the end of the 19th century.

Not only does it have the attraction of being surrounded by vineyards, **Beaune** is a charming town with ancient walls, and a medieval town centre whose steeply pitched roofs, coloured tiles and gilded vanes are much photographed. The region is especially noted for its fine white wines, among them Montrachet, Meursault and Puligny.

A6 (MACON)

Etang Quinard

Bourg Teyssonge ★ ★

Organised activities for children at summer weekends. Point relaxe in a pleasant picnic area. Covered pedestrian access to the caféteria on the other side of the motorway.

Ceignes-Cerdon ★ ★

Relais du Bugey restaurant and snack bar, with tourist information and regional products shop, La Vitrine de l'Ain. Lovely wooded picnic site.

Le Lac ★

Drive down to this neat and tidy aire with superb views. On a promontory overlooking the Lac de Sylans is an interesting museum which tells you about the building of this motorway and some of the history of the region.

La Michaille

Small, with a view.

Valleiry

Access to the Arche caféteria is through a pedestrian tunnel.

Péage de Viry

Pay here

Péage de Nangy

Pay here; automatic toll, giving change if you have coins,to the left.

Bonneville

An attractive, well laid out aire. The Relais du Mont-Blanc caféteria is built in the style of a local farmhouse.There is a separate snack bar in the barn, and both have terraces with views to the Chaine du Bargy to the south, and to Mont Blanc to the east.

Péage de Cluses

Pay here; automatic toll, giving change if you have coins, to the left. Beautiful setting.

AIRES A6 (MACON) ~ CHAMONIX (PASSY)

	km	from Passy
		Macon Centre
		Replonges
Etang Quinard	197	**St Andre de Bage**
		Macon Est
		St Genis
		Bourg en Bresse Nord
		Viriat
Bourg Teyssonge ←	163	→ **Bourg Jasseron**
		Bourg Sud
		A42
		Gorges de l'Ain
Ceignes Cerdon	130	**Ceignes Haut Bugey**
		St Martin du Fresne
Les Monts de l'Ain		*Nantua*
Le Lac	116	**Neyrolles**
		Sylans
Plateau de Retord		*Tunnels, Viaducts*
La Michaille	103	**La Semine**
		Bellegarde Ouest
		Eloise
Le Vuache		*Le Grand Cret*
		Monts Jura
Valleiry ←	79	→ **Valleiry**
Péage de Viry	=	**Péage de Viry**
		Le Genevois
		St Julien
Le Salève		*Genève*
		Archamps, A401
		Annemasse, A411
Péage de Nangy	=	**Péage de Nangy**
		Thonon Evian
		A41
		Haut Chablais
		Bonneville Ouest
Bonneville ←	35	→ **Bonneville**
		Bonneville Est
		Scionzier
		Cluses Centre
Chaine du Bargy		*Le Faucigny*
Péage de Cluses	=	**Péage de Cluses**
		Sallanches
St Gervais les Bains		
		Passy
Mont Blanc		*Chamonix*

CHAMONIX (PASSY)

St Andre de Bage
Well screened from the road by a bank.

Bourg Jasseron ★★
The wooded picnic area, with point relaxe, is very pleasant. Relais de Bresse caféteria.

Ceignes Haut Bugey ★★
The picnic area is beyond the fuel station in a lovely wooded site, stretching back up a hill.

Before the Tunnel de Chamoise, which cuts through the Monts d'Ain, the road, still motorway, becomes single-lane, with no central reservation for about 1km. before the tunnel and then through the tunnel. There must be a more-or-less permanent traffic jam here. Unless you are in a great hurry, you wont mind, for it is all so spectacular, and the jam melts away as you emerge at the far side. It is well advertised in advance, and can be avoided by turning off the motorway to Nantua. Lunchtime is not a bad time to go through.

Les Neyrolles
Take the exit for Nantua, and the aire is well below the level of the road, to make it as inobtrusive as possible in this lovely setting. It is very neat and clean.

La Semine
Very small aire, but with quite a view!

Valleiry
Arche caféteria and sandwicherie at the end of the site. When we went the latter was not open, and the caféteria, serving both sides of road, must get very crowded. There is no picnic area, and no way back to the fuel station by car once you have passed it.

Péage de Viry
Take a ticket. Good view of Jura mountains.

Péage de Nangy
Pay here; automatic toll giving change if you have coins, to the left.

Bonneville
There is a footbridge to the caféteria on the other side of the motorway. Picnic area with quite a view, and a Gendarmerie.

Péage de Cluses
Pay here; automatic toll, giving change if you have coins, to the left.

Poet Lamartine was born in **Macon**, and, on his first visit to Europe, Turner painted here.

Cars from **Bourg en Bresse** have the distinction of the 01 suffix on their numberplates! There is a nice tale concerning its suburb, Brou, which has led to it becoming a symbol of married love to the French. In 1480 Philip of Bresse had a serious hunting accident. His wife Margaret of Bourbon promised that, if he recovered, she would transform the priory at Brou into a monastery. Recover he did, but Margaret died before she could carry out her promise. Twenty years later, her son Philibert died unexpectedly, and his wife Margaret of Austria remembered the promise and decided that her husband's death was a punishment. So that his soul could rest in peace, she carried out the promise of her late mother-in-law. The tombs of the two Margarets and of Philibert are in the church at Brou.

Look to the north at the eastern entrance to the Tunnel de Chamoise for a view of the **Lac de Nantua**. The town of the same name developed on the site of a 7th century abbey. Both scenery and engineering are spectacular on this stretch of motorway, with its successive **tunnels** and **viaducts**.

The Département de **l'Ain** takes its name from the river and the mountains. This was a centre of fierce resistance to the Occupation during the last war.

The **Viaduc de Bellegarde** crosses high above the Rhone as it winds its way down from Lake Geneva. To the west of Bellegarde, at more than 1300 metres, is the Plateau de **Retord**. The engineers had no other option but to tunnel through **Le Vuache**. As you leave the tunnel, travelling east, there is quite a view down the plain towards Geneva. **Le Grand Cret** is the ridge of the **Jura** nearest to the motorway, separated from the Montagne de Vuache by the pass through which the Rhone flows.

The area around Geneva is **Le Genevois**. The mountains beyond **Mont Salève**, the imposing rock face to the south of the motorway, used to be given that name, but they are now known as Les Aravis. There must be quite a view of Geneva from the top of the **Télépherique**!

Chablais being the limestone massif to the east of lake Geneva, **Haut Chablais** is that higher part of it with Morzine its centre of tourism. **Le Faucigny** is the series of limestone ridges to the north of Cluses. South of the motorway between Cluses and Bonneville, its highest peak in the **Chaiñe du Bargy** is the Pointe Blanche, 2437 metres. **St Gervais les Bains** is a spa town as well as a skiing and mountaineering centre. A summer and winter resort, **Chamonix** is the gateway to **Mont Blanc**. The Autoroute Blanche offers splendid views of the massif, 4807 metres at its highest point. You can see the peaks by taking the spectacular cable car crossing the Vallee Blanche from Le Palud to Chamonix; or you can climb Mont Blanc itself. Queues form in the height of the season to make the final ascent, and how to deal with the litter left by walkers and mountaineers has become a serious problem.

Evires

Groisy
Good views.

Péage de Villy le Peloux
Take a ticket. Good aire after the barriers, with a motorway information centre, open in summer.

Fontanelles ★
Relais caféteria with terrace, and pleasant picnic area.

Albens

Drumettaz ★ *i*
Route Napoléon tourist information board.

Péage joining A43
Pay here.

Granier *i*
There is an Arche caféteria, with terrace. The aire is dominated by Mont Granier, on the north-eastern edge of the Chartreuse; a spectacular setting.

Péage leaving A43
Take a ticket.

Chapareillan
Small aire in a splendid setting.

La Terrasse ★
Small but pretty aire.

Péage de Brignoud *i*
Pay here.

Bois Claret ★
Views of the Belledonne massif.

AIRES A40 (SCIENTRIER) ~ GRENOBLE

A40 (SCIENTRIER)

	km	from Grenoble
		Massif Chablais
		La Roche S/Foron
Evires	154	**Etaux**
Col d'Evires		*Plateau des Glières*
Ponts de la Caille		*Tete du Parmelan*
Groisy	144	**Les Crets Blancs**
		Cruseilles
Péage de Villy le Pel.	=	**Péage d'Allonzier**
		Annecy Nord
		Annecy Sud
		Lac d'Annecy
Fontanelles	126	**La Ripaille**
		Montagne du Semnoz
		Rumilly
Albens	111	**St Girod**
		Aix les Bains Nord
Drumettaz	98	**Mouxy**
		Aix les Bains Sud
Péage	=	**Péage**
Dent du Chat		
		Chambéry, A43
		Challes les Eaux
		Vallée de l'Isère
Granier ←	46	→ **L'Abis**
		Les Marches
Péage	=	**Péage**
		A43
Chapareillin	37	**Les Marches**
		Pontcharra
		Pontcharra
La Chartreuse		*Chaine de Belledonne*
		Le Touvet
La Terrasse	21	**Chonas**
St Hilaire		
Plateau des Petites Roches		
Péage de Brignoud	=	**Péage de Brignoud**
		Brignoud
Bois Claret	10	**St Nazaire**
		Montbonnot
		Meylan Est
Le Vercors		
		Meylan Ouest

GRENOBLE

Etaux
Good views.

Les Crets Blancs
Bar/buffet in shop. Good views.

Péage d'Allonzier *i*
Pay here. Motorway information centre.

La Ripaille ★

St Girod
The Table d'Orientation shows the mountains which we have just left behind us.

Mouxy
Le Petit Café, with terrace, at fuel station. There is a pleasant but small picnic area.

Péage leaving A43
Take a ticket.

The road through Chambéry, the capital of Savoie, is not a motorway, but it is a fast 2-lane highway and includes the 1km long Tunnel des Monts.

L'Abis
There is a covered footbridge to the facilities on the other side of the motorway.

Péage joining A43
Pay here.

Les Marches

Chonas
Small, with a good view and quite a nice grassy area.

Péage de Brignoud
Take a ticket.

St Nazaire

Travelling towards Geneva, the motorway descends from the Aire d'Etaux, and a vista of limestone mountains, the **Massifs du Chablais et de Faucigny Giffre**, opens up ahead, north of the river Arve which the Autoroute Blanche A40, follows. The **Col d'Evires** is to the north of the motorway.

Haute-Savoie was the first of the Départements of France to be liberated from German occupation without Allied help, but the human cost was high. At the end of the forest road up from Thorens, at the Col des Glières, is a **Monument de la Resistance** commemorating those who died in action on the **Plateau des Glières** in 1944.

The **Ponts de la Caille** are a 19th century suspension bridge and a modern single-span bridge crossing the Usses gorge side by side. The distinctive **Tete du Parmelon** escarpment is visible to the north-east. The signs tell us where the **Lac d'Annecy** is, but it is not visible from the motorway. Between Chambéry and Annecy the motorway follows the slopes of Mont Revard and then of the extensively wooded **Montagne de Semnoz** which dominates Annecy.

At the northern end of the Mont du Chat is the **Dent du Chat** the cat's tooth, overlooking the lac du Bourget (the largest and deepest in France) and Aix les Bains.

Challes les Eaux is a spa town. The **vineyards** of Savoy stretch along the wide sunny valleys; on the slopes around Montmélian are the villages which produce some of the finest wines of the region; Apremont, Myan and Chignin.

Between Grenoble and the A43, the motorway follows the wide **Vallée de l'Isère**, one of the most fertile regions in the Alps. The **Chaine de Belledonne** is to the east of the motorway between Montmélian and Grenoble. At the Grenoble end is Chamrousse, a host of the Winter Olympics; further along is the Massif des Sept Laux and the peaks of Belledonne and Le Frene.

The Chevalier de Bayard, described by Francois I as 'sans peur et sans reproche', the perfect medieval knight, was born near **Pontcharra** at the Chateau de Bayard in 1476. His success in the joust and finally in battle (he is said to have defended a bridge single-handed against 200) have earned him a place in French history books.

Two towers remain from when the **Chateau du Touvet**, north of the motorway, was fortified; the gardens have a remarkable Italian waterfall. Driving south, the **Vercors** beyond Grenoble looms into view after the Aire de la Terrasse. A funicular railway, the steepest in Europe, climbs from the N90 in the valley up to the small resort of **St Hilaire du Touvet**. International parapente competitions are held here, from the **Plateau des Petites Roches**.

The A41 between Grenoble and Pontcharra passes between Pre-Alpes and Alps, between the limestone Chartreuse and the cristalline Chaine de Belledonne. The highest peak in the Chartreuse the Dent de Crolles towers above the plateau and the valley.

Les Brotteaux ★ ♿ ⛺ 🌳 📞
The best place for a picnic is at the far end of the site.

Lyon Montluel ⛽ ♿ ⛺
Fuel station shop is small; minimal WC outside. Picnic area beyond, quite pleasant, with mature shrubs, and a grassy area; no WC there.

Péage de Beynost
Pay here.

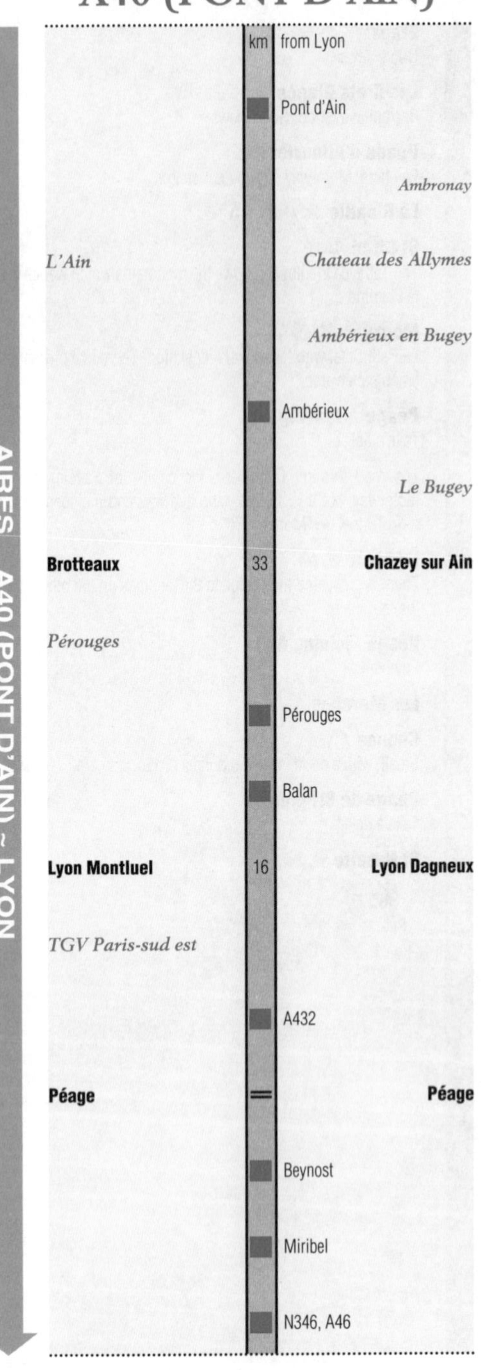

Chazey sur Ain
Quite a pleasant picnic area.

Lyon Dagneux
Bar-buffet in fuel station shop.

Péage de Beynost
Take a ticket. There is a nice sculptured waterfall, La Cascade, to look out for here.

A quiet motorway, crossing gentle terrain, in contrast to the spectacular scenery of the A40 from Geneva from which it branches towards Lyon.

There is a well-restored Benedictine abbey in the village of **Ambronay**. **Le Bugey** is the area of wooded hills to the east of the motorway.

The motorway crosses the **Ain** twice, the first time high above it, the second surprisingly close to it.

On the slopes of Mont Luisandre is the partly 13th century **Chateau des Allymes**.

So typical a medieval town, **Pérouges** has featured in several historical films, including The Three Musketeers. There is a fine view of the town and its ramparts from the motorway. Threatened by a decline in its trade and prosperity in the 19th century, when it was bypassed by the railway, it owes its continued existence to admirers of its charms who, for many years, have been buying and restoring its houses, to avoid them falling into decay.

Coming from Paris, the **TGV Sud Est** line is carried on an extraordinary viaduct across the motorway, to follow the A432 to Satolas airport, where there is an underground terminal, and beyond.

A43

LYON

AIRES LYON ~ ALBERTVILLE

St Priest
Separate caféteria at the end of this slightly neglected looking site.

Péage de l'Isle d'Abeau
Take a ticket. Free tyre pressure check after the barrier.

L'Isle d'Abeau
Arche restaurant, caféteria and snack bar with terraces; all very nice indeed. Motorway and traffic information; cash dispenser. Ibis Hotel beyond main aire, and test-your-reflexes driving centre at end of this pleasant aire. Strongly recommended for a meal; food and service are excellent.

Le Vernay
Table d'Orientation showing the Alpes de Dauphiné et Savoie; small and pleasant, beside a stream.

Les Marouettes
Small; good views of mountains, especially on leaving the aire.

Romagnieu
Picnic area and games at end of site. Backdrop of mountains.

Le Lavaret
Quite small, beautifully landscaped, well kept aire, with a view of, and possible access to, the Lac d'Aiguebelette. Very pleasant.

Granier
Arche caféteria with terrace. Overlooked by Mont Granier on the north-eastern edge of the Chartreuse.

Péage

Val Gelon
Access at exit to St Pierre d'Albigny. Bar/buffet with terrace in fuel station shop. Good planting. Panorama des Sites Olympiques.

Péage
As the motorway ends. Pay here. The A430 goes on 18kms to Albertville; the A43 will eventually continue through the Alps to Turin.

	km	from Lyon
		Porte des Alpes
		Bron Aviation
		N346, A46
St Priest	8	**Manissieu**
		Aeroport de Satolas
		A432
L'Isle d'Abeau		*Crémieu*
		Le Bugey
Péage de l'Isle d'Abeau	=	**Péage de l'Isle d'Abeau**
		L'Isle d'Abeau Villefontaine
L'Isle d'Abeau ←	28	→ **L'Isle d'Abeau**
		L'Isle d'Abeau Est
		Bourgoin
Le Vernay	39	**Coiranne**
		A48
		La Tour du Pin
Les Marouettes	53	**Les Sitelles**
		Les Abrets
Lac de Paladru		
Romagnieu	63	**Le Guiers**
		Belmont Tramonet
Le Lavaret	78	**L'Omble**
		Lac d'Aiguebelette
Lac d'Aiguebelette		*Lac du Bourget*
La Chartreuse		
		Chambéry Nord, A41
Le Granier		*Challes les Eaux*
		Granier
Granier ←	100	→ **L'Abis**
N. D. de Myans		*Les Alpes*
Péage	=	**Péage**
		A41
		Montmélian
Val Gelon	120	**L'Arclusas**
Péage	=	**Péage**
Eglise de Chamousset		*Forteresse de Miolans*
		Frontenex
Mont Blanc		*Confluent de l'Arc et l'Isère*
		Aiton

Manissieu
There is a Croissanterie/grill in the fuel station shop. At the end of the site is a table d'orientation and good views over Lyon.

Péage de l'Isle d'Abeau
Pay here, keeping to the right. There is a Gendarmerie 1000 metres beyond the barriers.

L'Isle d'Abeau ★
The snack bar is open in summer only. Most of the facilities are on the other side of the motorway, across a covered footbridge; no disabled access.

Coiranne ★
Small, open site, but some shade, and a stream running along the back.

Les Sitelles

Le Guiers

L'Omble ★
Views over Lac d'Aiguebelette.

L'Abis
Covered footbridge to Arche caféteria on other side of motorway, but no access for the disabled.

Péage
Pay here.

L'Arclusaz
Bar/buffet in fuel station shop, with terrace. Lot of planting, quite pleasant.

Péage
Take a ticket to join the motorway.

On a clear day you can glimpse the Alps ahead from soon after Lyon. **Satolas** is a busy international airport with a TGV station under it.

L'Isle d'Abeau is a new town to the south of the motorway; the aire of the same name is nearer the old town 5kms to the east, on the north side.

The western edge of the limestone plateau L'Ile Crémieu is a line of characteristic cliffs. The town of **Crémieu**, once a stronghold defending a route into Dauphiné, overlooks the Lyon plain.

Excavations in the **Lac de Paladru** a water sports centre, have revealed the existence of a neolithic farming village. Medieval villages built around the lake were abandoned as the waters rose, but vestiges of these remain, too.

Le Bugey is an area of wooded hills to the north of the great meander of the Rhone as it sweeps down from Lake Geneva. Its southern edge is visible from the A43 after La Tour du Pin.

As the road approaches Chambèry, it nears the north-east edge of the **Chartreuse**, and there are stunning views of the Montagne de l'Epine, and further ranges beyond, as you reach the Tunnel de Dullin (1600 metres long). The construction of Alpine motorways has been a remarkable feat of engineering.

Where the Montagne du Chat meets the Chartreuse Massif, is the **Lac d'Aiguebelette**. There is an excellent view of the lake just before you enter the Tunnel de l'Epine (3200 metres long), going towards Chambéry. The **Lac du Bourget** is the largest and deepest natural lake in France.

Until the 16th century Savoy was a sovereign state, and **Chambéry** its capital. Today Annecy disputes the leadership of the region. Chambéry's geographical position rivals that of Grenoble; using up almost all the space in the deep valley between the Montagne du Chat, the Chartreuse and the Bauges massif.

Challes les Eaux is a spa town on the slopes of the Bauges massif. The northerly peak of the Chartreuse massif is **Le Granier**, magnificent from the motorway. **Notre Dame de Myans** is the church of a village among the vineyards.

At **Montmélian** the motorway enters the Combe de Savoie, one of the great valleys of the High Alps, and offers marvellous views and different perspectives of the mountain scenery and villages. You should be able to see **Mont Blanc** ahead; coming in the other direction, from Albertville, the **Massif de la Chartreuse** and the **Granier** are in view. Quite a site to defend, the **Forteresse de Miolans** is a chateau on a rocky outcrop above the valley. For 200 years before the French Revolution it was a prison with a fearful reputation.

Close to the motorway is the **Eglise de Chamousset** a Romanesque church with a pretty bell tower.

Look out for the Pont Royal, just below the confluence of the **Arc and Isère** rivers, and **Miolans** on the hilside above.

A46

The Lyon western ring road is excellent.The section of dual carriageway road between the junctions with the A42 and A43, is of motorway standard.

Mionnay Ouest
There is a car wash at the fuel station. The shop is exceptionally well-stocked. No bar/buffet, but plenty of snacks are available in the shop, and there is a microwave to heat them through. Very good toilet and shower facilities downstairs.

Communay Nord ★★
A well-landscaped picnic site and good play area.

A6 (ANSE)

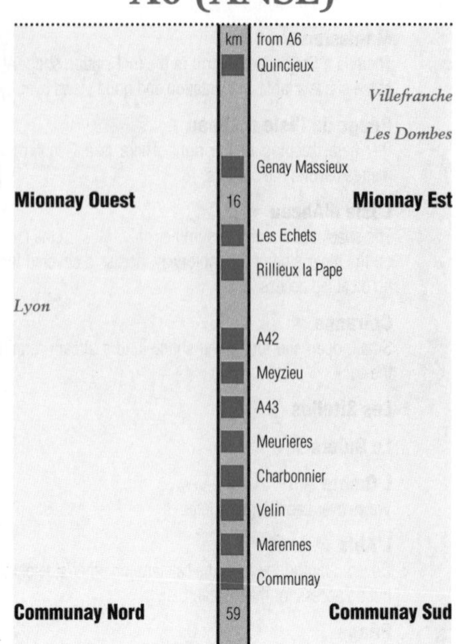

A7, A47

A47

The A47 is a non-toll motorway which explains the relative lack of services and the fact that its older section, the Givors end, is winding and narrow in places , with frequent speed restrictions. The St Chamond end is a well designed motorway with attractive concrete bridges decorated with symbols reminiscent of South American art, imaginative sound barriers and good landscaping.

St Romain *i*
There is a restaurant at one end of the fuel station shop, but it is close to the road and noisy.

Le Pays du Gier *i*
A smart and cheerful La Crocade restaurant and a picnic area with views over to the Mont du Pilat; the best place on this motorway.

A7 (LYON) ~ A72 (TERRENOIRE)

A7 (LYON)

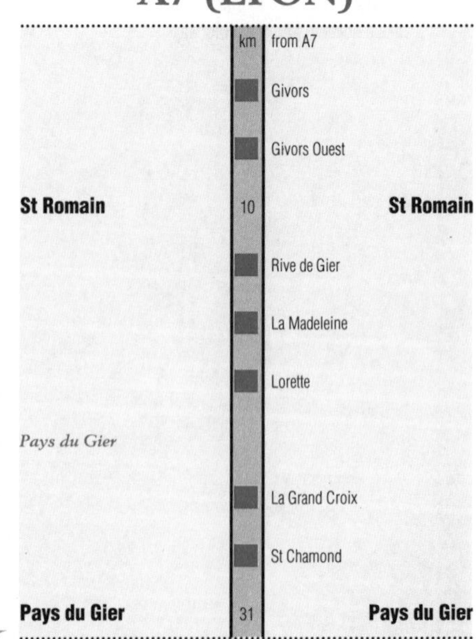

A72 (TERRENOIRE)

AIRES A7, A47 ~ A6 (ANSE)

Mionnay Est
Same as west

Communay Sud
Good facilities here including a well-stocked caféteria and shop. On the terrace there is a small fenced play area, with seats provided inside for parents.

The Saone valley between **Villefranche** and Macon is bordered on the west by the slopes of the great Beaujolais vineyards.

Lots of water birds in the flat, marshy area of **Les Dombes** its fertile fields interspersed with woodland and lakes (étangs) of all sizes. It's delightful, but you have to leave the motorway to see it; the bird sanctuary at Villars les Dombes is worth a visit if you have time.

The third largest city in France, **Lyon** is built on a beautiful site at the confluence of the Rhone and the Saone, a natural crossroads linking north, south, east and west. There used to be no way of avoiding its centre where traffic was frequently at a standstill, and the A46 has brought much needed relief.

A7 (LYON) ~ A72 (TERRENOIRE)

A72 (TERRENOIRE) ~ A7 (LYON)

St Romain
Bar/buffet in fuel station shop.

There is an 8 km section of good dual carriageway road, the N488, linking the motorway with the A72 at St Etienne. There are fuel stations on this. Travelling from St Etienne, take care not to miss the turning off the A72 onto the N488.

Le Pays du Gier
You will notice the red and white of the services on the other side of the motorway. Go off at exit 15 to St Chamond, over the bridge, round the roundabout, and you are there.

The industrial corridor along the valley is the **Pays de Gier**, which separates the Monts du Lyonnais from the Massif du Pilat. There are metallurgical and glass industries, with coal mining at Terrenoire, which means Black Earth.

Ponteray

Burcin

Space was obviously limited on this stretch of motorway; another very small site. The play area looks fun. I like the murals on the walls of the WC blocks on the A48.

Le Chatelard ★

The best place for a coffee break on this stretch of motorway. It is small but rather nice. A walnut grove runs alongside, and the views are superb.

Péage

Pay here.

L'Isle Rose *i*

The tourist information office is open in summer only.

AIRES A43 (BOURGOIN JALLIEU) ~ GRENOBLE

A43 (BOURGOIN)

	km	from lyon	
		A43	
Ponteray	48		**Chanses**
Burcin	61		**Oyeu**
Trouée de Colomb			*Lac de Paladru*
Plaine de Bievre			*Viaduc du Fure*
		Rives	
Le Chatelard	70		**Réaumont**
		Champfeuillet	
		A49	
Péage	=		**Péage**
		Pont de Veurey	
Isle Rose	85		**Voreppe**
		Voreppe	
		St Egreve	
Le Vercors			*La Chartreuse*
Grenoble			*Chaine de Belledonne*

GRENOBLE

Chanses ★

Drive round to the back of the site where there are steps up to a further shady picnic area.

Oyeu ★

Small, but set well back from road and pleasant.

Reaumont

A small, but very nice aire.

Péage

Take a ticket.

Voreppe

There is a bar/buffet in the fuel station shop.

There is evidence in the surrounding landscape, trees flattened or at crazy angles, that the **Trouée de Colomb** is a pretty windy spot!

West of Voiron, is the fertile **Plaine de Bièvre**, ancient bed of the Isere, where cereals are grown.

Excavations in the beautiful **Lac de Paladru**, a popular water sports centre, have revealed the existance of a neolithic farming village. Other villages built around the lake at the beginning of the Middle Ages had to be abandoned as the waters rose, but vestiges of these remain, too.

You may go to the **Chartreuse** to visit the famous monastery and try its liqueur; you may instead be captivated by the scenic beauty of the region, its majestic rock faces, summits, forests and gorges.

The rivers of the **Vercors** carve their way through gorges from the great limestone plateau to join the Isere. From the motorway one is impressed by the seemingly solid walls of rock which enclose the region, a natural fortress. Little wonder that it became a stronghold of the Resistance during 1943 and 1944. After D-Day, with passions running high and liberation apparently imminent, a republic was proclaimed. This was too much for the Germans, and parachutists and troops specially trained in mountain warfare were sent in to restore order. By the end of August 1944 hundreds of resisters and local inhabitants, from old folk to babies, had been killed. Their deaths are recorded throughout the region on poignant memorials.

The motorway crosses the **Fure**, on its way from its source in Lake Paladru to the Isere, on a spectacular viaduct.

To the south-west are the Alps, the **Chaine de Belledonne**, whose peaks approach 3000 metres.

With mountains all around, it is hard to decide which is your favourite view! **Grenoble** fills the valley of the Isere at the point where the Chartreuse, the Vercors and the Alps converge. A marvellous position, an elegant town centre, but stiflingly hot in summer, and often with a haze of pollution in the air from its many industries.

A48 (GRENOBLE)

800 metres after the péage at Grenoble, the A49 branches off towards Valence. Beautifully landscaped and sensitive to the environment, it follows the Isère river, and is dominated by the steep cliffs of the Vercors. Look out for the interesting architecture - shape, colour, material -of its bridges and buildings.

Poliénas
Small but OK, with splendid views.

St Sauveur
A small site, surrounded by walnut trees.

La Porte de la Drome *i*
The road has just crossed a lovely bridge over the Isere. Go to the left of the fuel station for the pleasant picnic area and good views. The Relais Porte de la Drome is planned to open during 1995.

Péage de Chatuzange
Pay here.

AIRES A48 (GRENOBLE) ~ VALENCE (BOURG DE PEAGE)

	km	from Grenoble	
			La Chartreuse
			Grenoble
	■	Tullins	
Poliénas	15		
			L'Isère
	20		**L'Albenc**
	■	Vinay	
St Sauveur	29		**Chambaran**
St Marcellin			*Le Vercors*
	■	St Marcellin	
Porte de la Drome	45		**Royans Vercors**
	■	La Baume d'Hostun	
Péage de Chatuzange	=		**Péage de Chatuzange**
	■	Bourg de Péage	
Romans			*Valence*

L'Albenc ★★

With lots of space, very good landscaping and planting, a footpath through the trees, and a large grassy area in the middle, this is the best place for a picnic on this motorway. Again, there are lovely views as you leave.

Chambaran ★

There is a lovely view of the Vercors from this pleasant, well-planted aire, which is spoilt by being rather close to the motorway. There are spectacular views of the river Isère as you leave.

Royans Vercors

The entrance to the aire is actually on Exit 8 from the motorway. There is access to the Relais facilities on the far side.

Péage de Chatuzange *i*

Take a ticket. There is an extra-large parking area after the barrier.

Signposted 'Grenoble' from the A7 motorway at the Valence Sud exit, there is about 20kms of fast road, the N 532, before you join the A49 south of Romans sur Isère.

The river **Isère**, whose valley the motorway follows, gives its name to the Departement. Approaching Grenoble from the west, the **Chartreuse** massif is ahead. With mountains all around, it is hard to decide which is one's favourite view! **Grenoble** fills the river valley at the point where the Chartreuse, the Vercors and the Alps converge. It has an elegant town centre, but can be stiflingly hot in summer, often with a haze of pollution in the air from its many industries.

The town of **St Marcellin** gives its name to a marvellously creamy soft cows milk cheese. Good from the supermarket, even better bought at a local market stall.

The traditional industry of shoe-making continues today in **Romans sur Isère**; the Musée de la Chaussure contains an amusing range of shoes from the ancient and the modern world.

The rivers of the **Vercors** carve their way through gorges from the great limestone plateau to join the Isere. From the motorway one is impressed by the seemingly solid walls of rock which enclose the region, a natural fortress. Little wonder that it became a stronghold of the Resistance during 1943 and 1944. After D-Day, with passions running high and liberation apparently imminent, a republic was proclaimed. This was too much for the Germans, and parachutists and troops specially trained in mountain warfare were sent in to restore order. By the end of August 1944 hundreds of resisters and local inhabitants, from old folk to babies, had been killed. Their deaths are recorded throughout the region on poignant memorials.

Valence is an important fruit marketing town.

La Pomme

Le Pas d'Ouiller ★ ★

This is Marcel Pagnol country, familiar to those who have read his autobiography or seen films of his books, and the view at this lovely aire is breathtaking.

Péage de la Ciotat

Pay here.

Le Liouquet ★

A Greek goddess, an unforgettable view and a shady spot for lunch.

Péage de Bandol

Pay here.

Sanary

AIRES MARSEILLE ~ TOULON

MARSEILLE

	km	from Toulon
La Pomme	55	
		St Marcel
		La Penne
		Aubagne
		A52, A8
		Carnoux
		La Bédoule
Le Pas d'Ouiller	40	
		Cassis
Les Calanques de Cassis		*Massif de la Ste Baume*
Péage de la Ciotat	=	**Péage de la Ciotat**
Le Liouquet	28	**Les Plaines Baronnes**
		Les Lecques
Baie de la Ciotat		
Cap de l'Aigle		
La Ciotat Ile Verte		
		Le Castellet
La Cadière d'Azur		*Le Castellet*
Bandol Ile de Bendor		
Péage de Bandol	=	**Péage de Bandol**
		Bandol
Ile des Embiez		
Sanary	12	**Sanary**
		Camp Laurent
Fort de Six Fours		
		La Beaucaire
		La Seyne
Chantiers Navales		
		Pont les Gaux

Péage de la Ciotat

Pay here.

Les Plaines Baronnes ★

The Mobilburger seems to be no more than a microwave facility; there is nowhere to sit and eat. To reach the picnic area, and the view, drive well beyond the fuel station, to the end of the site.

Péage de Bandol

800 metres after the aire; pay here.

Sanary

Just before the péage; small and basic, close to the road. There is a lovely view across the bay if you risk crossing the lorry park to look at the colourful mosaic 'Le Roi des Poissons' and read the legend of the king of the fish.

French novelist, poet and writer of screenplays, Marcel Pagnol, was born in **Aubagne**.

As the A50 reaches a highpoint west of Le Castellet, there is a fine view over towards the **Massif de la Ste Baume**.

The **Calanques de Cassis** are the inlets along the coast to the west, where the white of the limestone cliffs contrasts with the blue-green of the sea. Cassis itself deserves a mention; a busy fishing port in a pretty setting.

A great view down from the motorway to terraced **La Ciotat**, on the western side of the bay.

From the wooded **Ile Verte**, the great rock on the headland resembles an eagle's beak, hence its name, the **Cap de l'Aigle**.

Just to the north of the motorway, and even more picturesque in its hilltop setting, is **Le Castellet**, its ramparts overlooking the vineyards.

The attractive hilltop town you see beside the motorway to the south is **La Cadière d'Azur**, with the vineyards of Bandol stretching down below it towards the sea.

You will have noticed the terraced vineyards; **Bandol** is renowned for its velvety red wine, but it also produces white and rose provencal wines.

There is nothing quite like sunshine, a blue sea and an island in a beautiful bay to tempt you to break a journey! The **Ile de Bendor** is just off Bandol.

Look over from the Aire de Sanary to see the **Ile des Embiez**, a popular resort.

Overlooking the town of **Six Fours les Plages**, the **fort** has views to east and west, to the bays of Toulon and Sanary.

The **Chantiers Navales** at **Seyne** have been producing plant and machinery for the Merchant Navy for more than a century.

Péage de Sisteron ♿
Take a ticket.

Aubignosc ★ ♿ *i*
La Maison du Département is quite an advertisement for the Hautes-Alpes region with its hydro-electricity and motorway services design. Ultra modern, striped black and white outside, the colour scheme extends impressively inside to a white central hall and spiral staircase up to a viewing gallery. To one side is a black exhibition room with a large illuminated relief map sunken in the centre showing the region, its rivers, lakes and dams from the Camargue in the west to Italy in the east and Briancon in the north. There is a choice of caféteria or restaurant, the latter a raised section in the centre of the former, both with panoramic views. The regional products shop, though small, sells a good selection of produce from the mountains, and the video tourist information in the central hall is user-friendly and very informative. Outside there is a small, well-planned picnic area and separate WC block.

Belvedere de Peyruis les Mées ★ ♿
A lovely, neat aire, not very big, on the top of a hill, with a marvellous view over the plain to the south- east. On the far side are the Penitents des Mées.

Prieuré de Ganagobie ★ ♿
The use of large pebbles in this aire is very attractive. The priory is on the hillside behind, not visible from the aire.

Volx ★ ★ ♿
Rockets around; this looks interesting! The fuel station here is automatic; French credit cards only, no service at all. Most of the facilities - and yet more rockets - are on the eastern side, with access via a pedestrian tunnel.

Jouques ★ ♿
Well landscaped, clean and verdant; Escota certainly keeps the grass watered. This aire is rather small, but there is a further picnic area at the end of the site. Follow the sign to the Aire de Détente.

Péage de Meyrargues ♿
Pay here.

Meyrargues ★ ★ ♿
The best spot for a picnic on this route; after the fuel station, which has a sizeable caféteria in it, drive to the end of the site where there is a pleasant, spacious, wooded area. No separate WC block, but the fuel station is not far back.

La Champouse ♿
Super views from the picnic area.

AIRES SISTERON ~ MARSEILLE

SISTERON

	km	from Aix en Provence
Péage de Sisteron	=	**Péage de Sisteron**
La Citadelle de Sisteron		*Tunnel de la Baume*
	■	Sisteron Sud
		Digne les Bains
Aubignosc ←	111	→ **Aubignosc**
	■	Aubignosc
Belvedere de Peyruis	102	
		Les Péniltents des Mées
	■	Le Peyruis/Les Mées
La Durance		
Prieuré de Ganagobie	94	**Ganagobie**
Haute Provence		
Forcalquier		
	■	Forcalquier Oraison
Volx ←	75	→ **Manosque**
Manosque		*Moustiers Ste Marie*
	■	Monosque
Parc Nat. Reg. du Lubéron		
		Gréioux les Bains
		Lacs et Gorges du Verdon
	■	St Paul les Durance
Jouques	52	
		Cadarache
	50	**Pont Mirabeau**
Tunnel du Pont de Mirabeau		
Péage de Meyrargues	=	**Péage de Meyrargues**
	■	Pertuis
Meyrargues	32	**Meyrargues**
	■	Meynargues
	■	Venelles
	■	Aix en Provcence Nord
		Aix en Provence
	■	Aix en Provence Sud
	■	A8
	■	Aix Centre
	■	Les Milles
	■	Luynes Gardanne
	■	Bouc Bel Air
	■	Luynes
La Champouse	12	**Les Chabauds**
	■	Bouc Bel Air Garadanne
	■	Plan de Campagne
	■	A7

MARSEILLE

AIRES MARSEILLE ~ SISTERON

Péage de Sisteron
Pay here. Gendarmerie, and tourist information in summer.

Aubignosc ★
A pleasant aire, with lovely views and a good play area. Cross the motorway on a surprisingly open-sided footbridge to the facilities on the far side.

Ganagobie ★
I like this attractively-landscaped aire but would not use it on a hot day.

Manosque ★
The Maison des Alpes de Haute Provence has a few exhibits showing the region's geology and ancient history, in a modern building which also houses an Arche caféteria with terrace and a well-stocked shop. Outside you can't fail to see the rockets; there is also a climbing wall, with instruction in using this, and in fencing and archery, at weekends in summer; a good play area, too. Cars cannot return to the fuel station from the main aire. The picnic area in the trees at the end of the aire is used as a VTT track in summer (mountain bikes) as part of the 'Halte, Sport et Détente' programme, and has suffered a bit as a result. An excellent choice for a break for the energetic!

Pont Mirabeau ★
A stone commemorates the start of work on this motorway in 1982. The aire is beautifully landscaped and green, and there is an Aire de Détente, with play area, at the far end.

Péage de Meyrargues
Take a ticket.

Meyrargues ★
The Signal des Alpes is an aluminium sculpture at the entrance to this large, shady site.

Les Chabauds
Good facilities and super views.

Napoleon stopped at **Digne les Bains** in 1815 (see A8). Digne marks a boundary between Alps and Provence; north you will find no more olive trees; south, you are below the snow line. A tunnel takes the motorway under the Rocher de la Baume; at its southern end, look back to see the **Citadelle de Sisteron**, a medieval masterpiece at the gateway between the Dauphiné and Provence.

Legend has it that **Les Pénitents des Mées** are really monks, turned to stone for looking too long at the pretty girls of the Durance valley. Rising near Briancon, the river **Durance** travels 324 kms to enter the Rhone at Avignon. The E.D.F canal (Electricité de France), which serves several power stations, diverts much of the river towards the Etang de Berre. Its great hydro-electric potential, and its use for irrigation in this great fruit-growing region, is thus being realised. Such a useful river, but with so much of its water diverted to the canal for so much of its length, it is not very beautiful. The motorway follows both river and canal down to Meyrargues before turning due south to Aix.

A town with an industrial past? **Forcalquier** means lime-kiln (furnus calcarius in Latin, fourcauquie in Provencal). The narrow streets, little squares and old houses of **Manosque** have been carefully restored; the pastel walls and pantiled roofs are quite Mediterranean.

Moustiers Ste Marie, famous for porcelain, has an extraordinary site at the foot of a gap in a great limestone cliff, with a monastery built higher up on the cliff. Now Notre Dame de Beauvoir, this used to be called Notre Dame d'Entreroches (between the rocks). It is said that the first monks lived in caves on the cliff side. From the town a road runs up to the **Grands Gorges de Verdon**. The Grand Canyon has been carved through the high limestone plateau by the river Verdon. Why it did that rather than flow round it, no one knows, but it has resulted in exciting scenery. There are roads with viewing points along each side of the gorge, the most spectacular part of the northern route having been completed in 1973. It is possible, though arduous, to walk down and along the bottom of the gorge using the Sentier Martel footpath named after the man who first explored the 21 kms of the canyon in 1905. The **Lac de Ste Croix** separates the Grand Canyon from the lower gorges, from where the river flows down to the Durance near Cadarache.

The inhabitants of Paris are Parisiens; of Marseille, Marseillais; at **Gréioux les Bains** we have Gryseliens! The healing powers of the waters here were known to the Ancient Greeks, and the town has prospered as a spa on and off ever since.

Skirted by the Durance, and by the A51 from Manosque to Meyrargues, the **Parc Naturel Régional du Lubéron** is a forested mountain region, with fortresses and villages perched on rocky promontories and spurs, and dry stone huts called 'bories'. Experimental prototype reactors for power stations are produced at **Cadarache**.

Peypin ★

Pleasant picnic area, with super views.

Péage d'Aubagne

Pay here.

A8 (AIX)

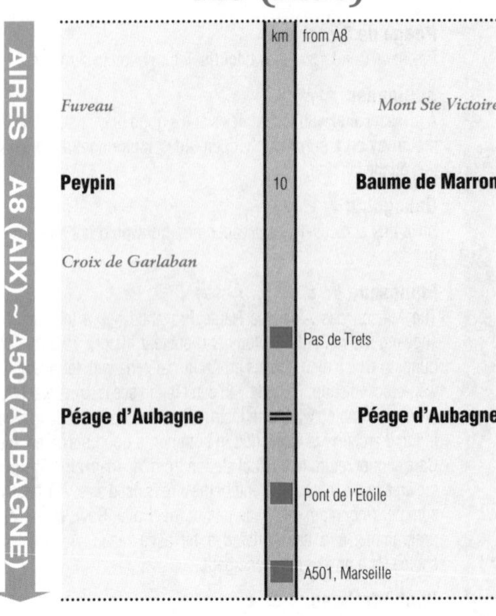

A50 (AUBAGNE)

Caissargues ★ ★

The twin viewing towers of the aires on each side of the motorway stand out as you approach this aire. There are picnic tables among olive trees and a car park near the simple exhibition hall, although the entrance to it is narrow and caravans will need to drive on to the second car park. Oleander, acacia and cypress trees line the path up to a small, beautifully presented exhibition portraying daily life in a Bronze age settlement, seen through the eyes of a young woman whose skeleton, adorned with a necklace of mussel shells, was discovered near here after 5000 years. I think you will be impressed, and entry (10h00 - 18h00) is free. Explanations are in French only, but it is above all a visual experience, so don't let that put you off; do make time to visit it if you are on this motorway. Afterwards walk over to see the fine set of columns from the old theatre of Nimes (built in 1827) which were rebuilt here in 1990, and stroll by the ponds with their fountains in the formal gardens which stretch away for perhaps half a mile. There are good views of Nimes, even if you don't climb the viewing tower. Floodlit at night, too; quite an impressive aire.

Péage d'Arles

Pay here.

A9 (NIMES)

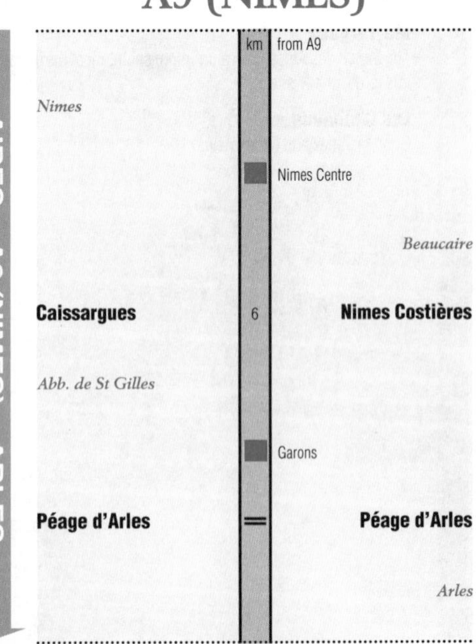

ARLES

Baume de Marron
Fairly minimal picnic facilities.

Péage d'Aubagne
Take a ticket here.

The view of the **Montagne Ste Victoire** from the A52 driving north is marvellous; the road is descending, and you see the mountain seemingly floating ahead of you across the valley.

Fuveau is a pretty village beside the motorway.

The reader of his autobiography will know that Marcel Pagnol, French novelist, poet and writer of screenplays, was born in **Aubagne**. Looking west after the town, you will see the **Croix de Garlaban** (710m) which loomed over the landscape of his childhood summers, described in his autobiography.

A9 (NIMES) ~ ARLES

Nimes Costières ★
A well-planned and spacious aire, part of it being the continuation of the formal gardens of the Aire de Caissargues. Climb the strange viewing tower to see how the gardens lead to the theatre colonnades on the far side of the motorway and to have good views of Nimes.

Péage d'Arles
Take a ticket. Tyre pressure check after the barrier.

Settlements surely existed on this plain, at the foot of the hills, for thousands of years before the Romans built a road, the Via Domitia, from **Beaucaire** on the Rhone to Perthus in the Pyrenees, thus linking Rome with the south of Spain, in 118 BC. It was under Augustus, who came here in 31 BC, that **Nimes** had its heyday, and many of the splendid remains you can see today were built at that time. By the fourth century, Arles became a more important town, and Nimes never really recovered, but its history contains several other periods of cultural and economic growth. It's textile industry, which flourished in the 18th century, has given us the word 'denim', a fabric 'de Nimes'.

St Gilles is a town on the edge of the Camargue, renowned for the Romanesque facade of its abbey church. In a commanding position overlooking the Rhone delta, the fortunes of **Arles** as a Roman capital owed much to having chosen the right general to support when it provided Caesar with ships for his campaign against Pompey's Marseille in 49 BC. The Roman amphitheatre, the twin of the one at Nimes, is used to this day for bull-fighting, a traditional Camargue sport. Van Gogh lived here for a short time towards the end of his life, painting non-stop, until approaching madness led him to enter an asylum at St Rémy de Provence where he died.

Gonfaron ★ ♿ /⊓\ ⌂ ☎ *i*

There is an excellent play area at the end of this small aire. The tortoise theme relates to the nearby Village des Tortues, where tortoises are reared for release into the wild to replenish a diminishing local population. They are, I believe, the same species once acquired by British gardeners who hoped that they would rid their crops of insects. The creatures, being, in fact, vegetarian, made a beeline for the lettuces and violas instead!

Les Lauvets ★ ♿ /⊓\

Up above the road; small, beautifully landscaped and colourful.

Péage ♿

Pay here.

La Chaberte ⛽ ♿

Underground traverse of Toulon will open in 1997 to join A57 and A50.

AIRES A8 (LE CANNET DES MAURES) ~ TOULON

A8 (LE CANNET)

	km	from Toulon
	■	Le Cannet des Maures
Tortues des Maures		
Gonfaron	45	**Les Sigues**
		N. D. des Anges
		Massif des Maures
Les Lauvets	31	**Le Suve du Vent**
Puget Ville		*Vignobles Varois*
Péage	═	**Péage**
	■	Cuers Nord
	■	Cuers Sud
	■	Ste Christine
	■	Les Terrins
	■	La Farlede
La Chaberte	9	**La Bigue**
	■	A570
Fort du Girardon		
Le Coudon		*Hyères*
Toulon		

TOULON

Les Sigues ★ ♿ /Π\ 🍴 📞 *i*
The same tortoise theme (see Gonfaron) is used in the excellent play area as you enter the aire.

Le Suve du Vent ★ ♿ /Π\
On this large, landscaped site there is information about Méditerrenean flora and a display of equipment used to fight fires, 'Lutte contre l'incendie'.

Péage ♿
Take a ticket

La Bigue ⛽ ♿
Fuel station planned near junction 5.

Two million years ago the vast continent that covered what is now the Mediterranean Sea broke up, leaving Corsica, Sardinia, the **Massif des Maures** and the Esterel; these two, then, are the most ancient lands in Provence. 'Maures' might refer to the Spanish pirates (Moors) who raided this coast for centuries, or come from a Provencal word for 'wooded'.

La Tortue des Maures is the oldest, and the most threatened reptile in France, and **Le Village des Tortues** near Gonfaron is doing its bit to protect it. Damaged and sick tortoises, brought in by the public, are cared for in its clinic and there is a successful programme of reproduction; between its opening in 1985 and 1993, 3500 tortoises have been returned to the wild in the Massif. You can visit the village by leaving the motorway at junction 10 and taking the N97 to Gonfaron; it is signposted from there.

Notre Dame des Anges: a priory with a view, high in the Maures.

On the lower slopes of the Maures are the **Vignobles Varois**, some of the main red-wine producing vineyards of the region.

Puget Ville is a pretty peaches-and-cream town nestling in the valley to the west of the motorway.

Hyères is a popular resort with the attraction of two islands off the coast, one having beautiful sandy beaches, the other a nature reserve with lovely shady walks.

The **Fort du Girardon** is at a high point (702m) on **Le Coudon**, the hill to the west dominating the motorway as it approaches the naval base of **Toulon**, not an easy town to traverse at the moment. Work on an underground throughway, linking the A50 and the A57, is in progress and is due to be completed in 1997.

Péage de Toulouse Sud
Take a ticket. Tyre pressure check after the barrier.

Toulouse
No picnic area.

Ayguevives ★★
Not a large aire but very well appointed. Picnic in the aire or walk up to the lock on the plane tree-lined towpath of the Canal du Midi.

Renneville ★★
Small, not a lot of parking, but pleasant if there is room. Situated by the Canal du Midi again.

Port Lauragais ★★★
Good picnic area, with tables beside the canal, and excellent services too, the main buildings being on an island on a man-made lake at the intersection of the motorway and the Canal du Midi. The architecture is most attractive, the exhibitions interesting and the regional products shop well stocked and displayed. There are boat trips along the canal in summer if you have time; try one of the many sports on offer, from sailing to skate-boarding; otherwise sit in the restaurant or the caféteria, where there are large windows overlooking the lake. A coypu climbed out of the water when we were there and sunned itself on a bank, and there are swans and wildfowl. You can return towards Toulouse from here; if the barrier is down, obtain a 'jeton' from the hotel.

Mireval ★
Rather close to the road, but you can walk down to a lake.

Montreal ★
Less developed than most on this motorway, there is a large grassy area, a nice lake at the back and a bit of a wood. A good bank of broom screens it from the road.

Carcassonne Arzens ★
Hidden behind the fuel station is a pleasant but small picnic area surrounded by vineyards, a little cloche-mur in the distance.

Belvedere de la Cité ★★
Up above road, a well laid out site with cypress and Mediterranean pines; not a lot of parking. The view of the fairytale city is quite spectacular.

Les Corbières ★★★
With the mountain of Alaric behind, and views over the valley and of vineyards all around, this is a delightful spot. On this side of the motorway is the fuel station, shaded parking and picnic areas and a parcours de santé which winds it's way up a hill. There is a nice wild area at the top with junipers, hellebores and pines. There is pedestrian access to the services on the other side.

Fontcouverte

Bizanet ★

Jonquières
A small site which extends up a hillside of scrubland, with views down towards the Mediterranean.

AIRES TOULOUSE ~ NARBONNE

TOULOUSE

	km	from Bordeaux
Péage de Toulouse Sud	=	**Péage de Toulouse Sud**
Toulouse	248	**Toulouse**
Clochc-murs toulousains		
Ayguesvives	256	**Baziège**
		Villefranche de Lauragais
Renneville	266	**Villefranche**
Canal du Midi		*Avignonet Lauragais*
Port Lauragais ←	274	→ **Port Lauragais**
Partage des Eaux		*Seuil de Naurouze*
		Castelnaudary
		Castelnaudary
Mireval	292	**Castelnaudary**
Montreal	303	**Bram**
Carcassonne Arzens	312	**Carcassonne Arzens**
		Carcassonne Ouest
		Carcassonne
Belvedere de la Cité	325	**Belvedere d'Auriac**
L'Aude		
		Carcassonne Est
Montagne d'Alaric		
Les Corbières ←	340	→ **Les Corbières**
Les Corbières		*Languedoc*
Fontcouverte	354	**La Peyrière**
		Lezignan
Bizanet	366	**Bizanet**
		Le Chemin des Cathars
Narbonne Joncquières	375	**Pech Loubat**
		A9

NARBONNE

AIRES NARBONNE ~ TOULOUSE

Péage de Toulouse Sud
Pay here.

Toulouse
Small picnic area.

Baziège ★
Medium size, not many tables, good grassy area at back.

Villefranche

Port Lauragais ★★★
As you approach the aire you will notice the canal converging from the right. Drive past the fuel station on the left, and follow the signs beside the lake and under the motorway to the main area. However,if you only plan a picnic, stay on this side, where there are tables and loungers, play area and WC block beside the canal. The swans here expect to be fed, but are cowards at heart if you decide to shoo them away!

Castelnaudary ★
A pleasant site with a limited play area. You can walk down to a lake at the back with coots on it and a grassy bank. No swimming!

Bram

Carcassonne Arzens
A medium-sized aire behind the fuel station, with a grassy bank at the back.

Belvedere d'Auriac ★★
A good view of Carcassonne from the terrace; oleander, junipers, Mediterranean pines all around. Then down some steps to a display of local archaeology, copies of artefacts which are in the museum in Carcassonne. This is the site of an Iron Age camp which overlooked the city.

Les Corbières ★★★ *i*
In regional style, grouped around a pleasant courtyard with an interesting sculpture by Alice Penalba (the winged woman is the nearest I can get to La Grande Ailée) on it, are the buildings of this fine aire, housing a shop with regional products, a rugby exhibition, 4 Pentes grill restaurant, Caféroute (24 hours in summer). The large picnic area has fine views over the valley, and shaded parking.

La Peyrière
Small, neat, surrounded by vineyards.

Bizanet ★★
The site extends a long way from the road, with woods at the back and a lovely view.

Pech Loubat ★★
'Le Chemin des Cathars' - an aire with fabulous views towards the Narbonne plain and the sea from strange concrete lookouts situated at the top of a hill. The road spirals up and round to the viewpoint, with picnic areas on the way, to the phallic monuments (3 giant horsemen, according to their sculptor, Jacques Tissanier) on the top. Plenty of parking, in all a fun place to visit.

Silhouetted against the skyline west of the motorway is a curious belfry, typical of the region, a **Cloche-mur toulousain.** Two towers are connected by a wall; there are three archways in each tower, a bell in each archway. It is in fact, the end of a church, built against but not as high as the wall.

Avignonet Lauragais is a small town on the hillside close to the motorway, dominated by its church.

The exhibition centre at Port Lauragais is named after **Paul Riquet,** the 17th century engineer who designed and built the Canal du Midi, and who died just months before the work was completed.

Paul Riquet's dream was to harness the torrents of the **Montagne Noire**, divert them towards the **Seuil de Naurouze**, which is the highest point (the **Partage des Eaux**) between the Atlantic and the Mediterranean along which the canal would have to flow, so that they could feed the slopes to the west towards the Garonne and to the east towards the Aude. You will notice the obelisk commemorating Paul Riquet's work on the hillside on the other side of the canal.

The pot on the brown sign for **Castelnaudary** contains cassoulet, the local casserole dish of beans, pork and sausage.

Travelling south the scenery has changed; from the fertile plain the road has climbed into the more arid region on the edge of the Corbières, with vineyards, poplars, broom and cypress trees. To the north are the rounded summits of the **Montagne Noire**. The vista as you approach **Carcassonne** is impressive. See the city from outside the walls, preferably at night, when it is floodlit; it is an astonishing medieval gem. What remains inside does not match the walls, apart from in one or two corners, and there are an awful lot of tourists.

Between the Romans and the Francs came the Visigoths, whose final stronghold was this mountainous south-west region, until Clovis the Franc, after a long campaign, succeeded in uniting most of Gaul by defeating **Alaric II**, leader of the Visigoths, in 507AD.

Les Corbières: the region between the Aude, the Pyrenees and the Mediterranean Sea; land of abbeys (Cistercian Fontfroide, Benedictine Alès, St-Hilaire and St-Polycarpe), chateaux (Peyrepertuse, Queribus) and vineyards, of which the finest, with an 'appellation controlé' is Fitou, in the south.

After the final Crusade against the Turks, a further reason to take up arms for medieval Christendom was found; the heresies preached by the **Cathars**. This is the region most sympathetic to Cathar views; where towns were burnt to the ground, their inhabitants murdered whatever their religious views. Only the best fortified towns survived the onslaught of the new Crusaders.

Péage de St Selve
Take a ticket. Tyre pressure check after the barrier.

Les Landes ★ ★ ★
Named after the region, a very large aire, with lots of picnic tables and childrens games among the pine woods. You can try archery or mountain biking here on summer weekends. An example of the efforts made by the authorities to keep motorway aires clean: in one section, we noticed 8 bins for 11 parking spaces! A Relais caféteria is due to open here soon.

Auros ★
Small and rather close to the road, its forest setting is pleasant.

Bazadais
A small wooded aire.

Le Chant du Coucou
The song of the cuckoo. A small aire; its setting, amongst the vineyards of Lot et Garonne, is pleasant.

Mas d'Agenais ★ ★
'Mas'is a langue d'oc word for 'house'; 'Agenais'the area around Agen. This aire is set well back from road, with a track back into the trees for cars. A large area of oak woods, interspersed with pine, to sit and walk in.

Queyran
Quite recently extended, this is still rather a small site.

Buzet sur Baize ★
A medium sized, well laid out and appointed aire with recently planted trees. There is a pretty, reconstructed 17th - 18th century pigeon house, typical of the region, in the corner of the site, which is overlooked by a fine 15th century chateau.

Bruch
A small site.

Agen Porte d'Aquitaine
Gateway to Aquitaine. A very large aire, with all services, apart from the fuel station, on the far side of the motorway, accessible to traffic from this side by means of a bridge. There is a museum of rugby, with mementos from the four nations (photos, shirts, etc), and a prune museum, with photos of plum picking, drying, and storage in times past. There is a Relais restaurant and snack bar. The Relais building is an interesting design, approached over water, with a lovely terrace, and stairs on the outside for climbing up to the top to have a fine view. Lots of greenery softens the effects of its concrete walls. The WC block is excellent, and includes a shower. The regional products shop has a tempting range of quality goods for sale. All so nice that I imagine it gets very busy at the height of the season. Outside, a lot of trees have been planted, and the games include table tennis. Baseball and archery are promised in summer. There is a bottle bank in the picnic area; you cannot return to Bordeaux from here.

AIRES BORDEAUX ~ AGEN

BORDEAUX

	km	from Bordeaux ring road	
		Martillac	
Chateau de Labrede			
		La Brede	
Péage de St Selve	=		**Péage de St Selve**
Les Landes	17		**Les Landes**
		Podensac	
Foret des Landes de G.			*Vignobles du Bordelais*
		Langon	
Villandraut			
Roquetaillade			
Auros	42		**Auros**
Bazadais	51		**Bazadais**
		La Reole	
			Sechoirs á Tabac
Le Chant du Coucou	62		**Le Chant du Coucou**
Lot et Garonne			*Marmande*
		Marmande	
Mas d'Agenais	77		**Mas d'Agenais**
Polyculture			*Bastides de Guyenne*
Queyran	86		**Queyran**
		Aiguillon	
Buzet sur Baise	97		**Buzet sur Baise**
Bruch	106		**Bruch**
Agen Pte d'Aquitaine ←	115		→ **Agen Pte d'Aquitaine**

AGEN

AIRES AGEN ~ BORDEAUX

At the Bordeaux Ring Road, follow signs for Begles and Bordeaux Centre. The road goes alongside the river. Take care to get into the left hand, Paris, lane, and then keep a sharp look out for directions to the ring road (Rocade), the small blue motorway signs and Paris.

Péage de St Selve ♿
Pay here.

Les Landes ★★
There is a bar/buffet in a temporary tent-like building, open only in summer; at the end of the site, beyond the services, there is a good wooded picnic area.

Auros ★★
Well back from the road, there are tables on the grass by the parking spaces, then a walk down into a small oak wood where there are more tables. There is a short walk laid out, through heather and bracken, among the pine trees.

Bazadais ★★
You can walk back into the woods from the picnic area which is situated beyond the fuel station.

Le Chant du Coucou
Quite a small site.

Mas d'Agenais ★★★
Set well back from road, with a good exercise circuit and walks in lovely woods.

Queyran ★★
There is a large wooded area behind the fuel station, and unusually good shelter for a rainy day in the WC block, where there are several tables by the drinking fountain.

Buzet sur Baize
As you approach, you will notice the 15th century Chateau de Buzet splendidly sited on the top of the hill on the opposite side of the road. The aire itself backs onto a small industrial estate.

Bruch
A small aire, situated in farmland.

Agen Porte d'Aquitaine
★★★ *i*
Good views over the valley of the Garonne from this very large aire. You cannot return to Toulouse from here.

From Bordeaux to Narbonne, the A62 and A61 link the Atlantic and the Mediterranean.

The **Chateau de Labrede** was the birthplace of Montesquieu, a man of letters who foresaw the Revolution, in 1689.

Hardly the moorland the name suggests, the **Foret des Landes de Gascogne** is a vast area of pine woods stretching from Bordeaux in the north to Bayonne in the south, it was created by drainage and planting only 100 years ago. Apart from the timber, the trees are an important source of resin. Much of the forest lies within a national park.

The motorway follows the Garonne; to the east of the river are the prettiest of the **Vignobles du Bordelais**, the vineyards of the Bordeaux region, in that area between the Garonne and the Dordogne known as Entre Deux Mers. To the west near Langon you will see the names of Sauternes and Yquem on the map.

Roquetaillade is a small town on the edge of the Landes, its chateau outwardly a medieval fort, its interior largely 19th century restoration by Viollet-le-Duc.

A little town in the Landes region, **Villandraut** has a ruined 14th century castle

You will have noticed unusual storage cabinets in the fields, and here is the explanation; they are **Sechoirs à Tabac**, drying tobacco leaves.

Lot et Garonne is the name of the 'département' around the confluence of the two rivers; the motorway travels past **Vignobles et Vergers**, vineyards and orchards, and you willl notice polytubes used for early fruit varieties.

The fertile valley of the Garonne produces a variety of arable crops, **polyculture**; the brown sign shows corn, wheat and clover.

As a gardener, **Marmande** means tomatoes to me; the brown sign shows that tobacco is produced there, too. Marmande is a town in the centre of the highly developed agricultural area of Lot and Garonne.

Guyenne is another name for Aquitaine; **bastides** were 13th and 14th century fortified towns, built by the English or the French in their struggle for control over the region.

A62

Moirax ★★
Once in this large aire, the road zigzags up a hillside to a viewpoint, from where you can see Agen and look out across the plain to the south east. There is a grassy slope which extends into oak woods, where the only shade is to be found.

Layrac ★
Fairly small, there is a steep bank at the back of this aire, with shrubs and trees planted on it, which is rather nice.

Les Dunes
A small, quite pleasant site.

Garonne ★
Named after the river. Recently extended to a good size, it will be better when trees have matured a bit.

Escatalens ★★
A pleasant, large, wooded aire, with a lake nearby. The exercise circuit is short, but OK, with nice carved signs. Not a lot of parking space.

La Foret de Montech ★★★
Well advertised in advance, this is a superb aire with an arboretum. It is set well back from road. The arboretum consists of a 500 metre walk amongst a variety of trees, all labelled (see appendix). There are benches along the way, as well as the seating in the large picnic area. There is a splendid selection of childrens' games, although it should be said that some of them look quite scary! Washing-up facilities at the WC block.

Naudy ★
Quite a small aire, with woods at the back, but no picnic area there. There are, however, some seating areas under little roofs on the grass.

Frontonnais ★★★
Extensive childrens games, outdoor table tennis and nice oak woods at the back of the site. The pedestrian tunnel to the Arche caféteria on the other side of the motorway is especially well-designed; gaps in its roof under the central reservation allow plenty of light to enter, and a variety of plants grow there. We also counted six bins in the tunnel! An alternative to the caféteria, if you are in a hurry, would be the mini-bar in the fuel station shop, which is larger than average.

Péage de Toulouse Nord
Pay here.

AGEN

AIRES AGEN ~ A61 (TOULOUSE)

	km	from Bordeaux ring road
	122	**Estillac**
Bastides et Chat. d'Albret		*Agen*
		Agen
Moirax	126	
Layrac	133	**Layrac**
Le Gers		
Les Dunes	143	**Les Dunes**
		Valence d'Agen
Auvillar		
Garonne	161	**Garonne**
La Garonne		*Moissac*
		Castelsarrasin
Escatalens	181	**La Foret de St Porquier**
Canal de Montech		
La Foret de Montech	187	**Lacourt St Pierre**
		Montauban
		Montauban
Naudy	197	**Campsas**
Frontonnais ←	207	→ **Frontonnais**
		St Jory
Péage de Toulouse Nord	=	**Péage de Toulouse Nord**
Toulouse		

A61 (TOULOUSE)

Estillac
Fairly recent tree planting, one covered table only, a few tables back among the trees.

Layrac ★★
This aire is rather close to road; drive round to the back where there is more space. A lot of planting has taken place.

Les Dunes ★★
The lorry park is close to the road; the main area is behind a little hillock, with shaded tables, a big grassy area, and more tables back among the trees. Broom has been planted on the slopes of the hill, and oak trees on the top. There is a rather nice water fountain.

Garonne ★
Beyond the fuel station there has been an expansion of a small picnic area.

La Foret de St Porquier ★★
Well back from road, a large aire, with a good screen of trees. There are footpaths, but no track for cars, back into the woods.

Lacourt St Pierre ★★
A good sized, wooded aire. The track for cars loops round the back, ensuring that the picnic area is well screened from the road.

Campsas ★★
Spacious aire, with footpaths back into the wooded area; very pleasant.

Frontonnais ★★★ *i*
One excellent feature of Arche caféterias is the separate coffee area, with a machine to get a jeton from to avoid queueing if you only want a coffee. The whole place is very smart, including the WCs, and there is a very nice terrace. The picnic area is delightful, with a little stream in a wooded area, and a vineyard at the side.

Péage de Toulouse Nord
Press the button to take a ticket. Tyre pressure check after the barrier.

Chateaux et Bastides de l'Albret refers to the Protestant Albret family which controlled a large part of south-west France in the 16th century; prudent marriage, having increased their power several times, led to one of them, Henry of Navarre, being crowned King of France, but only after he renounced his faith with the words 'Paris is worth a Mass'.

The exhibition at the Aire d'Agen shows that the greatest speciality of **Agen** is prunes; the finest of all plums suitable for drying comes from here. It is a busy commercial centre, and a market for other fruits grown in the region.

It used to be Gascony; now it is **Le Gers**.

Auvillar is a charming old hilltop village with a fine market hall in a triangular cobbled market square.

A fruit marketing centre on the Tarn, just before it joins the Garonne river, **Moissac** has had a turbulent past. Part of its fine Romanesque church and abbey remain.

The **Canal de Montech** links the Tarn to the Garonne.

A centre of Protestantism since the 16th century, and besieged during the Religious Wars on that account, the old fortified town of **Montauban** climbs up from the right bank of the Tarn, with more recent development on the left.

The **Ferme du 18ième Siècle** is a picturesque group of farm buildings to the west of the motorway.

Where Aquitaine looks to the Atlantic, its people sharing a history of three centuries of English rule, **Toulouse** had its roots more in Mediterranean civilisation and the 'langue d'oc' of the troubadours, and the Cathars. Partly as a consequence of this, the Cathar creed (preaching poverty and love, and against organised religion) flourished in Toulouse during the 12th century. The city was besieged for seven years during the Crusade led by Simon de Montfort against the Albigensians (the Cathars originated in Albi). When Toulouse eventually came under the authority of the Kings of France, the County was renamed Languedoc, after the language spoken here. There are still medieval streets, though the ramparts which checked the crusaders have gone, replaced by a ring of boulevards. A vital commercial and industrial town, Toulouse is known as a centre of high technology, and the French aerospace industry is based here.

Cestas

Les Gargails

Lugos

Le Muret
A useful aire with lots of facilities including a Caféroute, open 24 hours. Tourist information in summer only.

There is a gap in the A63 from north of Le Muret to St Geours de Maremme, linked by the N10.

Péage
Pay here; the easiest and quickest method on this motorway, at all the tolls, is to throw cash into a net.

Labenne ★
A lovely aire in the pine woods, with tables, loungers and climbing frames for the children among the trees. It is not large, but you can walk back into the woods where there is an exercise circuit. Apart from the open air shower, there is one in the WC block, which has proper toilets as well, unusual in a picnic area.

Péage
Pay here.

Bidart ★ ★
The pantiled roof and white walls of the service station are most attractive, and there is a bar/buffet in the shop. There is a limited view to the Atlantic from this small but very pleasant aire.

Péage
Pay here.

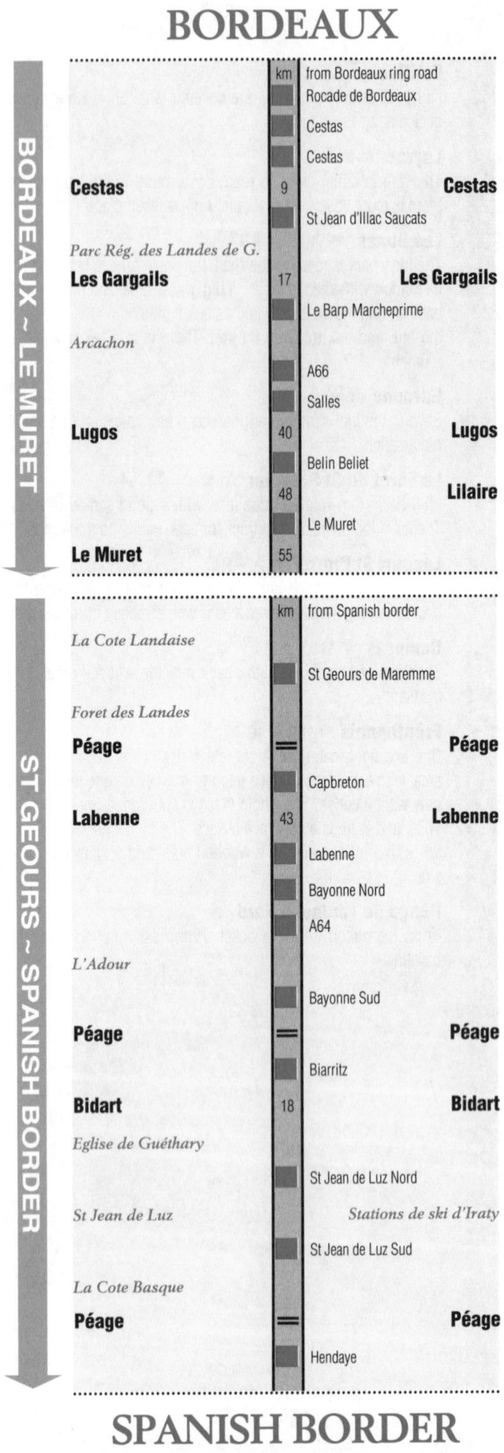

BORDEAUX

BORDEAUX ~ LE MURET

	km	from Bordeaux ring road	
		Rocade de Bordeaux	
		Cestas	
		Cestas	
Cestas	9		**Cestas**
		St Jean d'Illac Saucats	
Parc Rég. des Landes de G.			
Les Gargails	17		**Les Gargails**
		Le Barp Marcheprime	
Arcachon			
		A66	
		Salles	
Lugos	40		**Lugos**
		Belin Beliet	
	48		**Lilaire**
		Le Muret	
Le Muret	55		

ST GEOURS ~ SPANISH BORDER

	km	from Spanish border	
La Cote Landaise			
		St Geours de Maremme	
Foret des Landes			
Péage	=		**Péage**
		Capbreton	
Labenne	43		**Labenne**
		Labenne	
		Bayonne Nord	
		A64	
L'Adour			
		Bayonne Sud	
Péage	=		**Péage**
		Biarritz	
Bidart	18		**Bidart**
Eglise de Guéthary			
		St Jean de Luz Nord	
St Jean de Luz			*Stations de ski d'Iraty*
		St Jean de Luz Sud	
La Cote Basque			
Péage	=		**Péage**
		Hendaye	

SPANISH BORDER

LE MURET ~ BORDEAUX

Cestas

Les Gargails

Lugos

Lilaire
Bar/buffet.

Hardly the moorland the name '**Landes**' suggests, this vast area of pine forest stretches through **Gascony** from Bordeaux in the north to Bayonne in the south, and was created by drainage and planting only 100 years ago. Much of it is now in the national park.

There were no towns on the coast of the newly developed area; **Arcachon** rapidly grew from a fishing village to a prosperous resort, helped by the coming of the railway from Bordeaux and a visit from Emperor Napoleon III.

SPANISH BORDER ~ ST GEOURS

Péage
Pay here.

Labenne ★★
A pleasant place to stop. There is quite a demanding 'parcours detendu', exercise circuit, in the pine woods, including a steep slope. There is a bar/buffet in the well-stocked fuel station shop.

Péage
Pay here.

Bidart ★
Although in a built up area, and rather small, this is a very pleasant site on a hillside, with a panoramic view through to the Atlantic from the top. The architecture is attractive and of the region; pantiles and whitewashed walls. The coach and lorry park is down the hill. The buffet is open in summer only.

Péage
Pay here.

Less developed than the coast south of Biarritz, there are several pleasant resorts on the **Cote Landaise**. The largest of these are Hossegor and neighbour Cap Breton.

Reaching the sea at Bayonne, the river **Adour** forms the boundary between the Pays Basque and the Landes.

The two major cities of the region, **Bayonne** and **Biarritz**, have almost merged into one, yet each has its distinct character, formed through their very different histories. Bayonne, on the Adour, has been a prosperous port and Basque capital for 2000 years. Its neighbour Biarritz, a small fishing port 150 years ago, became a fashionable resort during the 19th century, largely due to its fine waterfront and sandy beaches, and to the arrival of aristocratic exiles from Spain who put it on the map.

St Jean de Luz is a lively resort at the mouth of the Nivelle river, with a sandy beach and a busy port. Its Basque name is **Donibane Lohitzun**.

The church of the small fishing port of **Guéthary** is in a commanding position, above the main road.

The forest of **Iraty**, on the border south of St Jean Pied de Port, used to provide the masts for ships of both the Spanish and French navies. Nowadays, skiers from both nations enjoy their sport in the resorts up there.

The main beaches south of Biarritz, **Les Plages de la Cote Basque**, are at St Jean de Luz, Socoa and Hendaye.

Péage de Sames
Take a ticket.

Hastingues
There is a bridge for traffic to cross to the services on the other side of the motorway.

Haut de Départ ★
The road has just come over the brow of a hill, and Orthez lies ahead. Some tables in this small but pretty aire have shades over them; others are among the trees.

Lacq Audejos
Modest exercise circuit around a central grassy area, and a summer bar/buffet.

Poey de Lescar

Serres Morlaas ★
Good wooded screen from the road, a small, pleasant aire with views of the Pyrenees.

Les Pyrénées ★ ★ ★
An imaginative, well-designed site, with the shop/snack bar building built of local, roughly-hewn stone, and good use of rock throughout. Food in the snack bar was simple but good when we tried it - my cassoulet was delicious - but it and the shop are small, considering they have to serve both sides of the motorway. Outside, the play areas are excellent, with table tennis and a wonderful dragon of a climbing wall (tuition on summer weekends) which separates the two good picnic areas, one for traffic from each direction. The Table d'Orientation explains the magnificent view of the Pyrenees.

Péage de Laloubère
Pay here. There is a Gendarmerie.

Les Bordes

Les Bandouliers ★
Set well back in woods, at a point where the mountains seem particularly close. A grassy bank screens the site from the road.

Péage de Cantaous
Pay here. This is the end of the motorway at present. The N117 is not a very good road until after St Gaudens, where it becomes dual carriageway.

AIRES BAYONNE ~ LANNEMEZAN

BAYONNE

	km	from Bayonne	
		A63	
Biarritz			*Bayonne*
		Mouguerre Bourg	
		Mouguerre Elizaberry	
			Les Plages Landaises
		Briscous	
		Urt	
Péage de Sames	=		**Péage de Sames**
			La Bidouze
Hastingues ←	30	→	**Hastingues**
		Peyrehorade	
Bastides et chateaux			*Dax*
Gave de Pau			*Les Landes*
		Salies	
Vignobles de Béarn			
Haut de Départ	64		**Magret**
Lacq			*Orthez*
		Orthez	
Lacq Audejos	80		**Lacq Audejos**
		Artix	
Poey de Lescar	94		**Poey de Lescar**
Lescar Pau			
		Pau	
Vignobles de Jurancon			
Serres Morlaas	111		**Serres Morlaas**
		Soumoulou	
Les Pyrénées			
Les Pyrénées ←	130	→	**Les Pyrénées**
			Collégiale d'Ibos
		Tarbes Ouest	
Lourdes			*Tarbes*
Péage de Laloubère	=		**Péage de Laloubère**
		Tarbes Est	
Viaduc de l'Arret Darré			
Les Bordes			**Les Bordes**
		Tournay	
Abb. de l'Escaladieu			
Les Baronnies			
Capvern les Bains			
		Capvern	
Les Bandouliers	172		**Lac St Martin**
		Lannemezan	
Péage de Cantaous	=		**Péage de Cantaous**

LANNEMEZAN

AIRES LANNEMEZAN ~ BAYONNE

Péage de Sames
Pay here. Gendarmerie after the barrier.

Motorway standard after you leave ASF; right down to A63 junction.

Hastingues
In the Middle Ages, four great routes led pilgrims from different parts of France to Saint Jacques de Compostelle in Spain; those from Paris, Vézelay and Le Puy converged at Hastingues. In this remarkable aire the large building you can see from the motorway houses an evocation of the pilgrimage, which was of enormous economic and cultural importance to the region; towns and villages along the route grew and prospered, pilgrims brought aspects of their own culture to the places they passed through and to their destination. In one area is the legend of St Jacques, in another the daily life of the medieval pilgrim, in a third the pilgrims' goal, arrival at the Cathedral, coupled with thoughts of the journey home. Outside, paths converge geometrically on a square, and all lead to the building whose circular form represents the cycle of arrival and departure. As for the pilgrim of old, so for today's traveller, who will surely be moved by this unusual and absorbing museum. A super place to stop, there is a snack bar in the fuel station shop.

Magret ★
A good bank of trees screens this small aire from the road; it is a very nice wooded spot.

Lacq Audejos ★
Modest exercise track around the central grassy bank of this small, but pleasant aire. Bar/buffet in the fuel station shop.

Poey de Lescar
A very small aire, without much parking space; nice climbing frame, though.

Serres Morlaas
A small site, but OK.

Les Pyrénées
Drive over the bridge to the services on the other side of the motorway.

Péage de Laloubère
Push button and take a ticket.

Les Bordes

Lac St Martin ★ ★
Drive back amongst the trees; a very pretty aire.

Péage de Cantaous
Pay here, no ticket needed.

Leave Toulouse by the A614, which becomes the N117. Regular laybys, emergency telephones, fuel stations and places to eat along this dual carriageway; not so good after St Gaudens.

Biarritz and **Bayonne** have almost merged into one city, yet each has its distinct character, formed through very different histories. Bayonne has been a prosperous port and Basque capital for 2000 years. Part of Eleanor of Aquitaine's dowry, it was English for 300 years, at its most prosperous during the 18th century. Biarritz, a small fishing port 150 years ago, became a fashionable resort during the 19th century, largely due to its fine waterfront and sandy beaches, and to the arrival of aristocratic exiles from Spain. There are several pleasant resorts along the sandy beaches of the **Cote Landaise**.

Gascony was part of the dowry Eleanor brought to her marriage with Henry Plantagenet. To achieve a stronger hold on their distant territory, the English built castles and walled towns, **bastides**, through the 13th century and retained power until the 15th century, when the French, inspired by Joan of Arc, drove them out. In **Dax** water still emerges at 64 degrees at the Roman baths from an underground spring. The pine forests of the **Landes** stretch from Bordeaux to Bayonne, created only 100 years ago by drainage and planting. **Béarn** is one of the ancient Pyrenean provinces; it's vineyards produce red, white and, in particular, rose wines. A lovely medieval bridge crosses the **Gave de Pau** at Orthez, and nearby is a woollen mill, Jerseys d'Aquitaine.

The motorway follows the river between Pau and its confluence with the Gave d'Oleron at Peyrehorade. The two rivers, now the Gaves Reunis, join the Adour a few kilometres west of the Péage de Sames. There is a beautiful bridge to cross.

One of the largest deposits of natural gas in the world was discovered at **Lacq** in the 1950s. Just west of Pau, **Lescar** is an ancient capital with a fine cathedral. Look out for the splendid Palais de Sports beside the motorway. During the 19th century, many wealthy British families came to live in **Pau**. Its popularity dated from the Peninsular war when British troops returned home and sang the praises of its mild climate and scenery. The sweet white wine produced in the **Vignobles de Jurancon** is one of the most remarkable of the region.

Lourdes has been a place of pilgrimage since the visions of Bernadette in 1858, and subsequent claims of miraculous cures at the grotto. Worth a visit, whether as a pilgrim, or to observe the way in which faith and commercialism co-exist.

Les Pyrénées are the home of the Basque people who have fought for centuries to be free of both France and Spain. The distant rugged peaks and the undulating terrain and pretty rivers of the foothills make for pleasant motoring. Ancient **Tarbes** was virtually destroyed during the religious wars of the 16th century; today it is a busy industrial and commercial centre. The **Collégiale d'Ibos** is the church with two dissimilar towers, in a small town just to the west of Tarbes. The **Viaduc de l'Arret Darré** crosses one of the region's oddly named rivers. Another is the **Arret Devant** (devant - in front, derriere - behind). Both flow into the Arros. **Les Baronnies** are the foothills south of the small spa town of **Capvern les Bains**.

A71

Bois de Bailly ★
Wooded site, in a lovely setting.

Chaumont sur Tharonne
Wooded picnic area beyond the fuel station.

Etang du Maras ★
Well back from road, a good sized aire with woods to one side, fields to the other. You will see the lake in the name (étang) as you drive out of the aire.

Les Marembert ★
Wooded, with a gravel track at the back of the site to drive down. Not large, but pleasant.

Salbris Theillay
Good snack bar in the shop, with terrace; small wooded area at back.

Les Croquettes
Being extended, but rather an exposed site.

Bourges Ste Thorette
Lively and popular Caféroute, open 24 hours, at one end of the shop, with a terrace. No picnic area.

Le Gite aux Loups ★
A large, wooded aire. The lorry park at the back is the nicest part; park round there if you can. There are a few shaded tables.

Centre de la France Farges Allichamps
Pass the fuel station to reach the Relais du Centre de la France where there is a restaurant and snack bar, both with terrace, and a shop selling regional products. There is a good play area nearby and very good WCs. At present these facilities have to serve both sides of the motorway and could get rather crowded on a busy day as they are not very spacious. I suppose a similar Relais will be built on the other side of the motorway when traffic levels increase. Meanwhile you may prefer to eat elsewhere if there are several coaches in the car park. Walk through to the rear of the main building and down some steps and you will find yourself in a museum containing artefacts found during the building of the A71 and showing the importance of the River Cher as the centre of European trade and communications in prehistoric times. It is very nicely done. You are directed up the same steps to a viewpoint on the roof.

AIRES ORLEANS ~ ST AMAND MONTROND

ORLEANS

	km	from Orléans
		Orleans Nord (A10)
		Orleans Centre
Cléry		*Parc Floral*
		Olivet
Bois de Bailly	10	**Bois de Télégraphe**
Chaumont sur Tharonne	27	**La Ferté St Aubin**
La Sologne		
		La Motte Beuvron
Etang du Maras	42	**La Briganderie**
Les Marembert	53	**La Saulot**
		Salbris
Romorantin		
Salbris Theillay	65	**Salbris La Loge**
		Vierzon Nord, A20
Vierzon		
		Vierzon Est
		Mehun sur Yèvre
Les Croquettes	93	**La Chaussée de César**
		Berry
Ste Thorette	100	**Marmagne**
		Bourges
		Bourges
Gite aux Loups	119	**Bois des Dames**
Champagne Berrichonne		*Jussy en Champagne*
Chateauneuf sur Cher		*Meillant*
		Noirlac
Centre de la France ←	146	→ **Centre de la France**
		St Amand Montrond

ST AMAND

Bois de Télégraphe ★ ♿
A wooded, medium sized aire in a lovely setting.

La Ferté St Aubin ♿
No picnic area.

La Briganderie ★ ♿
Drive down the gravel track to picnic among the silver birch trees.

La Saulot ★ ♿
Pleasant wooded site.

Salbris La Loge ♿
No picnic area.

La Chaussée de César ♿
No sign of a Roman pavement!

Bourges Marmagne ♿
Good sized shop, which includes La Croquade restaurant. Very nice terrace. No picnic area.

Bois des Dames ★ ♿
A pleasant, medium-sized aire, with point relaxe and a large grassy area.

Centre de la France Bruere Allichamps
♿
On this side of the motorway there is a picnic area. Drive across the bridge and pass the fuel station to reach the Relais du Centre de la France (see A71 south).

Romorantin is a former capital of **La Sologne**, a previously marshy region between the Cher and the Loire reclaimed for agriculture only 100 years ago. It is a region of forests and lakes (étangs), heather and broom. Look out for the flying ducks on the attractive three-shaded brown panels!

The **Parc Floral**, south of Orléans, is a showcase for local horticulture.

Apart from its square tower, the 14th century church of **Notre Dame de Cléry** was destroyed by the English, marching on Orléans in 1428. A year later the seige of Orléans was to be lifted by Joan of Arc and the future Charles V11; it was the latter, and his commander-in-chief, Dunois, who provided the funds to start rebuilding Cléry.

Vierzon is a meeting point, geographically (at the confluence of the **Yèvre** and the Cher, and on the border of the Sologne with Champagne Berrichonne) and of road and rail routes. It is also the centre of the porcelain industry of Berry. You will see the pretty Yèvre alongside the motorway between Vierzon and **Mehun**, where Joan of Arc once stayed, and which now produces 20% of all French table china.

Reminders of its rich and powerful past abound in **Bourges**; a 12th and 13th century cathedral, whose silhouette rises up from the surrounding countryside no matter which direction the traveller arrives from, palaces and houses which date from medieval and Renaissance times when the Duke of **Berry** was a close ally of the king. Bourges remains the commercial, industrial and artistic capital of the region.

One of the oldest agricultural areas of France, the limestone plateau of **Champagne Berrichonne** is a landscape of cereal cultivation, cattle and sheep rearing. **St Amand Montrond** is the centre of its dairy industry.

There are several interesting old chateaux, churches and abbeys in the region; **Ainay le Vieil, Jussy en Champagne** and **Chateauneuf sur Cher** are nearby. The recently restored **Abbaye de Noirlac** was founded by St Bernard. The chateau at **Meillant** was acquired by the Amboise family in 1464, and restored, as was Chaumont in the Loire Valley, on the profits of Charles II of Amboise' Governorship of Milan.

The **Cher** flows through Berry, close to the chateaux and never far from the motorway, irrigating the fertile land. It joins the Loire at Tours. The **Bois Chaut** is an area of small cattle farms in Berry.

Le Grand Meaulnes ★ ♿ /Π\ 📞
A pleasant, neat aire with a point relaxe. There is an interesting concrete book celebrating the literary heritage of this region of France, which includes Alain-Fournier, hence the name of the aire (the title of his most famous work). Have a look, too, at the picturesque old chateau/farm on the other side of the motorway.

L'Allier (Doyet) ★ ⛽ ✕ ♿ /Π\
There is a cafeteria, snack bar and regional products shop here, and beyond the fuel station there is a pleasant picnic area.

La Bouble ★ ★ ♿ /Π\ 📞
Attractive windmills of various shapes and a delightful walk through oak woods at the back of the site; the best aire so far on this motorway going south.

Les Volcans d'Auvergne
A fine single steel arch supports the bridge to the services which are all on the far side of the motorway.

Montpertuis ★ ♿ /Π\ 📞
Good climbing apparatus, nice site but not many tables.

Péage de Gerzat ♿
Pay here.

AIRES ST AMAND ~ CLERMONT

ST AMAND

	km	from Orléans
	■	St Amand Montrond
		Ainay le Vieil
Culan		*Foret de Troncais*
Bois Chaut		*Le Cher*
Le Grand Meaulnes	176	**Vallon en Sully**
	■	Vallon en Sully
		Moulins
	■	Montlucon
L'Allier (Doyet) ←	204	→ **Bourbonnais Sauzet**
Montlucon		
Néris les Bains		
	■	Montmarault
Le Bourbonnais		*St Pourcain*
La Bouble	233	**Chantelle en Bourbon.**
Gorges de la Sioule		*Vichy*
	■	Gannat
Les Volcans d'Auv. ←	255	→ **Les Volcans d'Auv.**
Chatelguyon		
Montpertuis	272	**Pessat Villeneuve**
	■	Riom
Riom		
Volvic		
	■	Gerzat
Péage de Gerzat	=	**Péage de Gerzat**
	■	Clermont Ferrand Nord
Parc des Volcans d'Auvergne		
	■	Le Brezet
	■	A720, A72

CLERMONT

Vallon en Sully ♿ ☎
Look out for crossing the Canal du Berry just before the aire.

Bourbonnais Sauzet
At the fuel station there is a free lights check. There is pedestrian access to the facilities on the far side of the motorway.

Chantelle en Bourbonnais ★
There is a small wood in the middle of this pretty aire and several points relaxes.

Les Volcans d'Auvergne
A volcanic landscape has been created beside the motorway as the extraordinary setting of this aire. There is a large tourist office, the Conseil Régional d'Auvergne, alongside the fuel station. Drive through to reach the parking area and access to the Relais des Volcans d'Auvergne. The building is luminous and classical; super architecture, rather cluttered with signs, displays and bins when we visited it which was a pity. A more serious criticism was the inadequate number of WCs; this may have been remedied. On the plus side there is a very good regional products shop. Both restaurant and cafeteria have terraces with exceptional views over the volcanic mountains; a lovely place to eat. Beyond the main building is the beautifully designed Forte Travelodge with similar panoramic views; a lovely place to stay, too! There is a lot of space for parking and picnicking beyond the main area but it needs time for trees and shrubs to become established, it is rather bleak at the moment. You can return towards Clermont Ferrand if you wish from this aire.

Pessat Villeneuve ★
Motorway always seems rather close, and car park rather crowded when we visited; the lorry park, in contrast, was empty, so why not use that.

Péage de Gerzat ♿
Take a ticket.

In the little town of Bruère Allichamps, where the N144 road crosses the D92, stands a Roman milestone; at this point, it is claimed, is the **Centre de la France.**

Culan is the site of a feudal fortress overlooking the Gorges of the river Arnon.

The pretty **Aumance** is a tributary of the Cher.

Southeast of Berry is the small province of **Le Bourbonnais.** To the east of the motorway is the **Foret de Troncais,** its largest wooded area whose oak is used to make casks which are transported west to the Cognac region for the storage of brandy. **Moulins** used to be the splendid capital of Le Bourbonnais, and home of the powerful Bourbon family.

Bourbon L'Archambault and **Néris les Bains** are ancient spa towns.

The industrial basin which includes **Montlucon** and **Commentry** is a large area of foundries, rubber and chemical works on the banks of the Allier.

Said to be the most fashionable spa in France, **Vichy** was the headquarters of the Petain government from 1940-1944.

The motorway crosses the **Sioule** flowing from its source in the Auvergne and cutting gorges through the foothills on its journey to join the Allier just beyond **St Pourcain.**

Travelling south, you will have distant but splendid views of the Volcans d'Auvergne after the **Col de Naves.** The conical shape of the extinct volcanic 'puys' becomes clearer as you approach the **Parc Naturel Régional des Volcans d'Auvergne.**

Volvic is a centre of quarrying of the dark volcanic lava used in the building of the towns of the region, notably **Riom** where there are some stately 18th century mansions. **Chatelguyon** is on the site of a castle built by Guy of Auvergne, hence its name.

Péage des Martres d'Artière
Take a ticket. Tyre pressure check and Gendarmerie after the barrier.

Le Branchillon ★ ★

A pleasantly landscaped, wooded site. The road winds around, overlooking a lake at the far side of aire. A further parking area at the far end of the site is described as a Zone de Détente; the main aire is better.

Limagne ★

Bar buffet in the shop; fenced play area behind fuel station.

Les Pins ★ ★

A well-landscaped site, with a variety of wooded and grassy areas. Turn right beyond the WC block to reach the picnic area. There is a further area for picnicing around the lorry park.

Haut Forez ★ *i*

Straight ahead for fuel; go right, past the 'Etape Sportive' to the parking, picnic and petanque area. Organised boules or mountain biking on summer Sundays might appeal to you; choose another aire for a picnic stop if not, for this is not a very attractive site.

Les Bruyères ★

La Plaine du Forez ★ ★

At the far end of the site, in the woods, is the 11-exercise 'parcours de santé'.

Chante Perdrix ★

A neat, tidy, well-landscaped site. At the back, on a small mound, is a look-out point, (a hide?), with pleasant views over fields where, who knows, there may be partridges.

Péage de Veauchette

Pay here.

AIRES CLERMONT FERRAND ~ SAINT ETIENNE

CLERMONT

	km	from Clermont	
		A75, A71	
Le Mont Dore			*Clermont Ferrand*
Puy de Dome			
		Lempdes	
Auvergne			
Péage de Martres	=		**Péage de Martres**
Plateau de Gergovie			
Le Branchillon	12		**Les Pacages**
			Plaine de la Limagne
Limagne	21		**Limagne**
			Vichy
		Thiers Ouest	
Thiers			
Les Pins	36		**Le Lac**
		Thiers Est	
			St Rémy sur Durolle
	49		**Les Suchères**
Les Monts du Forez			
		Noiretable	
Chateau d'Urfé			
Haut Forez	57		**Haut Forez**
Les Bois Noirs			*Monts de la Madeleine*
		St Germain	
			Pays Roannais
Les Bruyères	82		**Les Ardilliers**
		A89	
			Monts du Lyonnais
		Feurs	
La Plaine du Forez	102		**La Plaine du Forez**
Montbrison			
		Mont Brison	
Chante Perdrix	111		**Les Chaninats**
			La Loire
Péage de Veauchette	=		**Péage de Veauchette**
		Andrezieux Boutheon	
		Veauches	
		Boutheon	
		Firminy le Puy	
			St Etienne
		St Etienne Centre	
			Massif du Pilat

SAINT ETIENNE

Péage des Martres d'Artiere
Pay here. Gendarmerie after the barrier.

Les Pacages ★ ★
Drive on to find extra parking at the back of this lovely, neat site.

Limagne ★
There are woods at the back of this site; covered tables give some shade in the main area.

Le Lac ★ ★ ★
Drive past the main car park for there is a lot of parking space further back in this super aire. There are picnic tables among the trees and beside the lake. If you want seclusion park near the sign for 'Zone de Détente' and walk up some steps and along the shady path where an extensive woodland walk and a 20-exercise 'parcours de santé' have been laid out. There are a few tables in clearings along the way. Absolutely delightful. There are lovely views as you leave this aire.

Les Suchères ★ ★ *i*
There is an extraordinary work of art, Colonnes des Suchères, as you enter the aire; you can't miss it! Walk down a slope from rather a small parking area to the picnic area, which is surrounded by forests. There is a plan of the region.

Haut Forez
In a lovely forest setting, a modern, but very small aire.

Les Ardilliers ★
There is a nice grassy area at the back of this site.

La Plaine du Forez ★ ★
Bar/buffet in shop, and a very nice picnic area including one of the best covered areas I've seen. Good views over to the hills.

Les Chaninats ★
A little shade at the back of the site.

Péage de Veauchette
Take a ticket.

The Romans built a town on the site of **Clermont Ferrand** in preference to Gergovie. In 1832 a small factory began to make rubber here; the Michelin tyre business developed from this. The industrial town is on the hill, its older houses clustered round the cathedral. Vertingetorix, leader of the the Gauls, had his headquarters on the **Plateau de Gergovie** in his campaign against Julius Caesar in 53BC. Popular as a spa town and for winter sports, **Le Mont Dore** is among the 'puys', with the **Auvergne**'s highest peak, the Puy de Sancy, 1885m, just to the south. A toll road spirals up to the summit of the **Puy de Dome** which dominates Clermont Ferrand. Advantage has been taken of the fact that there is no crater to build an observatory, a radio mast and, no great surprise, tourist shops at the top.

The most fashionable spa in France, **Vichy** was the headquarters of the Petain government from 1940 1944. The fertile plain of the river Allier, where sunflowers, wheat and corn are grown, is called the **Plaine de Limagne**.

Thiers is in a pretty, wooded location on a hillside overlooking the Durolle. As the name of one of the main streets suggests, Rue de la Coutellerie, the town produces cutlery. On the hillside ahead as you leave the Aire des Pins is **St Rémy sur Durolle**. Its church has a nice clock on its tower.

The motorway passes through the northern part of the **Monts du Forez**. The hills are heavily wooded, (these are the **Bois Noirs**) largely pine and beech, and there is an important logging industry. **Les Monts de la Madeleine** are a northern extension on whose slopes, the Cote Roannaise, are vineyards producing rose wines. The highest point on this magnificent stretch of motorway is the **Col de Cervières**, 806 metres. The **Chateau d'Urfé** can be seen on the hillside ahead as the road descends towards exit 4 to **Noiretable**, travelling west. There once was a chateau at **Montbrison**, on a volcanic mound, surrouded by a few houses. The chateau, seat of the Counts of Forez, has long since gone, but the town remained. **Le Pays Roannais**, the region around Roanne on the Loire, is a centre of the French textile industry. The range of hills from St Etienne to Lyon are the **Monts du Lyonnais**.

Between the Rhone valley and the Loire basin, a watershed influenced by both the Mediterranean and the Atlantic, the **Massif du Pilat** is on the northern edge of the Cevennes. Long renowned for its flora and fauna (Jean-Jacques Rousseau collected plants here in 1769), it forms part of a Parc Naturel Régional. **La Loire**, the longest river in France, rises high in the Massif Central. The A72 crosses it near the Péage de Veauchette. The sewing machine was invented at **St Etienne** in 1830 by a poor tailor making army clothing. He remained poor until the day he died, for he never managed to market his invention. A student at the Ecole des Mines here had better luck; in 1833 Fourneyron won a prize for producing the first water turbine, a 50h.p. machine, and went on to become a highly successful engineer.

A75

Veyre
Bar/buffet in fuel station shop.

Le Val d'Allier

Cézallier *i*
Information kiosk only open in summer

Lafayette Lorlanges *i*
In the Relais Lafayette Lorlanges there is a caféteria, snack bar and shop. There is also a Forte Travelodge hotel.

Chalet

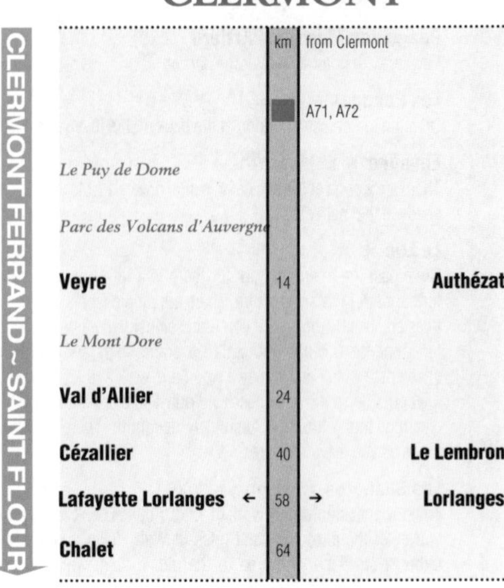

La Landrière ★ ★
Wooded and grassy; beyond the main aire, with its games for younger children, a second part going down a slope towards a lake, with tables among the trees and climbing frames.

Les Gripperies ★
Well back from road, medium sized site.

St Denis d'Orques
No picnic area.

Villeray ★

Laval Bonchamp
Bar-buffet, with small terrace, at fuel station shop. No picnic area.

Mayenne ★

La Paplonière

Péage de la Gravelle
Pay here.

Erbrée ★ ★ *i*
Drive past the fuel station, to the Relais Vert caféteria, tourist and traffic information, shop and Hotel Percival, all of which are well appointed and pleasant. Drive on around the back of the site to reach the wooded picnic area.

LE MANS

AIRES LE MANS ~ RENNES

	km	
		from Paris, A6
		A11
La Landrière	180	**La Chevallerie**
Les Gripperies	198	**La Coire**
		Joue en Charnie Sable
		Abbaye de Solesmes
St Denis d'Orques	211	**Thorigné en Charnie**
		Ste Suzanne
		Vaiges
Villeray	225	**Loriolet**
Laval Bonchamp	241	**Laval le Goudray**
		Laval Est
La Mayenne		*Laval*
Mayenne	248	**Chateau de Ricoudet**
		Laval Ouest
Fougères		
La Paplonière	259	**La Sorinière**
Péage de la Gravelle	=	**Péage de la Gravelle**
Vitré		La Gravelle
Erbrée	275	**Mondevert**

RENNES

SAINT FLOUR ~ CLERMONT FERRAND

Authézat
Information kiosk only open in summer

Le Lembron
Information kiosk only open in summer

Lorlanges
There is access to the Relais facilities on the far side of the motorway.

The conical shape of the 'puys' is typical in the **Parc Naturel Régional des Volcans d'Auvergne.** A toll road spirals up **Le Puy de Dome** west of Clermont Ferrand. Advantage has been taken of the fact that there is no crater to build an observatory, a radio mast and, no great surprise, tourist shops, on the summit. The Auvergne's highest peak, the Puy de Sancy, is just to the south of the spa town and winter sports centre of **Le Mont Dore**

LE MANS ~ RENNES A81

AIRES RENNES ~ LE MANS

La Chevallerie ★
Fenced play area, pleasant area of rough grass at back of site.

La Coire ★
Fenced play area and climbing frames.

Thorigné en Charnie
Bar/buffet, with small terrace, at fuel station shop. No picnic area.

Loriolet ★
Fenced play area towards end of site.

Laval le Coudray
No picnic area.

Chateau de Ricoudet ★

La Sorinière

Péage de la Gravelle
Take a ticket. Tyre pressure check after the barrier.

Mondevert
Boeuf Jardinier grill, Caféroute snack bar (open 24 hours in summer).

The **Abbaye de Solesmes**, on the banks of the Sarthe, is a Benedictine abbey, rebuilt in the 19th century in the style of the 12th, and in use today.

Sainte Suzanne is a walled hill-top village with a view.

Formerly a centre of a textile industry introduced by Flemish weavers, **Laval** is now involved in more general industry. In the Vieux Chateau, not much of which is old, is the museum.

Fougères is a really interesting old walled town. To reach the castle, and it is worth the visit, you walk down the hill, rather than up, for a change.

Vitré is an old flagmakers town on the Vilaine, with a castle, a regional museum and well-restored streets to walk through.

Appendix 1
Trees and shrubs

Arboretum at Foret de Montech, A62

Among the trees here are:

Chene Rouvre	Pedunculate oak
Cèdre de l'Himalaya	Himalayan cedar
Sapin Argenté	Silver fir
Pin Sylvestre	Scots pine
Sequoia	Californian redwood
Aubépine	Hawthorn
Néflier	Medlar
Alisier	Whitebeam
Pin Maritime	Maritime pine
Charme	Hornbeam
Méleze du Japon	Japanese larch
Cyprès de Lawson	Lawson cypress
Chene Pubescent ou Blanc	White oak
Sapin concolore	Fir
Sapin de Douglas	Douglas fir
Sapin céphalonie ou de Grèce	Greek fir
Thuya de Chine	Chinese red cedar
Cyprès commun	Halian cypress
Genevrier de Virginie	Pencil cedar
Sapin de Vancouver	Vancouver fir
Chataignier	Sweet chestnut
Pin de Lalissieu	Mediterranean pine
Chene écarlate	Scarlet Oak
Chene de l'Atlas	Atlas Oak

Arboretum at Aire du Lac, A72

Among the trees and shrubs listed are:

Genet à balai Scorparius	Broom
Fougère	Fern
Digitalis Pourpre	Purple Foxglove
Houx	Holly
Chene Rouvre	Pedunculate Oak
Chataignier commun	Sweet Chestnut
Saule	Willow
Abies	Fir
Sapin Argenté	Silver Fir
Hetre commun	Beech
Pin Sylvestre	Scots Pine

Appendix 2
Quote from the Museum at Port Lauragais, A61

L'autoroute parait aujourd'hui comme le grand moyen de communication du XXième siècle. Certains l'ont décrite comme un monde clos, évitant les villes, étrangère aux pays qu'elle traverse.

Pour sa part, la Société des Autoroutes du Sud de la France pense qu'il est dans son role de participer à une mise en valeur des richesses culturelles, économiques et touristiques des villes et régions desservies par ses autoroutes.Au-delà des services indispensibles, il s'agit de faciliter l'information des voyageurs et de leur permettre d'appréhender les cultures régionales par des centres d'acceuil et de promotion.

L'ensemble architecturel de Port Lauragais répond à ce souci, et tout particulierèment le Centre Paul Riquet qui est un hommage des batisseurs des voies actuelles à celui qui fut il y a 300 ans le constructeur du canal du Midi.

De telles créations, dues au succes d'une concertation étroite avec les partenaires régionaux renovent la conception de l'aire autoroutière, ainsi appelée à devenir le point d'ancrage de l'autoroute dans la région.

The motorway appears today as the great means of communication of the 20th century. It has been described as a closed world, avoiding towns, a foreigner in the world it travels through.

For its part, the ASF thinks it has a responsibility to publicise the cultural, economic and touristic riches of the towns and regions served by its motorways. As well as providing essential services for drivers, there are tourist and regional products centres.

Port Lauragais, and, in particular, its Paul Riquet centre, paying hommage from today's builders to the man who, 300 years ago, constructed the Canal du Midi, meets this responsibility.

Such creations, due to close cooperation with local partners, renew the idea of the motorway service station, which becomes the anchor point of the motorway in the region.

Acknowledgements

I am indebted to P&O European Ferries for generously providing me with several Channel crossings; to all the French motorway networks for information and in particular SAPRR, ASF, COFIROUTE, ESCOTA and SANEF for travel assistance; to Relais restaurants, in particular the manager and staff at Relais Dijon Cote d'Or at the Aire de Dijon Brognon and Relais de l'Artois at the Aire de Wancourt; to Arche restaurants, in particular the manager and staff at the Aires de Venoy Soleil Levant, L'Isle d'Abeau, Lorraine Sandaucourt and Verdun St Nicolas; to Loiredis, and in particular the manager and staff at Caféroute at the Aire de Bourges Ste Thorette; to Julian, Liz, Vicky and Chris, for sharing the driving, and for their splendid company on my travels; to Vicky also for allowing me to use her photographs.

Readers Suggestions and Comments

If you have any comments on what I have written, or about any French motorway services you have used, I should be most grateful if you would pass them on to me, to supplement my own research and help keep the book up to date. Please say if you will allow me to use your name.

Write to: Anna Fitter, Anthony Nelson Ltd., PO Box 9, Oswestry, Shropshire SY11 1BY, England.

Index

Note: The towns listed are those at the start and end of sections of motorway.